Mapping Tourism

Mapping Tourism

Stephen P. Hanna and
Vincent J. Del Casino Jr., Editors

University of Minnesota Press
Minneapolis • London

Parts of the Introduction and chapter 7 were originally published in earlier versions in "Representations and Identities in Tourism Map Spaces," *Progress in Human Geography* 24, no. 1 (2000): 23–46; reprinted with permission from Arnold Publishing.

Published by the University of Minnesota Press
111 Third Avenue South, Suite 290
Minneapolis, MN 55401-2520
http://www.upress.umn.edu

Library of Congress Cataloging-in-Publication Data

Mapping tourism / Stephen P. Hanna and Vincent J. Del Casino Jr., editors.
    p.   cm.
    Includes bibliographical references.
    ISBN 0-8166-3955-8 (hc : alk. paper) — ISBN 0-8166-3956-6 (pbk. : alk. paper)
    1. Heritage tourism.   2. Geographical perception.   3. Maps, Tourist.   I. Hanna,
Stephen P.   II. Del Casino, Vincent J.
    G156.5.H47 M28 2003
    338.4'791—dc21

2002153734

12 11 10 09 08 07 06 05 04 03   10 9 8 7 6 5 4 3 2 1

Contents

Acknowledgments

This project began almost seven years ago when we met at the University of Kentucky as graduate students. Over the years, we have continued to develop our individual and collective interests in representational and identity politics, tourism studies, and critical cartography. This edited volume is just another step in our ongoing efforts to more fully understand the complex material and discursive processes that structure the maps and spaces of tourism. We have drawn our inspiration for this work from numerous sources, including the intellectual contributions of scholars in geography and beyond that take seriously critical social theory. We have also benefited from numerous seminars and conferences where we have presented and shared our work with others. And we have been encouraged along the way by our positive intellectual and collegial relationships with the contributors of this text, along with numerous others in the field more generally.

Obviously, a project like this is not possible without the support of both institutions and individual colleagues. We would like to begin by thanking our current institutions, Mary Washington College and California State University, Long Beach, which provided us with resources to complete this project. We would also like to thank John Paul Jones, who advised both of us through our Ph.D.s and added his "two cents" worth on earlier versions of the paper that is the basis of the Introduction and chapter 7. Intellectually, this text also owes thanks to a number of other people, most of whom we shared a pint with at Lynagh's in Lexington, for their insightful contributions to our thinking about space, representation, and identity. Those individuals include, in no particular order, Carole Gallaher, Mary Gilmartin, Susan Mains, Sarah Dewees, Jim Hanlon, and Matt McCourt. We must also thank Carrie Mullen (and the University of Minnesota Press), who supported this project from its inception and who has been diligent in her efforts to see the book to completion. Finally, we thank Arnold Publishing for allowing us to reprint revised versions of parts of our article "Representations and Identities in Tourism Map Spaces," originally published in *Progress in Human Geography,* in the Introduction and in chapter 7.

Introduction: Tourism Spaces, Mapped Representations, and the Practices of Identity

Stephen P. Hanna and Vincent J. Del Casino Jr.

Tourism maps are everywhere. They are materially produced by tourism organizations and woven through the conversations people have when asking for directions. We are greeted by examples of these popular cartographies in mass mailings, at highway rest stops, and, of course, on the Internet. While stopping for a meal near an interstate off-ramp, we may, for example, find a tourism map under our breakfasts or dinners (see Figure I.1). Whether intended to inform and entertain, to distract the customer from slow restaurant service, or merely to collect grease and crumbs, this place mat/map lays out Virginia's tourism attractions for consumption. From the Stonewall Jackson Shrine to Virginia Beach, from George Washington's birthplace to Skyline Drive, the state's nature and history are represented as points of interest. In fact, between the blue icons representing tourism sites and the red text accompanying these icons, Virginia appears to contain nothing but sites for the tourist to explore.

But what does a tourism map produced by a restaurant supply company tell us? As we sip our coffee we may learn, or be reminded, that Virginia is "The Old Dominion" and that despite being named for a virgin queen, she *is* the "mother of presidents." If we are tourists, perhaps one of the icons will jump out at us, leading us to consider making a detour to see Thomas Jefferson's home or the site of Lee's surrender at Appomatox.

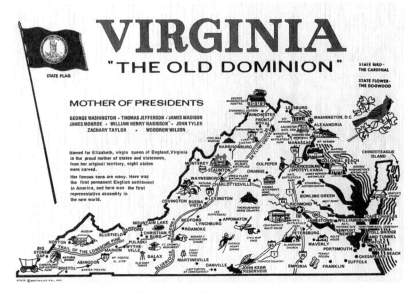

Figure I.1. Virginia on a place mat. Smith-Lee Co., Inc.

If we are not, the map may give us ideas for future travels. In other words, like any other map, a tourism map conveys information to us about places. And it represents a particular way of socially and spatially organizing places of consumption for tourists and nontourists alike (Urry 1995). Thus, we interpret and use map information to plan our travels, to learn about places, or simply to help us pass the time while waiting for the check.

At first glance, the relationships among tourists, tourism maps, and the spaces of tourism seem unproblematic. Produced as advertisements, these maps are used by tourists to find their way to and through tourism spaces where they experience the history, the culture, the nature, or the leisure practices represented on the map. Yet, this simple model tells us nothing about how tourism maps and the social actors deploying these representations *construct* tourism spaces and identities. The Virginia map does not simply present the state to us. Instead, it embodies (Crang 1999) Virginia cartographically and acts to guide a visitor's gaze and actions to help her or him experience *that* Virginia (Urry 1990). The icons and text are produced specifically to place before the tourist sites/sights that define the state's history, geography, and identity. In so doing, the icons reference, reinforce, or ignore a whole realm of texts and knowledges that also take and lend meaning to the spaces represented on the map. These *intertextual* connections, which often exist "below, above, or beyond the surface" of the map, provide frameworks of discipline as well as moments of resistance to hegemonic readings of tourism maps and spaces.[1] The map's authors and readers, for example, go to such places with a working knowledge of who Patrick Henry was or how a tourist should act while visiting Arlington National Cemetery. Reciprocally, without such intertextual moments neither author nor reader could conclude that the map helps to naturalize a heroic and romantic version of Virginia's Confederate history, or that the map denies that this history remains a site of struggle between groups identified by race or political leanings. Thus, as a material representation of space that is produced and interpreted in changing social contexts, this tourism map is complexly and intertextually interrelated with the spaces and identities it strives to represent (DeLyser 1999).

In this volume's essays, the authors argue that tourism maps, such as the Virginia place mat, are key sites through which we can construct a critical study of the relationships among space, identity, and representation. The relationships that emerge from the interrogation of tourism maps provide insights into how tourism is not only represented but also practiced by tourists, tourism workers, the state, global capital, and other social actors. *Mapping Tourism,* therefore, has two intertwined goals. First, the chapters in this book investigate how tourism maps *work* as integral parts of the production of tourism spaces and concomitant practices of identity. These popular cartographic representations are regularly used by tourists not just to guide their ways to and through tourism sites but also to learn about the histories, cultures, and environments represented as parts of these places. Neither critical cartographers nor tourism studies scholars have taken these particular sets of representations seriously, however. It is our contention that the chapters that follow help us understand how these representations work to construct and reproduce the spaces and identities that inform our histories and heritage, our environmental perceptions, our urban and rural landscapes, our languages and political actions, and our racial, sexual, gendered, and ethnic identities. In short, tourism maps interact with tourism spaces and identities to reproduce people's knowledges about their worlds.

Second, tourism maps provide a concrete site through which different disciplines and subfields, including cartography and tourism studies, can be woven together, breaking down the artificial boundaries that often mark disciplinary sites of inquiry. These cultural artifacts make themselves available to multiple theoretical and methodological approaches. Theoretically, our authors address issues regarding the interrelationships between space and representation and space and identity, the processes of social spatialization, the selling of place, the intersections of heritage and memory, the tensions that mark the "boundaries" between subjectivity and power, and the contested reproduction of landscapes as texts. Methodologically, these authors use multiple approaches—ethnography, textual analysis, interpretivism, deconstruction—to interrogate tourism maps as spaces. In so doing, they contribute to the ongoing interdisciplinary discussions about the intertextual and material relationships among and between representations, such as tourism maps, and the spaces and identities the maps claim to represent. Thus, as geographers, we (the editors) hope this book suggests ways in which spatial theories of representation and identity can be used by scholars working in the fields of cultural and race studies, women's studies, and anthropology and sociology. In turn, we demonstrate the influence these disciplines continue to have on the development of critical geographic thought.

An introductory chapter covering the relevant work in all the aforementioned disciplines, however, would be either too shallow or too long to be useful to most readers. In the remainder of this Introduction, therefore, we provide an entry point to the chapters that follow by reviewing parallel developments in the two literatures most immediately relevant to the study of tourism maps—cartography and tourism studies. Even within these two more limited bodies of work, the range of perspectives on the complex relationships between space, identity, and representation allows us to provide a useful background for the key conceptual arguments made by each of the volume's authors. We conclude with a brief review of the contributions, as well as a set of suggestions on how this volume might be read, to emphasize that there is a variety of connections among these essays. We want to encourage the reader to reproduce the book's meanings as she or he reads.

Theorizing Tourism Maps, Spaces, and Identities: Critical Cartography

Throughout geography's modern history, cartography has occupied a crucial place in a geographer's education, and certainly mapping is still an integral part of geographic methodology. In cartography and, increasingly, Geographic Information Science classes, geographers are trained to overcome the technical limitations of scale, projection, and generalization to produce maps theorized as simplified mirrors, or models, of reality. There is a history within both geography and cartography that notes the technical and, to a lesser extent, social limitations of this scientific cartography (Monmonier 1991; Peters 1990; Wright 1942). These internal critiques, however, are little more than refinements to the dominant paradigm of cartography: the science of accurately modeling the world. In such a model, representations of real space have no impact on the space they claim to represent. Throughout the past century geographers have depended on this conception of cartography in order to delimit regions, map landscapes, and plot patterns. Although this theorization certainly produces useful results, it ensures that any critical reading of a tourism map is limited to a listing of cartographic miscues or crimes that distort the map's accuracy and, therefore, mislead the defenseless map reader. It also ignores other forms of mapping that may not result in a material map product or artifact.

As has been noted (Del Casino and Hanna 2000), the profound challenges to positivist human geography beginning in the 1970s were largely lost on cartographers. As marxists, feminists, and humanists critiqued the spatial science paradigm as ahistorical, irrelevant, and/or blind to social relations of gender, race, sexuality, and class, most cartographers refined their methods to both rationalize the cartographic process and perfect their ability to model space (for critiques see MacHaffie 1995; Ryden 1993). Harley (1989: 1), among others, laments the widening gap between human geography and cartography and focuses blame on mapmakers for operating "in a tunnel created by their own technologies without reference to the social world."

Fundamental critiques of cartography have sought to unveil the social constructedness of the map and/or to explore and critique the discipline's role in the histories of the state, capitalism, and Western colonialism (Belyea 1992; Black 1997; Duncan and Gregory 1999; Edney 1993; Gregory 1994; Harley 1988, 1989, 1990; Harley and Zandveliet 1992; Livingstone 1992; Pickles 1992; Ryden 1993; Sparke 1995, 1998; Wood and Fels 1986; Woodward 1991). Working along and across these lines and employing a variety of disciplinary perspectives, an increasing number of works force us to reexamine the relationships between map and space, between map production and use, and between the discipline and the world it claims to represent.

J. B. Harley's "Deconstructing the Map" (1989) remains one of the most influential critiques of traditional approaches to maps and cartography and thus serves as our entry into this literature. In this and later works, Harley constructs a critical cartography not as a science of mapmaking but as a fully socialized and politicized analysis of the discipline's history, discourses, and practices. Harley presents a way of understanding the map and cartography as both parts and products of social discourses and, therefore, as employments of power. Importantly, Harley's definition of the map is *not* confined to the area being mapped, but includes titles, legends, pictures, and descriptive text usually placed at the margins of the page (Harley and Zandveliet 1992). By looking for absences and paying attention to the margins of maps as texts, the map critic can read between the cartographic lines and reveal how a particular map represents and reproduces the social and spatial status quo. Indeed, such an approach is a starting point for all of the authors in this volume.

For Harley, social power is inscribed in maps by cartographers operating within dominant discourses and institutions. This focus on the map's immediate production context, however, blinds him to other factors affecting the relationship between map, author/user, and space. He does not seem to realize that maps are intertextual. They are made and used in the presence of a broad range of existing representations of the place being mapped. As many of the chapters in this volume illustrate, disconnects in the intertextual contexts of users and producers raise the possibilities that map users may reinscribe maps with new meanings, an example of de Certeau's (1984) consumption as production. Karen Till, in chapter 3, for example, examines this very process in her analysis of tours of the "New Berlin," as does Mary Curran, in chapter 6, in her dialogical analysis of tourism and environmental hazards–based mappings of Butte, Montana.

Harley's incomplete dialectic between space and representation is another limitation of his critical cartography. Although he seeks to break the mimetic and unidirectional link from space to representation that dominates cartography, his flawed deconstructionist method seeks to find the real power relations in some space that is outside of and concealed by the map (see Belyea 1992; Sparke 1995 for a critique of Harley's methodology). Thus, there are no ambiguities in Harley's cartography, no possibility that the meanings of the spaces and identities represented in maps may be continually reproduced with changes in context. Owen Dwyer, in chapter 2, and Dydia DeLyser, in chapter 4, offer case studies of how these ambiguous processes operate in both the American "South" and "West," in an analysis of civil rights memorials, on the one hand, and in an ethnography of tourism in a ghost town, on the other. John Gold and Margaret Gold, in chapter 5, also find ambiguities in the changing meanings of the Culloden battlefield and how this mapped landscape of regret has been incorporated into the tourism spaces of Scottish nationalism.

Denis Wood's critiques of cartography and maps cover much the same ground as Harley's project and offer a way for our authors to extend their critiques of tourism maps (Wood 1991, 1992, 1993). He recognizes the social constructedness of maps, the powerful interests they serve, and the importance of all the symbols on these representations. Perhaps more than Harley, however, Wood focuses on how maps *work*. In *The Power of Maps* (1992) and other writings, Wood explains how maps "make present" the past, the future, and places other than that of the map's reader. In other words, maps are always linked to the spaces to which they give meaning. As Del Casino and Hanna point out in chapter 7, this has important methodological implications for investigating the intertextual relationships between space and representation. Similarly, Rob Shields provides a methodological and conceptual framework in chapter 1 for studying how maps and social practices mutually reproduce each other. For Wood himself, however, the appreciation that maps work through their ability to link themselves and map users to space does not extend from production to interpretation. While calling for an anthropology of map use (Wood and Fels 1986), he simply ends *The Power of Maps* by exhorting people to become their own cartographers—to make maps to serve their own interests.

In his critique of Harley, Matthew Sparke (1995) seeks to move past what he terms Harley's "demythologization" of cartography by employing Derridean deconstruction. Recognizing that cartography—and by extension the map—are "dynamic components of wider social dynamics," Sparke (1995: 4) urges cartographic critics to stop claiming that their deconstructions or demythologizations lead to the final and full understanding of any map. Rather, he suggests we continue to go back and "look for other ways in which the map, and what is supposed to lie outside of it—power relations, interpretation, the 'real' world, etc.—

might actually be still more complexly interrelated" (ibid.). It is this very complexity that the authors of this volume seek to address.

Complementing and often incorporating these efforts to retheorize the map, Duncan and Gregory (1999), Gregory (1994), Godlewska (1995), McClintock (1995), Belyea (1996), Livingstone (1992, 1999), and others have shown that cartography, as a discourse and practice, was central to the goals, justification, and administration of Western colonialism and imperialism. Godlewska (1995), for example, places cartography at the center of the Enlightenment's goals to accurately and objectively represent the world and attaches this science to colonialism in the context of the French attempts to conquer Egypt in 1803. Specifically, she discusses how the topographic maps in *Description de l'Égypte* "succeeded" in proving the superiority of European science and technology, in "writing out" modern Egypt in order to bring ancient Egypt to the fore, and in "bestowing" the gifts of modern and universal scientific knowledge to the inferior Egyptians (see also Duncan and Gregory 1999; Gregory 1994; Mitchell 1988). This cartographic validation of a European identity steeped in the ideals of the Enlightenment is complemented by Belyea's (1996) analyses of the interaction between European explorers and native peoples in Canada. She examines the fundamental incompatibility between native and Western mappings of the terrain and notes how the dominance of Western cartographic practices erased non-Western concepts of space. Considering the links between colonialism and modern Western tourism, these works provide valuable historical contexts for several of this book's case studies (e.g., Shields, chapter 1; Del Casino and Hanna, chapter 7).

These most recent critiques of cartographic discourse and practice provide one of the starting points for the essays in this volume. Sparke's works point a way toward challenging the boundaries between tourism maps and spaces, while Godlewska, Belyea, and other postcolonial theorists remind us that cartography is a practice always entangled with the material application of power (Sparke 1995). Furthermore, the link between cartography and colonialism provides one path toward understanding the complex interrelationships between the tourism map and identity. After all, as a part of the colonial project, cartography served to demarcate the Western, objective, rational, and modern (male) subject from the inferior, Oriental or African, traditional other. As we note later, modern tourists' experiences and gazes reproduce this demarcation as well. In the next section, we review similar developments in theorizing the relationships between space, identity, and representation in the tourism studies literatures.

Tourism Geographies

Unlike cartography, the study of tourism has not been a central object of analysis in the field of geography. There is an obvious reason for this absence: tourism was not a significant component of local or global economies for the first half of the twentieth century and thus it was neglected as an object of inquiry until after World War II. A second and more important reason, however, why tourism has remained on the margins of geographic inquiry is related to the internal dynamics of the discipline and the position of tourism studies within that field. Tourism geography emerged as a subfield in the 1960s and 1970s in conjunction with the rise in quantitative geography. As a result, tourism geography focused on a neoclassical economic approach of studying tourism supply and demand and, like mainstream cartography, operated within a rigid framework that neglected the critical turn (Mitchell and Murphy 1991 provide a comprehensive review of tourism geography in the 1980s).

By the 1990s, therefore, tourism geography was located in a few key universities and was limited in its scope of analysis. Britton (1991: 451), in a summary of tourism geography, laments the rigidity with which geographers have examined tourism:

> Although oversimplifying, we could characterise the "geography of tourism" as being primarily concerned with: the description of travel flows; microscale spatial structure and land use of tourist places and facilities; economic, social, cultural and environmental impacts of tourist activity; impacts of tourism in third world countries; geographic patterns of recreation and leisure pastimes; and the planning implications of all these topics.

In tourism geography, the major theoretical question to be overcome is similar to that for cartographers: what is the most accurate approach to modeling, or representing, the current tourism environment?

After Britton's critique of positivist tourism geography, some tourism geographers made the turn toward more "critical" approaches to studying tourism (e.g., Kinnaird, Kothari, and Hall 1994; Shaw and Williams 1994). Other geographers also began to engage the work of tourism studies scholars outside the field, such as MacCannell (1989) and Urry (1990, 1995), and have further developed approaches to studying tourism that take seriously questions raised by critical social theory (e.g., Shaw, Agarwal, and Bull 2000 provide a review of tourism geography in the United Kingdom; Crouch 1999b also includes a series of tourism-focused case studies). What has resulted is an unclearly demarcated boundary of "tourism geography" despite the continued existence of institutions that train geographers in the neoclassical approach to evaluating tourism. Indeed, most of the authors in this volume would not identify themselves as "tourism geographers" per se, and are more likely to align themselves with the subdisciplines of cultural, social, feminist, and/or historical geography. The interdisciplinary nature of tourism studies has meant that geographers have become an important part of the dialogue around the nature and social construction of tourism spaces, representations, and identities (e.g., Crang 1997). As such, tourism is now seen as a critical area of study for geographers as evinced by new tourism-oriented journals such as *Tourist Studies* and *Tourism Geographies*.

The engagement with tourism studies, and anthropology and sociology more broadly, has produced a plethora of work by geographers that interrogates tourism and leisure as a set of consumptive practices (e.g., Valentine 1999), as a means of socially constructing identities and subjectivities (e.g., Kayser Neilson 1999; Johnston 2001), and as a way in which places are sold (e.g., Gold and Ward 1994; Kearns and Philo 1993). Themes that have emerged out of the tourism studies literature, such as the critical examination of "authenticity," are now part and parcel of the discussions by and with geographers, particularly in the area of heritage and cultural tourism (e.g., Crang 1996; DeLyser 1999; Hoelscher 1998; Johnson 1996). In many ways, all of our authors examine "authenticity" to a certain extent, and Dwyer (chapter 2), Till (chapter 3), DeLyser (chapter 4), and Gold and Gold (chapter 5) focus on this concept quite explicitly.

The interrogation of "authentic" tourism has its roots in the work of Dean MacCannell, who published *The Tourist* in 1976 (reprinted in 1989). Working within a marxist tradition and drawing from the Frankfurt School, MacCannell articulated a "theory of the leisure class" in which he argued that the tourist is engaged in a modern form of religious ritual. The tourist seeks out an "authentic" other in an attempt to order and structure the world. Authenticity can never be fully realized, however, because it is constantly staged through the process of creating representations for tourists. MacCannell argues that these material and social practices banish the real or authentic to the backstage, outside the sight and reach of the tourist. Therefore, spaces of tourism hide the reality of everyday life under a myriad of representations that cover "the endless spherical system of connections which is society and the world" (MacCannell 1989: 56). Unfortunately, the causal arrow for MacCannell is largely unidirectional—representations point toward and simultaneously hide authentic spaces from the tourist, who can only be tricked by the representation or experience disappointment and alienation (see Taylor 2001 for an extended critique of MacCannell's theorization of authenticity).

Some of the limitations in MacCannell's work can be addressed through the work of John Urry (1990, 1995) and Chris Rojek and John Urry (1997a). Central to Urry's work is the "tourist gaze." This gaze is formulated in part through the collection of already existing representations of the tourist's destination—representations that promise a contrast from the tourist's everyday routines of work and home. Armed with such a set of "preconceived notions," the tourist travels to seek out and collect the representations that define a particular tourist gaze. The gaze becomes a lens through which the tourist experiences sites, cultures, and identities as different from her or his own (Urry 1990). Rojek and Urry extend Urry's earlier analysis, offering a theory of "travel" that examines how cultures are constructed through migration and interaction. What their work reveals is that tourism sites and representations are always contested. As they explain, "there are various possible readings of the same heritage" (1997a: 13), and thus any tourism site is always open to interpretation. As Gold and Gold point out in chapter 5, interpretations are dependent on the choices made by the organizers of tourism (and perhaps tourists themselves) about what is "authentic" and "inauthentic." Authenticity, as they argue, is not an a priori fact, therefore, but a cultural process (see Edensor 1998 for an excellent discussion of the cultural processes defining symbolic tourism sites). The meaning of the contested process of tourism is thus quite clear: "the 'culture' which is produced and consumed by tourists may not be as obviously artificial or contrived as once was thought. [And] It should not receive the denigration that tourism typically receives since all cultures are inauthentic and contrived" (Rojek and Urry 1997a: 11). Arguing further, Rojek and Urry aver that "all cultures get remade as a result of the flows of peoples, objects, and images across national borders, whether these involve colonialism, work-based migration, individual travel or mass tourism" (ibid.).

What emerges out of these critiques is that tourism is not simply an economy or a set of sites/sights, but is in itself a set of cultural practices (Crang 1996; see articles in Rojek and Urry 1997b). As Dwyer argues in chapter 2 of this volume, "The symmetrical authority of maps and monuments—in one case generated via claims to scientific accuracy, in the other by recourse to weighty materiality—stands in stark contrast to the inherent instability of the messages they bear." Therefore, the identities claimed through and represented by the production of such artifacts remain unstable and are contestable, which is what Curran argues in her reading of the mining landscape of Butte, Montana, in chapter 6. Thus, in the act of practicing and performing tourism, both tourists and non-tourists (tourism workers, "locals," etc.) construct and reconstruct social and spatial identities (Butler 1988, 1990; Natter and Jones 1997). As Crouch (1999a: 4) explains:

> To make a spatial practice is to engage in a transformation, not to return or imagine a past, but to creatively enliven, to repeat only the possibility of a new, unique moment. Agencies that represent tourism and leisure can only provide structures into which our imaginative practice enters and through which it explores its desires, and their promotional message that inflects these structures may not be ours. Crude consumption figures do not reveal very much of spatial practice. Indeed, those structures may deflect or deaden interest.

As a practice, tourism (and leisure and travel more generally) is inextricably linked to social and spatial identities. The identity categories constructed through tourism practices are always partial, however. They never capture the complex differences that constitute a particular social actor (Natter and Jones 1997). This allows, and is caused by, individuals who perform their identity within and beyond these categories (Butler 1988, 1990). In tourism spaces, tourism workers perform and thus reproduce the tourism space and their identity as "host" through their actions. As individuals, they are to "become" the site, thus hiding what is, for them, work. In chapter 4, DeLyser examines the practices or performances of tourism workers explicitly in her analysis of Bodie, and

Del Casino and Hanna in chapter 7 interrogate the ways in which host and tourist identities are formulated through representative practices. All such social actors "embody" identities through social and representational practices; and the tensions that are part and parcel of tourism and leisured spaces are materially present in bodily inscription and performative action (see Bassett and Wilbert 1999; Jarlov 1999; Laurier 1999 for a discussion of embodied social practices in tourism spaces). This becomes a crucial moment in chapter 1 of this volume, where Shields argues that bodies are integral to the processes of social spatialization, and again in Till's examination of the bodily practices of touring Berlin in chapter 3. At the same time, performances by tourists and tourism workers expose the partiality of the representational action through, for example, resistance to the acts themselves. Ad-libbing by tourism workers rewrites scripts and regulated work norms (Crang 1997; Warren 1999). Thus, identity categories only imperfectly capture the identities of social actors performing within and beyond these categories, making the relationship between the category and any actor ambiguous and open to contestation.

In the spaces of tourism and leisure, social and spatial identities collide and elide, creating moments of "uncertainty." The uncertainties expose the margins of categories, such as tourist and nontourist, and make present the struggles that arise as tourists and nontourists try to either reinforce or break down the tenuous social and spatial borders made possible through the practice of tourism. Curran's analysis of the contested representational regimes vying to produce Butte, Montana, is an excellent example of how maps are representative of tensions and conflict in and of the cultural landscape. As tourism and leisure continue to blur with work and other forms of travel, tourism spaces are changed and (re)arranged. In some cases, tourism has become almost unrecognizable as activists in Canada (Shields, chapter 1) and locals in Berlin (Till, chapter 3) both engage in tourist-like practices, further blurring the boundaries between tourist and nontourist. According to Shields (1991b: 81), such contestations to tourism identities and spaces create a "discontinuity in the social fabric, in social spaces, and in history" or moments of liminality. These liminal spaces and moments exist within and between space-fixing regulatory frameworks, creating tensions between the everyday and the exotic, the modern and the traditional, work and leisure, discipline and freedom. These tensions are defined by the particular regulatory regime the tourist is "escaping" through the practice of tourism.

Tourism spaces are thus tension-filled because they exist at a set of constructed boundaries between the exotic and the everyday, between resistance and regulation. Further, tourist entrepreneurs and government officials depend on the maintenance of these dualisms in order to market such spaces as "unique" to the tourist. But while particular representations, including maps, appear to fix such dualisms, their ambiguous relationships to social actors performing their identities in tourism spaces ensure that maps and other representations may both legitimate and destabilize identity categories. This destabilization is possible because no one is merely a "tourist" or a "tourist worker," but is instead a multiple subject constitutive of many discourses and identities. Each actor exists in a variety of social spaces simultaneously—at the "center" of one category designation and at the "margins" of another (hooks 1991; Blunt and Rose 1994).

Tourism Maps, Spaces, and Identities

Tourism maps, and the spaces they (re)present and (re)produce, are one place where we can explore the production of category designations and the tensions constituted by their ambiguous relationships to social actors attempting to "perform" or "practice" particular identities. Here we would like to suggest two things. First, the collision of identity categories and the blurring of their boundaries are both enabled by and constitutive of tourism maps and spaces. The everyday/exotic, modern/traditional, and disciplinary/resistance dualisms are definitive signs not merely of tourism, but of the individuals who perform within, reproduce, and destabilize these spaces and categories. Second, the tourism map represents the tensions among these supposed dichotomies through its depiction/creation of certain identities as parts of tourist sites, its imperfect concealment of other social actors (especially tourism workers), and its images of the tourists themselves.

The title of this volume, *Mapping Tourism*, expresses the intentions of our authors to destabilize the assumption that tourism maps and other popular cartographies are marginal texts that tell us little about everyday social and spatial relations. Rather, we argue that mapping is a dynamic process and tourism maps deserve our critical attention for they expose the ways in which identities are constructed and (re)produced. As intertextual objects, tourism maps are sites through which we can investigate the complex relations and flows of power that bring meaning to maps and the spaces they claim to represent. Tourism spaces, like the maps themselves, are also fluid processes that are intertextually related to the myriad representational practices that partially construct boundaries around particular places, thereby identifying them as "tourist" or "nontourist." As Shields points out in this volume, "The purpose of these texts [tourism maps] is to allow a past to be actualized in part by giving direction or illustration, and in part by fitting together with other tourist texts. This crucial quality of both intertextuality and of seamlessness informs itineraries, re-enactments, observed restagings of historical events and drama on site." In *Mapping Tourism,* our authors address these very issues. It is these interrogations of the interrelationships between past and present, tourist and nontourist, practice and identity, materiality and discourse that give life to the provocative analyses that follow and that animate the objectives of this volume. Thus, this volume is *not* simply about the lines, points, and images that, at first glance, seem to comprise tourism maps. Rather, *Mapping Tourism* is about the broader social and spatial contexts in and of which such objects are materially produced and consumed as people map tourism spaces through representational and social practice.

Reading the Text

The chapters that follow interrogate the multiple, contested meanings, inclusions/exclusions, and representations that constitute tourism maps and spaces. By focusing on the practices of mapping and (re)mapping tourism space, the contributors to this volume explore both the tensions that exist at the margins of various overlapping spaces and the intertextual linkages among and between representational practices, spaces, and identities. Such a strategy demands that the authors investigate text and context, history and geography. The practices of mapping space are thus not considered to be isolated processes, and maps are not examined as final products. Central to the discussions that follow is that maps, in the broadest sense of the term, are in a constant state of (re)production and are mediated by how they are deployed in relation to particular contexts and spaces.

We begin with Rob Shields's investigation of the multiple mappings of Québec in relation to the international politics that marked the Free

Trade Area of the Americas (FTAA) meeting in the summer of 2001. Working through the concept of social spatialization, Shields examines the ways in which recent political protests in Québec, and the rather harsh state-led reactions to those protests, have challenged the boundaries of Québec's historic tourism center and created new place images and myths in and of the city. Shields introduces many themes found in later chapters—most notably the relationships among place, memory and heritage, and bodily practices—and, therefore, provides a link between the theoretical arguments outlined in this Introduction and the rest of the case studies.

In similar fashion to Shields's analysis of Québec, Owen Dwyer's analysis of maps and monuments explores the tensions that surround the inclusion and exclusion of particular representations in the memorial landscapes of Alabama. Although separated from Québec by thousands of miles and numerous layers of contexts, Dwyer's Alabama is as contested and political as Shields's Canada. Dwyer examines the interplay of text and context, materiality and discourse, and how the relations between these processes reproduce memories of particular places and actions. As he argues, "This [theoretical] perspective allows memorial texts to be conceived of as in the process of becoming rather than in a static, essentialized state." Dwyer thus works to destabilize the sedimented discourses that have reproduced civil rights in the U.S. South in ways that fail to seriously consider the complex social and spatial relations that made such a movement possible.

Karen Till also examines the politics of mapping and memory. She does this through a discussion of how tourism maps of Berlin's process of construction (and reconstruction) expose the tensions and interrelations between the "front" and "back" stages of this "(future) global city." The maps of Berlin's reconstruction, and the tours that work in conjunction with those maps, allow those who participate in the tours to become part of the tourism site itself. Locals become part of the "selling of place" that often marks the reconstruction process. But Till's interviews with "local tourists" also illustrate the contested nature of the narratives of Berlin's reconstruction and of tourism more generally. Are the people visiting the "New Berlin" really tourists? Her analysis thus exposes not only the political nature of mapping, but the intertexuality that defines tourism practices and their concurrent representations. In so doing, Till interrogates how "locals [use the tours] to move out of their local networks and daily routines into 'unfamiliar' parts of the city."

Dydia DeLyser's discussion of Bodie, California, also engages narrative strategies, intertextual linkages, and discussions of memory. Unlike Dwyer or Till, however, her contribution is methodological; she provides an ethnography of the tourism map. DeLyser places her work relative to Wood and Fels's (1986) call for anthropologies of maps and focuses her ethnography on a major lacuna in tourism studies—how tourists use the maps and brochures intended to guide visitors to and through tourism spaces. DeLyser thus examines how maps work to reconstruct the past from the perspective of the present. "While some visitors," she observes, "depart from the brochure's text to create descriptions meaningful to their own lives, others draw intertextual connections that are more broadly held, linking life in Bodie to life in the American mythic West." She thus considers how such mapped representations constitute a limited reading of Bodie, for both the representation itself and the use of that representation are often marked by partial readings of Bodie's longer history and geography.

Disentangling historical narratives as well, John Gold and Margaret Gold investigate the historical production of Culloden, a Scottish war memorial site. Employing textual analysis in their investigation of how mappings of Culloden change in relationship to the history of Scottish nationalism, Gold and Gold focus on the narratives that have moved this battlefield from a place of obscurity to a site of tourism. As a "landscape of regret," Culloden, like Shields's Québec, Dwyer's Alabama, and DeLyser's Bodie, becomes a site of memory with intertextual connections to the spaces and identities of nationalism, language, and culture. Through their textual (re)reading of Culloden's changing narrative, Gold and Gold examine the process by which "Culloden has been mapped and remapped . . . as different generations contest its cultural meaning." In ways similar to Curran in chapter 6, Gold and Gold investigate the competing meanings of places of tourism and the mapped representations that selectively (re)present tourism history and memory.

Mary Curran's provocative analysis of two mappings of Butte, Montana, juxtaposes the efforts of two organizations (the Butte Chamber of Commerce and the Environmental Protection Agency) in trying to map Butte as a place of tourism, on the one hand, and as a place of ecological disaster, on the other, with the local, working-class definitions both maps seek to erase. As she deftly argues, reading the maps in conjunction allows one to expose the partiality of each map and reveal in one map what the other seeks to exclude. Curran's reading of these maps offers a distinct methodological contribution to our investigation into the social and spatial relations that constitute tourism maps. As Curran argues, "It is not enough . . . to deconstruct the historical narratives that inform these maps. Instead, the intention . . . is to destabilize the maps' representational regimes by indicating how these texts try to subvert 'the multiplicity and possibility of alternative voices' (Massey 1999: 281)." Curran continues: "Reading the maps against each other, we begin to disentangle the complex webs of social and spatial relations that have produced these images for popular consumption."

In chapter 7, Del Casino and Hanna also present a method for the critical examination of tourism maps. In their investigation of how tourism maps *work* to reproduce and represent the identities and spaces of sex tourism in Thailand, they focus on the complex intertextual connections that make maps integral parts of the intertwined processes of identity formation and the production of space. Employing the concept of "map space," Del Casino and Hanna argue that maps, as intertextual objects, are materially interconnected to other spaces and texts, both past and present, and are thus rich sites for the critical interrogation of tourism practices and spaces. "Therefore," they argue, "we read maps not just as texts but as spaces. As such, a map space is not bound by the margins of the paper on which it is printed, but is inscribed with meaning through its intertextual linkages with other texts and spaces. In addition, map spaces are sites through which we can examine the processes of identity construction, and the historically and spatially contingent social relationships that constitute identity categories."

Throughout these ethnographic and textual analyses of tourism maps, tourism spaces are marked by ambiguity, instability, and tension. All of these characteristics are (re)produced and (re)presented through the complex intertextual relationships between tourism maps and tourism sites, as well as with other texts, spaces, and identities. Mapping tourism space is concomitant with the mappings of bodies, performances, and various tourism practices. After all, maps are materially produced and practiced. They work with bodies by guiding, reconstructing, writing, concealing, and representing spatial identities. Thus, tourism maps are neither innocent nor simple. Their seeming fixity as power-imbued products of crass commercialism or weighty memorialism is destabilized when they are considered in relation to the unfinished and potentially undisciplined practices that are part and parcel of everyday tourism spaces.

Because we are bound by certain publishing conventions to number and order the following pages there might be a tendency to reproduce this book in the fashion that we have chosen to deliver it to the reader. In reality, there are a number of different orders and paths a reader might take to explore the many interconnected themes in this volume. The tensions between local heritage and globalization, for example, are front and center in Shields's work on Québec, but also lurk in Del Casino and Hanna's chapter on sex tourism spaces in Bangkok. Alternatively, a reader interested in methodology could group the chapters into sections on ethnographic (chapters 3, 4, and 6) versus textual (chapters 1, 2, 5, and 7) approaches. Or, another person might be interested in reading the chapters on heritage tourism by Dwyer, DeLyser, Gold and Gold, while contrasting those with the current political and social tensions examined by Shields, Del Casino and Hanna, and Curran. We mention these merely to encourage readers to make their use of this book in much the same way that tourists and tourism workers make their own uses of the mapped spaces of tourism.

Note

1. We use these multiple metaphors in order to distance our own perspective from that of structuralism, which would place the structures "underneath" or "below the surface." Instead, we want to argue that the intertextual moments are not embedded in deep structures (see Sayer 1985 for a discussion of realism in geography).

1. Political Tourism

Mapping Memory and the Future at Québec City

Rob Shields

This paper examines the political and cultural mapping of an Economic Summit on the Free Trade Area of the Americas and anticorporate globalization protests onto Québec City as a famous tourist destination. This "new tourism" brings political purpose and engagement to the traditional notion of travel and tourism. "Activist tourists" have become an important issue for customs and immigration practices at national borders, and political activist tourists have been vilified in the media, whether discovered among mercenaries in Afghanistan, working volunteers in Calcutta, observers in Chiapas, or en route to a protest rally in Canada. This might challenge most students of tourism, but the manner of travel, demands on services, and activities outside of protest rallies per se are all common elements with many other types of tourist and forms of tourism.

Québec City is one of the premier tourist sites in North America, known in brochures for the "medieval," touristy charm of walled "Old Quebec" and for its historic significance as a decisive site in battles between France and England over the possession of North American colonies. In English, the accent of the proper spelling appears when people wish to "accent" the politicized history and identity of the place. But for Anglophone tourists, it is always the less challenging, unaccented "Quebec" that is referred to in promotional literature. Vieux

1

Québec, in contrast, is the capital of the Province of Québec and, therefore, the capital of the French language in North America—a site of language politics, of memory, and of rituals of commemoration. Overlaid on this, in April 2001 Québec City played host to the Summit of the Americas, where the leaders of Western Hemisphere states (all, save Cuba) discussed a Free Trade Area of the Americas (FTAA). In part because of the grim precedent of the North American Free Trade Agreement (NAFTA), after which FTAA is patterned, hundreds joined protests against neoliberal, corporate globalization and what it represents: the lack of labor mobility, the loss of local control and of sovereignty over health and safety, environmental, and labor practices of multinational businesses.[1] In anticipation of the protests, a 3-meter (9-foot), 3.8-kilometer chain-link fence was erected—almost a parody of the eighteenth-century Ramparts surrounding the inner city of Vieux Québec. Up to sixty thousand participants in protest marches traveled from across Québec, Ontario, and the United States to join an international group of anti-neoliberal globalization activists and labor representatives.[2] They were denigrated as "protest tourists" and the media attempted in vain to find veterans of protests at similar meetings at Seattle, Prague, or Buenos Aires in the crowd—hooligans who might be labeled "fans" of protests. We will not, therefore, speak of "protest tourists" but of "activist tourists" and the interaction between the tourist image and tourism maps and new maps and cartographies of power and public assembly at Québec City.

As a walled and nostalgically European outpost of the sixteenth-and seventeenth-century conquest of North America, "Old Quebec," as the tourist brochures call it, has been the subject of centuries of tourism maps and guides. A new layer to this representation has now been added by the extensive international media coverage that included not only photographs of two breaches of "the Fence," the protesters, and the more than eighteen million U.S. dollars in tear gas and rubber bullets dispensed on them, but also maps of the central area of Québec City showing the Fence, routes of marches and assembly areas, and the location of breaches and battles. These new maps put a new face on "Old Quebec," showing a cordon sanitaire that supplements the ten-meter city walls and formidable escarpment and ramparts that once made the city an almost impregnable stronghold, guarding the access to the North American interior via the Saint Lawrence River. Access to private resi-

barrier put up around an area

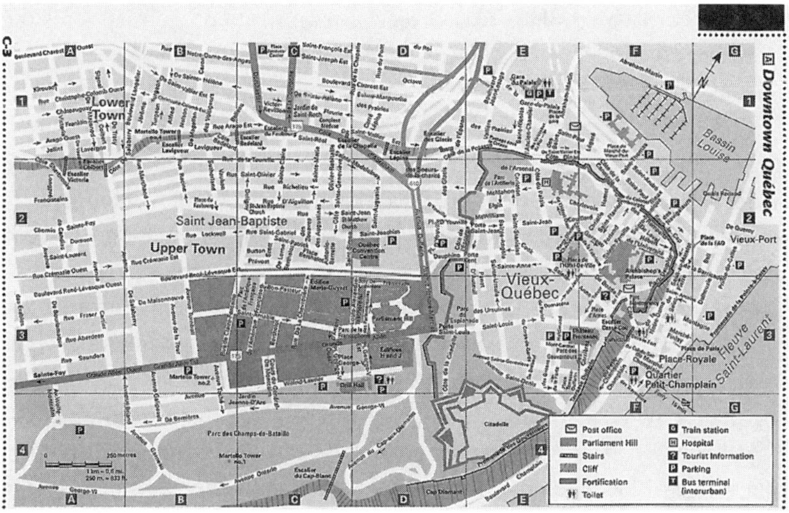

Figure 1.1. Tourism map, "Downtown Québec." *Where,* 2000.

dences and businesses was restricted. Public spaces inside the Fence were unilaterally privatized by being put under exclusive police control and use for the conference.

Like the narrow streets of the walled city, this article twists and turns through the maps of tourism guides and media coverage to place tourism maps and tourism practices within the theoretical context of social spatialization to explain their contributions to the creation and maintenance of place-myths of unaccented "Old Quebec City." A new layer of complexity is then added, for history and memory are political and in "Quebec City" they occupy physical spaces, such as battlegrounds, monuments, and city walls. These reminders of the history of Québecois in North America and of the city Vieux Québec as a site of struggle threaten to overwhelm the more comfortable, touristic "Old Quebec." This historical instability was pushed into the present during the events and protests of the summit. More than merely a question of the past, and even an issue of the present, I argue that place and memory hold a key to futures; spatializations operate not merely in, say, a Foucauldian panoptic present; spatializations have a future-oriented force. An "anticipatory spatialization" promises a Ville de Québec that is a national, not a provincial, capital. More darkly, through free-trade images and rhetoric exemplified by a recent postage stamp, the Québec

similarities btw. old + new city with fences, battlegrounds, etc.

Foucau talked about panopticon: tower with prison cells in the bottom and a look out at top of tower, and can see into every different cell from top. Basically - way of controlling space through controlling people who are in it by always watching and observing. If tourists are always watching a city, they will change what happens in that city.

summit is the birthplace of a project for a "unified" hemisphere, the "Americas"—the "Free Trade Area of the Americas."

Mapping Québec

Tourism maps of places such as "Old Quebec" are quite distinct from wider spatial representations such as a map of the Western Hemisphere or driving maps and road atlases. Significantly, tourism maps are rotated off of the North–South vertical axis, thus violating the "North is up" convention (see Figure 1.1). Particular features of the environment are picked out or selected for various forms of visual overstatement, such as inserting axonometric images of key landmarks or adding shadows to the plan view of historic buildings. In the tourism maps of unaccented "Quebec City," the cartographic grid is instead determined by coverage of a range of key sites and aesthetic issues such as the alignment of the principal streets horizontally across the page. The grid is a matrix for referencing sites (addresses) and areas identified in the accompanying text or listed in legends. The map itself is presumed to be docile—a neutral reference that relates the whole and the parts.

A map torn from *Where* (2000), a guidebook of current events and tourism-related commercial establishments in Québec City (see Figure 1.1), is centered on the business and political precinct of the Upper Town. It indicates historic buildings and the Walls and Parliamentary district in gray. Landmarks such as the historic Château Frontenac and the nineteenth-century Parliament facing the Place D'Youville (a prominent site of political protests over the centuries) are identified and numbered. Parks such as the Plains of Abraham battlefield (Parc des Champs-de-Bataille, Battlefield Park) are in bright green, the river is in blue, and major roads in red and streets in white are set against a background green tone. The Escarpment that separates the walled Upper Town from Lower Town and the river is an earthy brown. However, the dull green background tends to flatten the topography so the unfamiliar tourist will often not realize that there is up to a 260-foot difference in height between the Lower Town on the riverfront and Upper Town or anticipate the steepness of streets. Certainly, the Escarpment is steep enough to make the funicular that connects them a worthwhile ride.

Mapping the Fence

As a result of the summit, new maps of Québec appeared showing the Fence alongside other prominent touristic elements of the city (see Figure

1.2). But this new map, like all tourism maps, as Alistair Bonnett demonstrates in his pioneering article "Landranger 168" (1996), merely continues the braiding of politics and history with topography to reinforce the preservation of a walled city center and to maximize its French "European" character. Québec is often advertised and widely conceived as "a little piece of Europe." Tourism maps indicate the sites and itineraries of ritualized, spatial practices that bring the past into the present. They spatialize or "cast" Québec City as a site of present-day difference.

The tourism maps' orientation to convenience is continued in the maps of the Fence, dubbed the "Wall of Shame" by demonstrators, politicians, and many local residents alike (Figure 1.2; see also Glassman, Prudham, and Wainwright 2000). In mapping the exclusion zone, this map differentiates the Fence from the perimeter lying along the "Falaise" or Escarpment, and the Ramparts of the Upper Town and Citadel. The key hotels and workplaces of the heads of state are picked out with numbers (the Hilton, Centre des congrès, and so on). These are overlaid on a map showing the local landmarks such as the Parliament, convents, the outline of the Citadel, and others. The historic, symbolically all-powerful site of the battle of the Plains of Abraham (Parc des Champs-de-Bataille) is also enclosed, preventing demonstrators from congregating in the largest open space of the city and occupying what is both a symbolic site of Québecois identity and, in the eighteenth century, a decisive point of hemispheric struggle between empires. This vast area has been cleared of its nineteenth-century buildings and industry to create a park or large field to the west of the Citadel where British infantry faced off with the French garrison after slipping past the fortress and scaling the Escarpment under cover of night.

Although the map of the Fence is intended to report and inform, it became a required text for protesters who needed local knowledge (see Lachance and Norcliffe 2001, who include their own excellent map) to find not only the Fence but strategic points and sectors along it. The large gathering of protesters reflected many agendas. Some groups, such as labor unions, were seeking a seat at the table; others objected to neoliberal globalization or to capitalism in all its forms, while others simply objected to the Fence itself. These cleavages were reflected in a diversity of tactics. Different groups traveled on different routes and congregated at different points along the Fence. Moderate mainstream unions and nongovernmental organizations sponsored marches that avoided going near the Fence. Many others participated in a pre-summit "People's Summit"

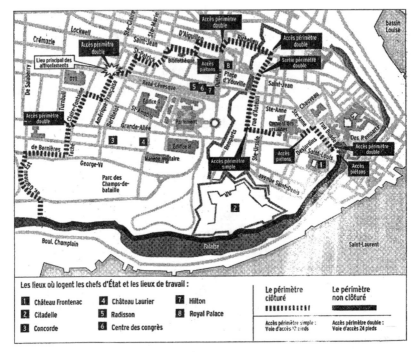

Figure 1.2. The Fence. *La Presse,* April 21, 2001.

in the parliamentary district, while the "black bloc" of anarchists and proponents of direct action attacked the Fence and succeeded in pulling a part of it down on Friday, April 20, when heads of state arrived (see "Lieu principal des affrontements," Principal site of clashes, Figure 1.2). Peaceful protesters were only a few meters away, singing and chanting. The Fence became a linear political strip along which flowers were laid at some points while activists attempted to chain themselves to it at other points. But this information is lost on the map. The newspaper maps of the Fence are close relatives of the political cartoon. Although in some cases the routes of marches were noted, maps of the Fence caricature the protests by highlighting only the most violent sites of protest, making the power of cartography to shape understanding obvious by the maps' incompleteness and blandness.

Tourism and Social Spatialization

These maps reveal the extent to which, if the site is already remarkable, the topology is overwritten with "place-images" (Shields 1991a, 1991b) that make up a "place-myth" that is both touristic and political. What might merely be notable or strategically advantageous topography is only the geological foundation of a mythic and site-specific landscape of historic national events, memory, and Québecois-nationalist history. This overlay sits in an imperfect and ambiguous relationship to the empirically verifiable city that one can encounter, smell, taste, and interact with. As a result, the tourism maps are accompanied with detailed instructions on how the materially real is to be related to the representations (texts, maps, images), all of which we are assured are true, "accurate," and equally "real."

Any site is interconnected into an overall relational network of similarly mythified sites and regions in which each place is distinguished not only by its proper place-myth but by its distinctiveness and contrasts with other sites. Tourism maps of one place are related to other, smaller-scaled driving maps, which take us to other places that are presented in their own tourism maps at a detailed scale. This *geography of difference* is socially constructed over the long term and constitutes a spatialization of places and regions as "places for this" and "places for that"; that is, each site or area is construed as appropriate for certain social activities and behaviors—and this is central to its identity. The places, are cast—or *spatialized*—as certain types of place: romantic, harsh, warm, boring, polluted, foreign, and so on. The "first nature" of topology is reconstructed as a "second nature" (Lefebvre 1991).

This second nature is not merely a fixed system of coordinates; it is a relational network of differences that provides the principle and rationale for movement between places and regions. Rather than a fixed structure, the process of *spatialization* is a process and a horizon of meanings. To contrast with most tourist literature that refers to the elements and crowds assembled at a site to create its ambiance, spatialization theory equally stresses what is excluded and what remains elsewhere as contrasts and as distant places—such as a tourist's home—in relation to which the tourists' and protesters' experience of Québec is constructed. Each of these place-myths is the locus of intense struggle over its meaning. Places are taken up from the raw topological diversity of the land and integrated into a meaningful human geography that is nonetheless contested. This *social spatialization* lies at the core of tourist destination choices (Shields 1991b) and is the basis of our geographical sense of the world as a space of difference and distance.

It is in part because of the geographic prominence of the walled, historic center of Québec City that it has been possible to maintain the illusion of a city frozen in history. This is true both visually, in terms of the skyline, and in the close-focus experience of tourists and residents' image of the city. Newer neighborhoods dating from the late eighteenth century, the suburbs of the late nineteenth, not to mention the post–Second World War sprawl of neighborhoods now form a continuous urban agglomeration stretching along both the north and south shores of the Saint Lawrence River. The literature and images of these neighborhoods are widely known to French-speaking and English-speaking audiences alike through the work of popular writers such as Roger Lemelin, whose 1948 novel *Les Plouffes* (English trans. Lemelin 1950) has been made into a film and a television series. These areas are much more typical of the urban morphologies of other North American cities, but in the English television version they are not connected with the almost museum-like tourist image of "Old Quebec," as the walled center is known.

Intense media coverage and a legacy of maps of the protests at the Québec summit added another layer and tension to the place-myth of the city. But after the fact, even the graffiti has been painted over. The newspaper maps and media texts are the sole remaining testimony to the Fence, which was constructed so as to be disassembled in time for the summer tourist season. Key sites of conflict, such as near the Grand Theatre at the corner of Boulevard René-Lévesque and Ste-Claire, become embedded more into local memory as the place where the Wall of Shame collapsed, rather than into tourism texts and maps.

Tourism maps contribute to maintaining touristic place-myths by simply leaving out details or entire cities that do not conform to the touristic myths, however much the narratives of guidebooks may be criticized or struggled over. In the case of "Old Quebec," the city clearly extends off the top and left-hand sides of the tourism map (Figure 1.1). But on the right, and in the top right-hand corner (map reference G1), the city blocks are not only not represented but a light green tone gives a pleasant and reassuring sense of nature. What is there (industry) is not relevant to most tourists. Absence or exclusion is the Achilles' heel of place-based research and too great a faith in the tourism map or the guidebook. Place cannot be studied apart from its embeddedness within spatialization or its relation to other places, to the absent, is lost.

In the process of social spatialization, places are not only overcoded but interrelated via classification schemes and reifying divisions into, for example, locals' and tourists' parts of a city, safe and dangerous areas, ours and theirs, work and leisure places. More than mere function is at issue. This "production of space" concerns social and cultural reproduction and interaction. People learn the comportment associated with a place as well as with their social status and gender. Spatialization is thus not only a matter of sites and networks of space, but exists at all levels to tie the micro scale of the body to the macro scale of the region. Bodies are "spaced": the performative carriage of the body, the gestures, actions, and rhythms of everyday routines deemed socially appropriate to a particular site, are etched onto place and into the somatic memory of individual inhabitants. Such a practical, somatic *hexis* is usually not recalled except with an awkward self-consciousness when one finds oneself "out of place," as the idiomatic expression puts it. Spatialization is thus both written and read practically by bodies as much as metaphorically through the conceptual operations of discourse. Goffman has referred to these as "meaning frames" (1974) and others have referred to habitual routines (Bourdieu 1977) and to "scripts" for everyday interaction—however contested or renegotiated "on the fly" (Smith 1987). At the core of spatialization is a process of simplifying for cognitive purposes, and of stereotyping as a pragmatic strategy for everyday life.

As a cognitive and practical habitus, social spatialization is a source not only of social algorithms (cf. Bourdieu 1977) but of allegorical solutions (attempting to solve new problems or cultural conundrums by metaphorically assimilating them to established routines or to the implied nexus of behavioral codings implicit in a place-myth), differentiating categories (for example, "right" versus "left" and "near" versus "far"), and conceptual shortcuts including stereotypes and "metaphors we live by" (Lakoff and Johnson 1979). Spatialization ties together the cultural conception of the environment with individual bodies to sediment, in a practical and physical manner, social reproduction in line with place-myths (however contested or only pretending to the status of the hegemonic). It embraces not only spatial patterns but temporal rhythms. *Place is a memory bank for societies.* It takes on this memory function by virtue of retaining and displaying the inscribed traces of rhythmic repetition of routines in time and space in a manner that is relatively difficult for a single individual to erase or for a small group to change in a short time without the investment of a great deal of effort (the wholesale and total destruction of a city, for example).

Tourism maps are part of tourist texts and media that might be classed along with guidebook narratives and a panoply of inscriptions ranging from arrows, plaques posted by heritage authorities, and indicators of what can be observed from scenic lookouts or in a panoramic view. Through quoting, summarizing, and imitating, these texts are closely related to full histories, paintings of famous events, "tourist art," and souvenirs. The purpose of many of these texts is to allow a past to be actualized in part by giving direction or illustration, and in part by fitting together with other tourist texts. This crucial quality of both intertextuality and seamlessness informs itineraries, reenactments, observed restagings of historical events, and dramas on site. Place-images depend on textual integration. A tourism map must work together with a guidebook narrative, which in turn must not clash with actors or animators in period costume describing their lives, the distances they might walk each day, and so on.

One of the major touristic aspects of a place is this embedded sense of historical and repeated routines—whether desirable or undesirable according to the tourists and tourism entrepreneurs. Places such as Québec City are also memory banks of cultural traditions and political events that bring tourists face-to-face with local culture and tradition. The touristic, promotional images of the city must necessarily fit tourism and leisure activities into the existing matrix of the physical and historical aspects of the place-myth. The preexisting elements of the place-myth must be recast as pleasurable if they are not already deemed so. In effect, this comes down to providing illustrations of possible pleasurable coordinations between tourists' bodies and the site itself—a spatialization that integrates the very bodies of tourists, in an advantageous manner. In this process, tourism maps, tourist itineraries, and illustrations such as postcards and media images are central.[3] If only by smoothing over the rugged contours of the city with a reassuring dull green, the tourism maps of "Quebec City" flatten the space of the city into a more welcoming format.

The Image of "Old Quebec"

The street names and toponymy of the city preserve its history. During the late nineteenth and early twentieth centuries, the touristic image of "Old Quebec" was constructed first from its reputation as an impregnable, natural fortress that took advantage of the high cliff of Cap

Diamant to control passage to the settled regions of the Saint Lawrence River and Montreal upstream. Samuel de Champlain established the first settlement below the cliffs in 1608 that was captured by the English in 1629–32 (an early Anglophone occupation of the site that is virtually erased in the "Frenchness" of Québec City's reputation). The new "Old City" on the cliffs above this "Lower Town" dates from 1633. The maps capture the manner in which the walls were an extension of European defensive theory and military architecture rather than the mobile forms of bush warfare practiced by native groups, and eventually by American troops. Together with the fortress of Louisbourg, Québec was intended to anchor France's claims on North America.[4] Both proved strategically ill-conceived: their remoteness from supply meant that when battles were fought around them, victory depended on whichever side was able to resupply and reinforce its troops first. Louisbourg fell after the siege of 1758 and Québec fell to the British in the famous battle of the Plains of Abraham in 1759 in which the commanding generals of both sides—Wolfe for the British and Montcalm for the French—were fatally wounded. The battle is often reduced to the status of a duel between these two figures. The city was then retaken by French reinforcements dispatched from Montreal. In turn, these troops retreated once British reinforcements arrived, leaving the continent in the hands of the British.

In the 1800s, as one of the major landmarks along the Saint Lawrence River, Québec was a natural stopping-off place for shipboard passengers. As a site of a battle popularly credited with deciding the fate of North America, it became an obligatory stop in the secular ritual of commemorative tourism in which travelers could view the topography of this "wonder of the New World," witness the site of historic decision, and savor, with (and often as) the victors, the dominating view over the river and the Francophone, Québecois countryside from the cliff-top promenade. The Canadian Pacific Railways' *Ancient City of Quebec* guidebook claimed:

> Here civilization first began to conquer savagery in this northern land, because here are the battlegrounds on which the best blood of Old France and Old England met in deadly combat and decided the fate of half a continent. (CPR 1926: 3)

From the Dufferin Terrace in front of the Château Frontenac, one still has one of the greatest views in any city.

> Jutting out along the brink . . . 200 feet above the roofs of the quaint
> "Lower Town" of the old city, is the Dufferin Terrace—a Government-
> built promenade which takes rank with the Hove Lawns and Esplanade
> at Brighton, England as the resort of beauty and fashion, and far sur-
> passes almost any promenade in the world in the tremendous pano-
> rama that it commands. At the eastern end of this promenade rises
> the beautiful pile of the Château Frontenac, which the western end
> is under the shadow of the grim fortress known as the Citadel from
> which flaps the Union Jack, symbol of Empire of which none are more
> proud than the people of Quebec [sic]. (Ibid., 12–13)

One popular manner of sharing the spoils of history with the victors is
to occupy, however momentarily, this position—literally and figuratively "above" the terrain of everyday life. The result is a vast still-life pano-
rama, a gesture that sees the land and inhabitants "laid out" for inspec-
tion in terms reminiscent of the objectives of the Ordinance Survey.[5]
The view was described to prospective tourists in grand terms that are
entirely lost in today's tightly focused and functional tourism maps:

> Clustered on and around rocky and precipitous heights that resemble
> Gibraltar in their frowning impregnability, this wonderful old city com-
> mands a landscape that takes rank among the great show places of the
> world. The "Upper Town" looks away out over the mighty St. Lawrence
> to where bustling cliffs as high as its own are dotted with the houses
> of the town of Levis and crowned by the immense forts erected by the
> British Government. Far in the distance beyond are outlying spurs of
> the ancient Appalachian Mountains that extend 1300 miles to south
> and east. Looking in the other direction, the bold outlines of Cape
> Tourmente forty miles away on the north shore can be seen, while back
> from the north shore line the eye is carried to where the crests of the
> Laurentians, the oldest mountain range in the world, fade away in bil-
> low upon billow of wonderful blues and purples that melt imperceptibly
> into the azure of the sky. Beyond that horizon lies a vast unpeopled wil-
> derness that stretches sheer to the Polar regions. (Ibid., 3–4)

European opinion makers, guides, and travelogue writers sought to
conjure up and place each city in a single aphorism so that it might, on
the one hand, be known, and, on the other, expected or anticipated.
Thus, Henry Ward Beecher called Québec "a populated cliff" (rather

oversimplifying) and "a small bit of mediaeval Europe perched upon a rock and dried for keeping—a curiosity that has not its equal in its kind on this side of the ocean" (cited in ibid., 6). Québec is cast as European, even if it has to be so in a patchwork of European fragments: "Strolling in Lower Town one might fancy himself in Amiens . . . and along the Grand [sic] Allée, running right across the Plains of Abraham, you might be in Brussels or Paris, only that Clifton Terrace seems to recall Kensington" (ibid., 7). Henri Lefebvre argued that such codings of places and regions are treated by social actors and institutional decision makers as nature—as a priori material objects. It is as if the historical place-myth were as solid as the high bluff on which the city walls sit (Lefebvre 1991: 89–90).

Charles Dickens, on his nuptial trip, which was to popularize the practice of honeymoons, wrote for his readers:

> The impression made upon the visitor by this Gibraltar of America, its giddy heights, its citadel suspended, as it were in air, its picturesque steep streets and frowning gateways and the splendid views which burst upon the eye at every turn is at once unique and lasting and make it a place not to be forgotten. (Cited in CPR 1926: 6)

The skyline and tourism guides of Québec City are dominated by four elements represented in all tourism maps, and today in the maps of the Fence. The Ramparts of the Old City follow the edge of the most famous element of the "first nature," the Escarpment (labeled "Falaise," Figure 1.2; shaded Figure 1.1). They were built by the French in the 1730s and 1740s and expanded under the British administration against American threats of invasion in the 1770s through the early 1800s. A Citadel (2 in the Legend, Figure 1.2; labeled Figure 1.1), built by the British in the 1760s on a classic defensive plan of angled walls, completes the Ramparts. The fourth element, the Château Frontenac (1 in the Legend, Figure 1.2; shaded, Figure 1.1), was constructed by the Canadian Pacific Railway as part of an ambitious plan to provide luxury hotels for rail travelers crossing the continent or doing the "Northern Tour."[6] The hotel was first opened in 1893 and expanded during the early 1920s (see Shields 1998).

In brochures of Québec City, history—the grand history of battles and discoveries at that—is the prime commodity offered, underlining the memory functions of Québec. The Upper and Lower Towns of "Old

Quebec" are presented as a sort of living museum—a site of tourist consumption overcoded by history. "Museumified" areas continue to function as urban infrastructure for an itinerant population of tourists and service workers who live away from the town. The provision of services is dominated by the infrastructure necessary to support travelers, while offering as many opportunities to consume as possible. At the same time, however, these are more than merely consumption sites: they claim an authenticity that differentiates them from theme parks, however clever. In addition, they support a modified form of urban activity: they make the past present, bringing an archaeological form of history—stones and material artifacts—forward into the symbolic culture, habitual practices, and routine rhythms of contemporary life. The significance of the Ramparts on every tourism map of "Old Quebec" is not only a result of their prominence as a barrier that must be negotiated (the Escarpment is much larger, and is itself presented as a tourist object through local archaeological and geological exhibits); they are *the* military artifact, far more tangible and visible than the battlefield.

The ritual aspects of a tourist's visit to Québec include taking in sites in the Upper Town, including the view from the Promenade des Gouverneurs (Figure 1.1) and walks along the Ramparts with their canons pointing riverward at an unseen foe; the steep descent into the Lower Town (identified as stairs, Figure 1.1) with its shops, historic squares, museums with their exhibits, the Citadel, and Plains of Abraham battlefield (Parc des Champs-de-Bataille, labeled both Figures 1.1 and 1.2 and also shaded Figure 1.1); and shopping in boutiques, including the unusual purchase of art—usually paintings depicting Québec city and people. Ironically, it is the Plains of Abraham battlefield that is more historically significant than the British-built Ramparts or Château (they were never actually tested in the defense of the city). Although not a clearcut victory, the battle fought is taught in English school texts as a victory by the British over the French forces, and as a decisive moment in the contest for control over the European exploitation of North American staples such as the fur trade and, it was hoped, gold and silver. However, the lines of the Ramparts and the battlements of the Château serve as icons that constantly remind the viewer of the "historical topography" of the city—"second nature" crowning the Escarpment. In tourist brochures of the 1920s, this is softened, but restated in classic nature–culture terms:

true historical importance

On summer evenings the military musicians from the Citadel . . . come down to the band stand here to play for the enjoyment of all who seek recreation upon the promenade. Then the scene is gay with life and laughter and romantic with the mysterious beauty of the night. . . . Looking down and out upon such far-flung distances as this promenade on the cliff-edge commands, the night unwontonly huge and grand, impresses the imagination with a new awe and mystery. *On the one hand is nature, silent, primeval and all-enveloping. On the other is life and music, soft light and an ever-changing picture of beauty and fashion.* They make a combination that is unforgettable. (CPR 1926: 14–15; emphasis added)

Sites of Memory and Tourism

"Tourism is not unrelated to the issue of history, because tourist sites are often either packaged as, or are indeed relics of this past" (Kugelmass 1996: 200). The cartography of tourism is, beneath the surface, political and religious territory. The interest of "Old Quebec"/Vieux Québec is not just staged authenticity (Urry 1991) or a site of quaintness or nostalgia. It continues to be a raw site of political struggle at the level of rival states and political institutions operating within the spheres of linguistic-religious identity. Because Québec is a place of both tourism and memory, it is a locale of not only residents and tourists, but also of a type of pilgrim who commemorates not the defeat of French forces but the lasting endurance of Québecois cultural and linguistic integrity. In effect, history remains paramount. Although Nora (1989) has referred to memory as itself a site *("lieu de mémoire")*, it is more directly apparent that sites are places in which history is embedded. Nora characterizes such sites as "remains, . . . embodiments of a memorial consciousness" (1989: 12).

In effect, these are sites at which the past is spatialized and its distance manipulated. It must not only be set into the lineage and progressive tale of some particular person's past but it must be brought near, made present in its glory, pathos, and tragedy. As such, the recall of socially and effectively charged events involves a social organization of a historical space as much as of a historical time (Kirmayer 1996). Memory is constructed through secular rituals of the systematic, often guided, tour in which the site is "framed" by discourse. Terdiman has commented that memory acts in the present to represent the past (Terdiman 1993).

Ricoeur identifies a dialectic of appropriation and distanciation (Ricoeur 1976: 43) in which personal and collective experiences are drawn together in a cluster of elements that is then presented as "a memory" of a thing, event, or person (Neisser 1982). The psychological, museum, and archaeological metaphors by which the past is conceived "tend to transform the temporal into the spatial and are intensely visual. Layers are excavated, veils lifted, screens removed. The position of the viewer is left in question, but there is always a space, a distance, between the spectator and her memory," a space within which the tourist gaze can be focused and the memory formalized (Antze and Lambek 1996: xii).

Whereas historians and archaeologists provide an academic account of historical change, guidebooks and tourism maps have an especially close relationship to oral history and bodily experience (somatic memory). Read while walking through a site, recited out loud to companions, or read out loud from plaques, historical information on the significance of places, monuments, and events is closely associated with clues for movement, directions for tours or itineraries. Such sources of guidance allow unfamiliar visitors to fit into a ritualized path (Shields 1991b: 128) while eliminating the necessity of asking directions from the locals. Tourism texts are props that locate the reader in terms of a *whole,* representing an entire city or a day's walk in a map. They *distance* the tourist, nose in a map, from the everyday interaction of residents. They also direct the experiential and embodied quality of the tourist visit—making the tourist *present* in a specific, tinted, touristic staging of the place. This is a matter of *being there* in all its ethical fullness and the attendant memories of others at the site (whether, for example, guides and tourism service workers or crowds of other tourists). However, it is a presence to place and to others that is partial, directed, and staged through tourism maps. In "Quebec City," for Anglophone and Francophone tourist alike, everyday life is made to recede in favor of the past. The tourism maps reproduced here direct one to sites where historical events "happen," not to places to make a phone call or buy stamps. Thus, the map enters directly into the comportment and itineraries of bodies and the spatialization of the site—indeed, the availability of a tourist text (map or guidebook) is one of the topologically distinctive and identifying features that allow a tourism site to "cohabit" with the everyday environment and infrastructure of residents or other "insiders" who eschew such guidelines and take the tourist quality of their material environment to be entirely *virtual.*[7]

Drawing on different sources, Kugelmass (1996) has also interpreted pilgrimage-like travel to historic sites such as Auschwitz as a form of secular ritual that performatively reconnects the past to individuals' lives. As part of individual memory projects and larger mythic frames of death, formative historical events, including periods of cultural genocide or repression, notions of cultural destiny, and essentialistic beliefs in cultural identity, are all part of the consumption of places of memory and cultural myth. Although Kugelmass warns that the reconstruction of the past in mythic terms robs history of its critical power to disturb, it must be noted that the orchestration of a constructed, mythic past is central to the motivation and manipulation of social energies through "prosthetic memory," for better or for worse (including the cataclysmic excesses of nationalism and xenophobia over the past two centuries). Québec City with its Citadel, canons, Ramparts, and Plains of Abraham battlefield is precisely such a place of memory. It retains the traces of historical action—on the battlefield, for example, traces of dikes and defensive earthworks remain, even though actual sites of encounter and thus of the defeat of French forces have been banished from the field itself into a politically cautious exhibit in a "Battlefield Interpretation Center." There is little to reconnect this historical event with personal biography, little to reinforce the canons along the walls and promenade as a prosthetic memory of battle. They are merely quaint props to a historic site, and almost effaced in tourism images. In 1998, I met a tourist searching the guidebooks, maps, and the city and tramping the battlefield in frustration looking for a monument to an English victory. There is none.

"Vieux Québec" is also such a site of memory: a mapping of a once and future state onto the topography of battlements. This mapping is a prophecy, an Anti-Canada counterposing the homeland of the *ethnē* to the expansiveness of the spatialization of Canada "ad mare usque mare." Even the tourism maps keep alive the space of potentials. Perhaps,

> Countries of memory that were once real countries again make their appearance: once erased from the map, they first reappear as ghost images, quickly draw substance to themselves, and soon are undeniably here. . . . the erased countries of the world emerge . . . to finish their unfinished destinies. . . . This is the geography of the victims of history returning via the imagination to possess the present. This map shows

no distinction between reality and dream: it's drawn to scale. (Codrescu 1990: 57–58)

"Je me souviens"—I remember—asserts the motto on every Québec automobile license plate. To understand what this motto refers to—and to understand the subtle differences in its interpretation—is a mark of insider status as a Québecois. But there is no generalized need to remember the past (Bloch 1996)—and certainly no need to record or remember it the way we do. Bloch has argued that different cultures constitute the relation of the person to history in very different ways and that peoples' views of themselves in history have strong implications for the form and content of their actual engagement with history—an engagement, we might add, that is often expressed in the form of cultural tourism. "Je me souviens" indicates a commemorative tourism diametrically opposed to the sort of tourism interpolated by English-language tourism brochures.

This cultural orientation to historicity affects the kind of interest members of different cultures have in long-term memory and the shape they will give to that interest (after Antze and Lambek 1996: 148–49). The motto is often thought to refer to the defeat of the Battle of the Plains of Abraham (which would mark the Francophone, state ideology of Québec as strongly negative). But this is to oversimplify and misunderstand that the injunction is not to remember a particular event but to "remember," to take up a particular stance with regard to the Francophone peasant-settlers' cultural history *(le patrimoine)* of Québec. Hence the ambiguity of the battlefield itself and the continuing importance it has for Québecois and foreign visitors to reconstitute a historic time and place.

> Ethnic groups have a unique and collective commitment to memory—indeed, one might take that as their most salient characteristic—but that memory should be understood less as a thing that can be passed intact from one generation to the next . . . or even as a constant force within the trajectory of a group (I would like to distinguish a sense of the importance of the past or tradition from the substance of tradition) than as a continual process of engagement and disengagement, of remembering and forgetting propelled in either direction by overarching social, political, and economic forces. (Kugelmass 1996: 200)

By contrast, the tourist site of "Old Quebec" is constituted to manage the political risks and cross-cultural difficulties of these very different tourist practices. It is a quintessentially Canadian gesture: neither monuments to bombastic victory nor to defeat. Potentially transgressive opportunities are normalized by restricting encounters and maintaining an orderly flow of tourist traffic within the walled city while most of the residents conduct their business in the adjacent central business district, the government quarter with its Parliament building and bureaucracy, and the surrounding neighborhoods. Nonetheless, the apparently seamless spatialization of "Old Quebec" as a prime tourist destination— "quaint" and premodern, "European," grand yet unthreatening—can be seen to be quite unstable and internally fragmented between the primacy of Québec as a politically charged site of collective memory and the leisure practice of tourist consumption of the sites for its "quaint" history, view, and activities (all those elements that make up the tourist experience). This instability is reinforced by the widespread knowledge of Québec City's political significance and the more recent return of the city to the global media and political stage during the Summit of the Americas.

After the Fact: Anticipatory Spatializations

Not only does Québec City stand out as the object of intensive efforts at creating a tourism image, but it is a particularly significant node within an overall spatialization of Canada and of Québec as the site of historic events. It is an exemplary site of French-Canadian settlement at which cultural history and nationalistic political projects are sedimented, like geologically layered events and sites of memory (Shields 1991a, 1997). Québec City—and, for that matter, the touristic "Old Quebec"—take on their importance in relation to other spaces and places. It is in relation to the people and territorial province of Québec, and of Canada, that the Québecois political history at Québec City is significant. This significance is, furthermore, an issue not merely of history, but of present governments and of the future. Traveling to "Old Quebec" as a tourist, one cannot but be aware of the political project, oriented toward a future "Quebec state," of which the city would likely remain the capital. Homi Bhabha captures the importance of this aspect of spatialization for our temporal expectations and anticipations:

"Beyond" signifies spatial distance, marks progress, promises the future; but our intimations of exceeding the barrier or boundary—the very act of going *beyond*—are unknowable, unrepresentable, without a return to the "present" which, in the process of repetition, becomes disjunct and displaced. The imaginary of spatial distance—to live somehow beyond the border of our time—throws into relief the temporal, social differences that interrupt our collusive sense of cultural contemporaneity. (Bhabha 1994: 4)

One might observe that even the ritualized practice of Québec as a site of memory is governed by an indexical structure in which archaeological traces, historic sites, and monuments refer off to another, vanished Québec. Centrifugal references and links point offstage, so to speak, to other places and spatial relations. The tourism maps' and guidebooks' emphasis on the military fortifications, strategic geographical location, and decisive historical events are constant reminders of the city as a truly grand "site of memory." One is aware that one might stumble across evidence of contradictory ambitions for the place. These are ambitions to respatialize "Old Quebec" vis-à-vis the past and in relation to other places, so as to create different futures, including nationalist ones. The place-myth developed in the pleasant tourist images of "Old Quebec" appears to loose its hold on the actual city, and its ability to purify the place of extrinsic, competing images and the distracting place-myths of other sites. In place of a coherent, locally focused place-myth is a dynamic, anticipatory spatialization in which relations to other places are primary. Rather than a relatively fixed identity, as constructed and commodified in both the historic and contemporary guidebooks (cf. CPR 1926; Livesey 1996), the character of spatialization shifts to one that is turned away, to other sites and toward the future, to those ambitions, to "what happens next," and what happens here in relation to other places in a larger context of relational social spatializations of North America and the world. In this geography, Québec is merely one relay in an overall circuit in which tourists, place-images, and capital never rest. Media images, maps, and tourist texts are all central to this circulation and congress of place-myths. As Lida Curti put it:

In every country the media pose the problem of the shifting boundaries between national and foreign, otherness and sameness, repetition and difference. Italian television shows sharply how different cultures mingle and blend on the national screen in a flow of fictions . . . *Dallas* is naturalized in popular Naples, how Californian-ness can become part of the imaginary of a Southern Italian housewife, how the proximity of a poor Roman *borgata* to a petty bourgeois household in Rio, to a mansion in Denver, Colorado, is made acceptable and plausible by its appearing on the same flat screen in the same household in close succession. (Cited in Chambers 1990: 52–53)

[handwritten marginal annotation: → underlying political struggle between French and English / giving different meanings between French and English.]

The tense dialectical spatializations of the touristic place-myth of "Old Quebec" and the political place-myth of Vieux Québec sometimes lose their purchase and control over the site and activities there as the stress shifts from intrinsic, fixed references focused on the site to extrinsic, "centrifugal" comparisons and contrasts to other sites. In temporal terms, this shift may be a reversal from the emphasis on the past into a future-directed projection of new spatializations—a new space of distance and difference. The historical linkages to hemispheric struggles between rival nations remains as a latent circuit that can be quickly brought back to life at times such as the Summit of the Americas. The result is a dialectical tension within the tourism maps and an unstable identity through its links to other sites. These elements make Québec into a particularly acute switching point, a liminal threshold between the local and the global, in which particular attractions and even the entire historical city center can find themselves caught betwixt and between everyday life and the historic drama.[8]

Thus spatialization is anticipatory and represents a form of *spatially projected discipline.* This can be understood as a specific form of power that supplements and expands on Foucauldian visions of panoptic, disciplinary power (O'Connor 1998). In the process of spatialization, the local is related to the distant by virtue of the interconnected quality of place-myths that depend on a structural principle of other, contrasting place-myths in order to take on a (comparative) significance. Place-myths circulate not only in media discourse and images but in the tangible manifestation of commodities brought from distant places and local people who bear the signs or colors stereotypically associated with distant regions. The motive structure that puts tourists into circulation is this principle of comparative difference. The promise that place-myths can be tangibly experienced by tourist bodies once they arrive at that destination motivates travel. Desirous anticipation and the promise of gratification both enter into the equation that produces that crucial *event*: the mobilization of the tourist.

Rather than remaining fixed, self-referential, and inwardly oriented, place-myths are even more in circulation within an increasingly global-ized flow of cultural information, commodities, and people. "Flow" is crucial for it is in the in-between moment of indexical referentiality and counterpoint between places that spatialization takes on its importance (Shields 1997). Thus spatialization is even less a fixed structure, but constitutes a virtual space of possible movements and anticipations of what follows from a given action in a given site, and what alternative courses of action are possible. Rather than a loss of the local, however, the importance of local place-images and myths as a counterpoint to the received images of other places and spaces is increased, along with the role of the physical environment as an anchor for the spatialization of the place as a certain kind or character of site.

Mapping the Summit of the Americas on the Future

A final map illustrates this process. A little map making a big claim was issued as a colorful postage stamp commemorating the summit at Québec City. Although depicted here in black and white, it is surprising that the opportunity to present an embossed topography of the stamp was missed. The stamp depicts the hemisphere in the lurid blue, greens, yellows, and browns of topographical atlases with the names of the par-ticipating states "chopping" up the blue surface of the oceans (Figure 1.3). Maps were central in the construction of the summit by public-relations specialists. This fictive view is more than a map, of course. It is a view imagined from space. These images of Earth, as McNaughten and Urry (1998) remind us, present us with a unifying visual metaphor, a "dialecti-cal image" (Benjamin 1999). In this case, it takes up all the distances and contradictory outlooks of a third of the planet and folds them into a new unity, "The Americas." Born out of a map in a neat sleight of hand, the hemispheric image suggests the obviousness of unified state policies ir-respective of local conditions, differences, and desires. This is what was at stake in the protests, and why the Fence came to be.

The implication of anticipatory spatialization lies in the observation that social spatializations connect the here and now, the "near," or the face-to-face and present-at-hand, to the "distant," the future, and the possible. They connect what could be called the *real* present-at-hand

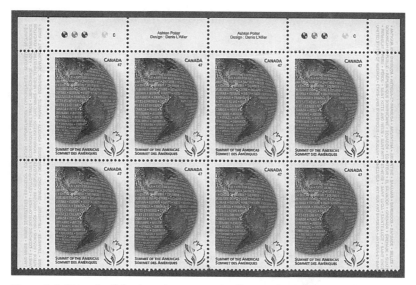

Figure 1.3. Summit of the Americas stamp, April 2001. Copyright Canada Post Corporation, 2001. Reproduced with permission from Canada Post.

with the *virtual* of the past and the *probable* of the future. As a synoptic network of place-myths and regional space-myths, far-off places (though not specifically experienced) are known by the contrast or similarity of their reputations and place-myths to other places. On the stamp, a popular cartography of unity reorganizes places by tightening the relationship between them, fitting them into a geographical logic of colorful continental topography. The stamp continues the imperial geography of conquest that created Quebec and that is still resisted in the counterspace of Vieux Québec and celebrated in the tourist spatialization and gaze of "Old Quebec." The ambitious stamp heralds a geography of industrial location decisions and marketing geomatics. It is performed via a cartographic representation of the hemisphere as a space to be consumed through the all-seeing eye of the philatelist and the public—a miniature tourist gaze (Urry 1991). One might imagine that at Quebec we stand not on a cliff-top promenade, but on some newly named "Summit of the Americas," looking down at this topographical map or portion of a globe. The complexity of the negotiations, the strange bilingual tensions between the local French hosts (willing or not) and the English of North America and of international business, are sublimated into the background noise of the names of states etched like ocean waves on the stamp.

This form of projection sheds little light on the obvious geopolitical issues raised by trade negotiations. These are masked by the representation of the hemisphere as topographical dance partners flung across the finite space of the globe. This cartographic stamp commemorates a political event hinted at in the maps of the Fence, with a map on which politics—national boundaries and the like—is not even present. Is it not a tourism map? A further irony is the resort to a map that uses the old cartographic conventions of a much-loved color scheme all but abandoned by commercial cartography today: the blue-green-yellow-brown topographical maps that hung next to a national flag in the schoolrooms of our childhoods. This stands in contrast to cartographic expectations formed in an era of global imaging systems (GIS) presentations of data in sophisticated formats, covered with bubbles, lines of trade flows, and other scaled representations of socioeconomic processes—the same era in which we see the world from space as a decisively *not* blue and green planet but one grayed and clouded over by ecosystemic traumas, or portrayed in the black and white of composite satellite radar, or in the red-green of infrared images. Clearly this is a stamp from fantasyland, not from a developed country with a space program such as Canada.

It is presumed that such an image would communicate globally the essence of a Free Trade Area of the Americas without the necessity of being literate (although the postal system remains dependent on literacy). The style of map presented on the stamp is commonly found in travel literature, and especially in the simplified onboard cabin brochures and videos of airlines' air routes and destinations. Although Quebec is not represented as a dot or a nation, this intertextual reference points to the readiness with which maps continue to be uncritically accepted as authoritative instruments that tell us "where we are," and "where we are going." Whereas the topography of such tourism maps is overworked, the bent lines of air routes, air traffic control zones, and reference radio beacons (which are actually a matter of interest and fascination for many) are completely oversimplified into a few understated great circle lines—lines on which tourists in aircraft blithely presume themselves to be traveling.

Ambiguously, this postage map does not locate the conference. "2001 Quebec" is written in small, almost illegible, characters beneath a logo.

As a rhetorical gesture, this map denies place in favor of hemispheric spatial extension and a coloring book fantasy of mountain ranges and cordilleras. Despite this, despite its tourist identity anchored in the city as the antithesis of the Americas, despite its political identity tied to the parochial Quebec state, this map interconnects with the tourism maps and the maps of the protests. All three map a shifting social spatialization at different scales and with different temporal emphases. In the example of tourism maps, historical significance and the battles for continental colonization are embedded within the geopolitics of imperial European rivalries. In the map of the protests, struggles over globalization are written in the street-corner scale of bodies tearing down the Fence at the summit. On the stamp, the proceedings at Quebec reach out to refigure the future of a third of the globe.

Tourism maps for the tourist gaze, with their violence to the actuality and complexity of the landscape and their orientation to convenience rather than to a North–South axis, are strongly intertextual illustrations. They form part of a larger tourist text that represents and reproduces a place-myth that is a fragment in a social spatialization. In their reference elsewhere and off-page to other places, they explicitly feature the geopolitical spatialization of a site, not simply its topography or its history. This is true as much for the pale green and gray areas of flattened disinterest on the tourism maps of Quebec City as it is for marked areas of interest, beauty, and significance. These absences speak of forgotten pasts not brought to light or memory, just as much as the didactic walking tours attempt to "stitch" tourist bodies into the weave of tourist sites, and to generate individual "prosthetic memories" of a collective history. Tourism maps, including the maps of protests and the Fence, interpolate individuals to local knowledge and distant views into a space of potentials, of desire and travel. At the same time, they position tourists, keeping them within a tourist frame. Maps locate the tourist in relation to the whole of a tourist site, and they distance tourists from locals by enabling them to follow itineraries and access a past that may be obscured to inhabitants or appear much more ambiguous and difficult to interpret. As an indicator of both a set of spatial relations between tourist and everyday sites and a set of temporal relations between a constructed past, a present, and a future, the tourism map is also a time machine for the tourist gaze. It is an anticipatory device, welcoming your visit, but suggesting a world that has been and a world that might come to be.

Notes

I would like to thank the editors, Vincent Del Casino and Stephen Hanna, as
well as many who commented on earlier versions of this essay, including the
Association of Canadian University Teachers of English, the Canadian Comparative Literature Association. Research on Images of Urban Sociability was
funded by the Social Sciences and Humanities Research Council of Canada.

1. "Neoliberal globalization" is a loose descriptor used by many nongovernmental and activist groups to describe a neoliberal and neoclassical economic agenda that eliminates local control and jurisdiction over the environment,
labor, and health in the name of reducing trade barriers and the "cost of doing
business."

2. The largest of these marches was held on April 21. Estimates are by the
newspaper *La Presse*.

3. As part of promotion of travel on its railway, and on the ocean lin-
ers that provided transatlantic and transpacific links, the Canadian Pacific
produced the first comprehensive tourism advertising for Canada. It covered
the country from coast to coast, and although it did not offer views of either
subarctic taiga or the arctic archipelago, it offered a romanticized vision of
North American wilderness and appropriate sports activities such as hiking,
canoeing, golf, hunting, fishing, and skiing. In embracing both winter and the
rough landscape of the West, the Canadian Pacific Railway (CPR) provided a
more or less authentic vision of the possibilities of the Canadian climate and
topography. Its advertising images and guidebooks also drew on some of the
diversity of indigenous inhabitants and settlers of various ethnicities, as well
as the white, English-speaking tourists who were the wealthy audience these
images were intended for. Far more than any state department of tourism, the
CPR—beginning scarcely five years after Confederation (the founding of the
Canadian state as a "British Dominion"—a quasicolonial prototype of its current transcontinental manifestation)—shaped a dominant image of Canada and
set the terms and costs of access to these landscapes both for the relatively small
percentage of literate, urban Anglo-Canadians at the time and for foreigners.
This promotional effort contributed a series of strongly marked place-myths
such as "Old Quebec" to the late-nineteenth-century Canadian spatialization
of the "True North," which consisted of natives and northern wilderness, snow,
mountains, "land for all" settlers on the prairies, and the railroad companies'
other great contribution—making the new nation's motto "From Sea to Sea"
into a traveler's reality.

4. Louisbourg was built as a fortress after the theories of the military architect Sébastien Le Prestre de Vauban. It included a town based on seventeenth-
century urban planning principles on Cape Breton Island, Nova Scotia, as a
base from which to control the cod fishery on the Grand Banks. It was occupied

from 1713 to 1758 and then abandoned, but is now rebuilt as a museum and one of the largest tourist attractions in the Maritimes.

5. This view remains, though now one looks downstream to the countryside of the Île d'Orléans, and across the river to the industrial and less tourist-oriented city of Lévis.

6. The "Northern Tour" was a circuit of Boston, Quebec City, Montreal, Niagara Falls, and Buffalo, popular with the wealthy of the Southern states from the early part of the nineteenth century (Shields 1991a; McKinsey 1985).

7. "Virtual" in the sense that, like a memory or dream, the tourist aspect of the local environment is real but ideal in that it is made up of historical events, not material events happening in the present moment that might be empirically verified. For more on the distinction between real and virtual, see Shields 2000.

8. For more on the concept of liminality, see Shields 1991b; Turner 1974.

2. Memory on the Margins

Alabama's Civil Rights Journey as a Memorial Text

Owen J. Dwyer

Over the past two decades, the American memorial landscape has been
reshaped to bear witness to the Civil Rights Movement of the 1950s and
1960s. Early efforts, undertaken through the 1970s and early 1980s, were
dominated by mourners and memorial activists seeking to (re)dedicate
streets, terminals, and other pieces of civic infrastructure to the memory
of Martin Luther King Jr. (see Alderman 1996, 2000; Foote 1997). Since
that time, capital-intensive tourist attractions have come to the fore.
Beginning with the unveiling of Maya Lin's Civil Rights Monument in
Montgomery, Alabama (1990), and the National Civil Rights Museum at
the site of Martin Luther King Jr.'s assassination in Memphis, Tennessee
(1991), no fewer than a dozen museums and monuments associated with
the Movement were produced during the 1990s (Auchmutey 1997; Lee
1998; Sack 1998). The Movement's most extensive memorial landscapes
are located in the South, extending from the site of lunch-counter sit-in
protests in Greensboro, North Carolina, to the National Historic Site
in Topeka, Kansas. Monumental memory works are being undertaken in
towns and cities synonymous with the struggle against white supremacy:
Little Rock, Arkansas; Jackson, Oxford, and Philadelphia, Mississippi;
Birmingham, Selma, and Montgomery, Alabama; Albany, Atlanta, and
Savannah, Georgia; Orangeburg, South Carolina. In all cases, the evolv-
ing built environment is both the medium and the result of a continuing

struggle to define the contemporary significance of the U.S. Civil Rights revolution.

Across the South, both local and state visitor bureaus have been instrumental in promoting Civil Rights tourism. An important component of the promotional activities undertaken by visitor bureaus has been the production of maps and guidebooks designed to entice and assist visitors. Among the promotional media associated with these sites, tourist maps enjoy a special symmetry with the monumental landscapes they represent. This chapter examines the discourses woven on and through one of these publications, *Alabama's Civil Rights Journey* (Figure 2.1). Produced by the Alabama Bureau of Tourism and Travel, this booklet, and the highly abstract map that lies at its centerfold (Figure 2.2), present in microcosm many of the issues that characterize the monumental landscape.

Of particular interest is the role of the map in the abstraction of places out of their local context and subsequent insertion into a generalized heritage-tourism space. Like many of the representational devices used at Civil Rights memorials, this process of abstraction produces a sweeping historical narrative, one that is marked by absences, inclusions, and marginalizations. Nevertheless, as one node in the network of practices associated with reproducing Civil Rights memorial landscapes, the map under study is ambiguous and suggests ways in which contemporary antiracist discourses may be reintroduced into the historical narrative. Investigating the social production of the "past" on and through mapped Civil Rights spaces serves as a reminder that the production of memorial spaces is never complete.

The Politicized Condition of Maps and Monuments

Despite the widespread perception of tourist booklets and maps as mawkish ephemera that, at best, aid way-finding and, at worst, brazenly commodify the past, this chapter calls attention to their condition as memorial texts—one among many of the media designed to facilitate remembering and forgetting, for example, holidays, books, parks, and plaques (Young 1993). As with other memorial texts, both maps and monuments are political resources, laden with authorial intentions, textual strategies, and readers' interpretations (Natter and Jones 1997). One aspect of their politicized condition stems from the common understanding of maps and monuments as impartial records of, respectively,

> Feebly sentimental brief.

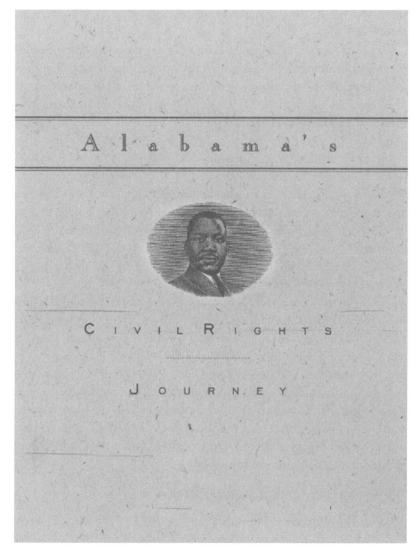

Figure 2.1. Front cover of *Alabama's Civil Rights Journey.* Alabama Bureau of Tourism and Travel.

space and time In the case of monuments, their location in public space, use of canonical media, and the enormous amounts of financial and political capital such installations require imbue them with an air of civic authority and permanence (Lowenthal 1975; Johnson 1995) Relative to personal and corporate media (e.g., television, books, films, music), public

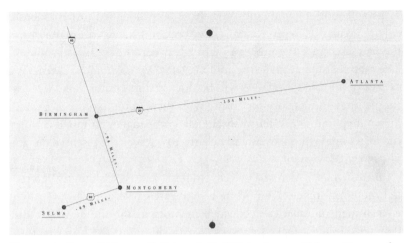

Figure 2.2. Centerfold map of *Alabama's Civil Rights Journey*. Alabama Bureau of Tourism and Travel.

monuments appear to be a lasting and official record of the past, above political bias, and worthy of civic admiration. Likewise with maps: the subtle claims to scientific authority that attend to cartographic products place them above the typical suspicions that confront other tourist literature (Harley 1988; Wood 1992).

Additionally, both maps and monuments constitute a situation for everyday activity, accruing to these representations the naturalizing power of time and place (Del Casino and Hanna 2000). For maps, this stems from their ubiquity →(presence everywhere) throughout tourist practices and the reliance tourists commonly place on them. For monuments, their weighty materiality and apparent permanence suggest the presence of something governed by geologic processes, beyond the vagaries of time measured on a human scale. The producers of monuments cultivate this appearance, seeking through the landscape a means of securing memory, to put it beyond the reach of time by etching it in the land itself. In turn, the impression of fixity conveyed by map and monument heightens the expectation of visitors that the real and authentic is within reach.

Finally, like maps produced by scientific cartographic methods, Civil Rights monumental landscapes are intended to present a mirror-quality image of the world from which visitors may gather their bearings. In contrast to the dominant trend in contemporary public art to produce objects that embody the practice of self-reflexive inquiry, Civil Rights

maps and monumental landscapes have been designed to be unabash-
edly referential (Dwyer 2000a). They seek to present in tangible form
the past itself, not the processes through which the "past" is produced.
The map that lies at the centerfold of *Alabama's Civil Rights Journey* is a
case in point (Figure 2.2). As will be discussed in greater detail later, its
simple lines and cursory text bring with them connotations of a hand-
drawn map found in a diary. Absent a larger spatial or temporal context,
the map's rigid simplicity silently claims to lay bare the essential geography of the Movement.

Birmingham, Alabama's, Kelly Ingram Park is a similarly referential memorial text. At one time a segregated park for whites only, it
is enshrined in America's collective memory as the site at which Bull
Conner's police attacked protesters with dogs and fire hoses in 1963.
The park, redesigned and rededicated as "A Place of Revolution and
Reconciliation" in 1992, is circumscribed by the "Freedom Walk," a
broad, slate-stone walkway along which large, dark steel sculptures have
been installed. The pathway is straddled by the installations so that visitors are confronted by a cordon of snarling police dogs, jailed protesters, and enormous water cannons, all of which they must walk between
and among if they are to complete their journey around the park. The
inscription on the base of one of the installations, showing two black
children behind a jail cell's bars, reads, when looking through the bars:
"We ain't afraid of your jail." From the children's perspective, looking
out from within the cell, the visitor reads along the top of the sculpture:
"Segregation is a sin." The overall effect conveyed via the sculptures'
figural realism and close, visceral presence on the walkway is that of a
spatial primer in the tactics of provocation and confrontation employed
by protesters to secure their rights.

Modernist criticism of referential memorial texts decries them for
presenting an unchanging, static version of history at odds with modernity's creative cycle of destruction and rebirth (Mumford 1938; Nietzsche
1985). This line of criticism charges that authorially rigid representations
follow from a sort of moral bankruptcy that places faith in backward-
looking facades and monuments rather than confronting the promise of
discontinuity, rupture, and change. More sympathetic criticism charges
that memorial texts displace the responsibility of remembering from
the living onto a totem-like structure that does the work of memory
for them (Nora 1989). As one observer has postulated, "once we assign

monumental form to memory, we have to some degree divested ourselves of the obligation to remember" (Young 1993: 5). For these critics,
the production of referential memorial texts raises the haunting question of whether they serve the purpose of remembering or of forgetting.

By attributing to monuments and maps an unchanging, static quality,
supporters and critics alike fail to consider the unsettled condition of
memorial texts that arises from the circuitous basis through which their
meaning is derived (Halbwachs 1980; Nora 1989; Sparke 1995). Whereas
authors may hope to imbue a sign with an essential meaning, memorial texts exhibit a remarkable plasticity of meaning: their ability to
"escape history" renders them susceptible to "the full range of possible
significations" (Nora 1989: 23–24). Originally written in the context of
monumental landscapes, Nora's observations are equally true of memorial texts more generally, including maps. Memorial texts have "no
referent in reality, or rather they are their own referent: pure, exclusively
self-referential signs" (ibid., 23). Map and monument alike possess no
intrinsic meaning but are known instead via references to other texts. As
such, their meaning is intertextual, in the sense of a hermeneutic circle
in which the basis for a particular interpretation is endlessly deferred to
other texts, and contingent upon the multiple interpretive canons that
readers bring to bear on a scene (Duncan and Duncan 1988; Duncan
1990; Sparke 1995). Rather than forming an inert backdrop for the un-
folding of historical narratives, maps and monuments are inextricably
entwined in the production of the past, not just simply reflecting it.

Understood as signifying systems—processes of making meaning
that are produced and reproduced rather than statically cast once and
for all—maps and monuments bear the impress of human activity and
exist as the tangible intersection of innumerable discourses. The result
is discourse materialized (Schein 1997: 675). Memorial texts, however,
do not simply bear the impress of human activity alone. By providing a
means for their articulation, map and monument are implicated in the
reproduction of discourses as well. The result is the mutual constitution of text and context (Duncan and Duncan 1988; Natter and Jones
1997; Jones and Natter 1999). In this formulation, a memorial text is
the articulated presence of numerous social discourses made manifest
through the actions of individuals and institutions. These actions are
both empowered and disciplined by the social discourses in which they
have meaning (Belyea 1992; Schein 1997). In turn, the memorial text is

reproductive of discourses of memory (among others). When individual actions produce a memorial text, the discourses embedded in the text are at once represented and reproduced.

This perspective allows memorial texts to be conceived of as in the process of becoming rather than in a static, essentialized state. Rather than possessing a fixed, established meaning, memorial texts are momentarily realized in a nexus of social relations as the result of attempts to define the meaning of representations, which nevertheless remain open to dispute and change. As a result, maps and monuments can be usefully known in relation to their connections with the ever-changing "outside," instead of being understood solely in terms of what is supposedly intrinsic and exclusively of the text (Sparke 1995). Through these connections, the individuality and the character of a memorial text are made known. The implication is that maps and monuments can be thought of in terms of their connections, rather than of what they contain. Thus, what a map or monument "contains" is its multiple and changing connections to an interwoven web of other sociospatial contexts (Duncan and Duncan 1988; Massey 1993; Sparke 1995; Schein 1997).

[margin note: changing meanings of maps + monuments as sociospatial contexts change over time.]

In line with this economy of meaning comes an understanding that once erected or committed to paper, the condition of the map or monument as a representation renders it susceptible to multiple, sometimes conflicting, interpretations. As they strive to set out an authoritative rendering of the content and meaning of the Civil Rights Movement, these memorial texts ironically and unintentionally create the possibility of countertransgressions (Laclau and Mouffe 1985; Cresswell 1996). Insofar as they put forward an understanding of *the* past, memorial texts present different audiences with the raw material for a new round of criticism regarding the "true" or "real" content and meaning of the Civil Rights Movement(s) (Jones 2000). The result of this authoritative visibility and radical impermanence of meaning is that representations dedicated to the Civil Rights Movement do not seal up and settle the Movement's meaning as much as they open a new chapter of struggle inextricably linked to its memory. They are sought out and contested by various groups because they are at once authoritative and yet susceptible to rewriting and appropriation.

[margin note: Those who write / erect these memorial text are authoritative in their ideas and try and present one view but others interpret differently.]

Thus, beneath the appearance of historical consensus and stability, memorial texts—and by implication the meaning and significance of the events they represent—are the product of and conduit for ongoing political debate (Gillis 1994; Foote 1997). From their inception, maps and monuments are designed and planned, with all of the narrative choices and biases this entails, <u>by those who have the time, resources,</u> and, <u>most importantly, the state</u> mandate to define the past (Harley 1988, 1990; Wood 1992). Their role as authoritative <u>arbiters</u> of temporal and spatial practice links them to the city, bringing into question their place in urban redevelopment, real-estate speculation, and <u>gentrification</u> plans associated with the "entrepreneurial city" and its selective appropriation of history (Harvey 1989b; Roberts and Schein 1993; Hall and Hubbard 1996). As part of the growing heritage tourism industry, the <u>history represented at monumental sites has been tailored to accommodate a broad range of interest levels</u> (Lowenthal 1998). Their reliance on state funding and corporate largesse makes them further susceptible to influence. Monuments "<u>do not arise as if by natural law to celebrate the deserving; they are built by people with sufficient power to marshal (or impose) public consent for their erection</u>" (Savage 1994: 135). The same can be said of <u>maps, that they are laden with interests, both served and denied</u> (Harley 1989; Wood 1992) The shared appearance of neutral objectivity obscures the partisan condition of maps and monuments and makes them potent political resources.

[margin annotations: "made by"; "→one who is chosen to judge or decide a certain issue."; "→purchase and renovation of stores/houses in poorly developed urban areas by middle/upper class, improving property value but displacing low income families."; "→ maps/monuments are partisan because people who construct have power/money. Presented in a way to look neutral/objective but in core, are not."]

Materialized Discourses

Relative to other pieces of tourist literature, *Alabama's Civil Rights Journey* is an exceptionally high-end product. The four by six-inch, twelve-page booklet is bound with a black ribbon and printed on high-quality card stock. The booklet's subdued narrative and monochrome photos establish a somber and dignified tone. Written in a close, intimate style, the text is reminiscent of a travel diary or a funeral memory book:

> Reaching Selma, we pass over the famous Edmund Pettus Bridge . . . We make a quick stop at Brown Chapel AME Church . . . We leave the church and head toward the only museum in the United States exclusively dedicated to the voting rights struggle, the National Voting Rights Museum.

The text is peppered with cues and subtle hints to the reader as to how to enact the place of the past:

> All paths in the park lead to the center, a place for quiet contemplation . . . We linger awhile, remembering.

The booklet's period photos show a determined King and equally determined marchers participating in the 1965 Voting Rights March from Selma to Montgomery. Working in tandem, the text and photos bring home the message that Alabama is a changed place in the wake of the Movement. After describing several harrowing scenes from the state's segregationist past, including the use of police dogs and fire hoses against protesters, the text reads:

> These powerful and shocking images from the '60s still flash into our minds when we hear the word 'Alabama.' As we travel through the State on our Civil Rights odyssey, we discover that Alabama in the '90s evokes powerful images of a vastly different kind. People of all races and creeds come together at the Civil Rights Memorial in Montgomery and the Birmingham Civil Rights Institute to participate in the healing process. Out of the ashes of Alabama's turbulent past, the phoenix of reconciliation and renewal is arising.

The final passage reinforces the twinned themes of accomplishment and renewal. Accompanied by a photo of marching feet, some of them wearing torn sneakers and others with dress shoes, the booklet concludes:

> As we come to the end of our Civil Rights journey, we echo the sentiment of an elderly woman during the Montgomery Bus Boycott who, when asked if she was tired, agreed that yes, her feet were tired. "But," she added, ". . . my soul is rested."

The overall effect is a solemn reflection on the accomplishments of the Movement.

The booklet's carefully cultivated mood is disrupted, however, when the reader catches sight of the Bureau of Tourism and Travel's corporate logo on the back cover (Figure 2.3). "Fun & games begin here," it proclaims. The clash between these moods—one steeped in solemn commemoration, the other smacking of shrill commercialization—serves as a reminder that memorial texts are as much about the future as they are about the past. In the case of *Alabama's Civil Rights Journey,* these tensions crystallize in the map that lies at the booklet's centerfold (Figure 2.2). The focus of the map is the distance between four cities, Birmingham, Montgomery, Selma, and, significantly, Atlanta. The booklet was produced in time for the 1996 Atlanta Summer Olympics, with the ostensible purpose of enticing tourists to make a side trip to

Alabama. The map's minimalist design accentuates the cities' connectivity. Stripped bare of the usual cartographic accoutrements, the map emphasizes the personal experience of the cities and the highways that connect them. Absent a compass rose and topographic features, the cities appear to float on an isotropic plane rather than the undulating hills of the Piedmont South. Further, the lack of any standard temporal identifiers—there is no title, date, or even the stylized patina of age—gives the map a timeless quality. The relative absence of details that would allow a reader to place these cities raises the question of whether it represents the past, the present, or the future. Resonating with the somber, introspective mood established by the text and photos, the journey this map traces is a timeless and personal one, removed from the details of time and space.

Alternately, the map's rigorous simplicity can be interpreted in the context of what the historian Glenn Eskew refers to as the "Won Cause" retelling of the Movement (Eskew 1998). Told in contrast to the Lost Cause of the Confederacy, the Won Cause represents the Movement as a story of sweeping cultural and political change. Condensed to a single, unified undertaking in pursuit of integration and voting rights, the Movement is presented at the sociospatial scale of heroic leaders

Figure 2.3. Back cover of *Alabama's Civil Rights Journey*. Alabama Bureau of Tourism and Travel.

orchestrating a national movement to overcome racist violence and official malfeasance. This interpretive frame emphasizes elite-led institutions (e.g., the National Association for the Advancement of Colored People [NAACP], Southern Christian Leadership Conference [SCLC]) and their leaders. It portrays the Movement as a series of key moments (e.g., the Montgomery bus boycott, the March on Washington) and is characterized by an overarching, if unstated, telos of inevitability that animates a regional transformation undertaken at seemingly preordained locales.

Ironically, this sweeping narrative constrains the Movement's political moment to electoral and legislative accomplishment. What remains is a sense of inevitability as to the time, location, and outcome of the Movement. Lost is a sense of the Movement as multiple "black freedom movements" striving to create and sustain antiracist identities (Morris 1984; Carson 1986; Hine 1986). Lost as well is a sense of the importance of local conditions for organizing, as well as the deeply ambiguous connections between local activists and national leaders and their institutions (Chafe 1980; Norrell 1986). Further, by casting acts of virulent racism as the sine qua non of the segregated order, the Won Cause confirms the popular genealogy of racism as an individual pathology grounded in unreasoning prejudice—the effect of which is to displace consideration of racism's more insidious institutional and epistemological manifestations. Broader consideration of the Movement—its shortcomings, its internal contradictions, its future—is displaced by a focus on its gains relative to the segregated past. The result is an essentialized vision of the Movement, one that fetishizes legislative and judicial victories to the exclusion of more enduring problems and achievements. Overall, the Won Cause is consistent with the style of history presented at many popular heritage sites—a mode of presentation that critics charge limits the possibility of progressive social change by captivating audiences with the simulated and hyperreal (Burnham 1995; Gable 1996; cf. Johnson 1996b; Porter 1996).

Seen in this light, the map's design reinforces the themes of accomplishment and transcendence that characterize the Won Cause. As an initial matter, it depicts the sites of Martin Luther King Jr.'s three most successful campaigns, all in Alabama and all within driving distance of tourists coming from Atlanta, King's hometown and base of operations. In fact, King plays a conspicuous role in the booklet as a whole. In addition to appearing on the booklet's cover, he figures prominently in the text and photos. The map's spartan design and the booklet's focus on King are part of a larger process of abstracting the Movement out of its local sociospatial context. Further, the commercial concerns of the map (i.e., the short driving distances between Atlanta and Alabama's attractions) cast the Movement at a scale removed from the regional and local dynamics of organizing for social change. In so doing, the map underscores the Won Cause's circumscribing of the Movement's aims and achievements by presenting a small selection of the many sites related to the Movement in Alabama and the region as a whole. Reminiscent of the teleological overtones of the Won Cause, the limited selection of cities reinforces a sense of inevitability that Important Things were predestined to happen in these places.

design or purpose inherent in nature.

Compounding the extraction of the Movement from its sociospatial context, the map presents the cities in the order they are encountered during a drive from Atlanta: the first stop is in Birmingham, then on to Montgomery, and finally Selma. By ignoring the chronological ordering of Movement campaigns in these cities (i.e., Montgomery 1954, Birmingham 1963, and Selma 1965), the map echoes the abstraction that characterizes both the text and the photos. As it narrates the visitor tour, the text follows the order laid out by the map: "Our journey begins in Birmingham . . . Our journey now takes us south to Montgomery . . . Reaching Selma. . . ." In so doing, the text represents each city in isolation, ignoring the vital connections between them. For their part, the photos, with the exception of a portrait of King, are all from the 1965 Voting Rights March. They are, however, not identified as such and a casual reader might get the impression that they represent images from each city. Thus extracted out of time and space, the Movement is set into orbit as a node in a network of tourist attractions.

spatialization between cities ignored by book and map.

This alternate interpretation raises a number of questions regarding the spaces depicted in and through the map, text, and photos of *Alabama's Civil Rights Journey*. Among them: Who are the intended subjects of this memorial text? What spaces is it designed to promote? What vision of the past and future is it intended to foster? One manner of investigating the tensions, omissions, and inclusions that arise from these questions is to examine the discourses that are woven on and through the memorial text of this booklet. In keeping with the understanding of memorial texts as materialized discourses, the following sections discuss a discourse that is materialized on and through *Alabama's Civil Rights*

Journey. These discourses, through the constitutive medium of the memorial text, both empower and discipline their subjects. The result is the mutual constitution of memorial text and memory, albeit in a fashion that promises their ongoing alteration.

Activism, Entrepreneurialism, and the Production of History

The growth of Civil Rights tourism that *Alabama's Civil Rights Journey* embodies is the result of a complex mix of memorial activism and entrepreneurialism (Alderman 1999). By turn complementary and contradictory, drawing clear distinctions between these commingled memorial impulses is difficult. The collaboration and accommodation of activists and entrepreneurs, sometimes working together, sometimes at odds, renders oppositional categories tenuous (Sandage 1993; Domosh 1998). Although oppositional categories may be used to call attention to conditions of unequal access to the means of representation, these same binaries restrict the time and place of politics to a single moment in which oppositional forces clash. The result is a view that unnecessarily solidifies the fluid lines of politics associated with coalitions and interest groups and imposes a filter through which events are narrated as definitive and epochal. Thus, neither *Alabama's Civil Rights Journey* nor the sites it promotes can be understood as purely the result of activism or entrepreneurialism, but rather as an ambiguous blend of alliances, conflicting sympathies, and co-optation.

In the late 1960s, many Civil Rights activists began pursuing their political agenda through the creation of cultural institutions. In the face of political defeats and white backlash, and in light of the positive results associated with voter education and the election of black mayors, activists identified cultural politics as a sustainable way of mobilizing local people for change. At the core of this memorial activism was a desire to exert a significant measure of control over the production of knowledge for and about African-American experiences. One of the key aspects of this effort was to contest the conflation of public history with the history of white men. In the wake of the passage of Civil Rights legislation, activists sought to further the Movement's goals by preserving the memory of the struggle and setting it in a broader historical and geographical context, especially with respect to the international aspects of antiracist and colonial struggles (Ruffins 1998a, 1998b).

One result of these efforts was the creation of more than ninety

African-American museums between 1950 and 1980 (Stewart and Ruffins 1986; Ruffins 1998a). Created alongside these museums were a large number of art galleries, performing arts academies, festivals, conferences, and academic departments. Separate from the existing cultural infrastructure of historically black churches and colleges, these new institutions envisioned themselves as facilitating the arrival of progressive racial identities. A defining feature of these new institutions was their efforts to develop talent and political consciousness rather than act as a vanguard setting standards of style and criticism. In contrast to elite institutions that reached relatively few people, these new institutions emphasized serving a broad audience. With initially small collections and staffs, they worked to foster strong networks of supporters, visitors, and volunteers—networks that have been crucial to developing collections, programming, and continuing operations in an era of decreasing federal funding for the arts.

Concomitant with the development of popular African-American cultural institutions has been the rise of heritage tourism (La Tempa 1993; Spritzer 1993; Mines 1998). This contrasts sharply with the previous neglect of blacks by the tourism and museum industries (Goodrich 1985; Spratlen 1986; Falk 1995). In a manner analogous to the social-spatial transgressions of the Movement itself, the public commemoration of its memory has opened the doors of museums and monuments to blacks, inviting them into places that heretofore were the domain of white elites (Floyd et al. 1994; Philipp 1994, 1995). Memorials to the Civil Rights Movement offer African Americans and antiracists more generally an opportunity to take part in a tourist experience that recognizes their impact on American history (Woodward 1988; Philipp 1993; Taylor 1993). Further, survey research conducted at Civil Rights memorials notes that African Americans often visit with family, especially children, highlighting the welcome afforded them and suggestive of the sites' relative importance among cultural attractions (Travel Industry Association of America 1993, 1996; National Tour Association 1997; Dwyer 2000b). Significantly, the same survey research indicates that visitors often shop and stay overnight when visiting heritage sites.

It was in this context that Frances Smiley, director of group travel for Alabama's Bureau of Tourism and Travel began promoting black heritage tourism via such publications as *Alabama's Civil Rights Journey* (Smiley 1998). The first African-American professional at the bureau, Smiley was initially assigned the task of promoting group tourism. With the support of her immediate supervisor, she organized an effort to spread the message that the state had changed since the Movement. The intended effect of this message was to entice the many African Americans who had left the state to consider returning for a vacation, or longer. Importantly, she strove to promote a nuanced rendering of the African-American past, one that did more than simply highlight the birthplaces of athletes and entertainers.

As a result of her efforts, Alabama produced the country's first statewide guide to African-American history, *Alabama's Black Heritage* (Ahmad 1993; Alabama Bureau of Tourism and Travel 1993; American Visions 1993). Its publication in 1983 caught the attention of newspapers across the country. Alabama's governor at the time was George Wallace, and the press savored the irony of the former archsegregationist promoting African-American history. Illustrated with maps, color photos, and suggested tour routes, hundreds of copies of *Alabama's Black Heritage* were requested during the first week and, after four months, the first print run of 18,500 copies was exhausted (American Visions 1993; Sherman 1998; Smiley 1998). Since then the guide has gone through four more editions, the number of sites listed has increased from fifty-four to 163, and 650,000 copies have been distributed worldwide, in the process refuting the claims of detractors who believed there was not a significant market for black heritage tourism (Clark 1993; Sherman 1998).

Although it is decidedly reserved in comparison to *Alabama's Black Heritage*'s magazine-style layout of glossy color photos and tour-book text, *Alabama's Civil Rights Journey* shares a central attribute with its literary predecessor and the Won Cause more generally: a dichotomy between the past and the present. As discussed earlier, *Alabama's Civil Rights Journey* opens with the evocative juxtaposition of past racist violence and contemporary racial harmony. *Alabama's Black Heritage* begins with a similar sentiment:

> When an unassuming seamstress, tired from a long day at the sewing machine, refused to give up her seat on a Montgomery city bus, little did she know that forty years later she would be revered as a hero by a world of admirers.

The narrative thrust of both publications is to cleanly separate the past from the present, with the past forming a benchmark from which today's

progress can be measured. The contemplative tone of the text and photos of *Alabama's Civil Rights Journey* reinforces this dualism through al-
lusions to a personal journey into the past. The map, however, bears a
more ambiguous relationship to this dualism. Interstate expressways link
the cities to one another. Their presence, and the absence of the older
state highways that King and his Movement contemporaries traveled,
place this map in the present. Yet, the absence of less easily overlooked
chronological markings infuses the map with an element of ambiguity
as to its temporal coordinates. This ambiguous relation of the map to
time has a number of contemporary, and contradictory, implications.
For some, the placement of these events in the distant past, a journey
conveyed by *Alabama's Civil Rights Journey* via personal introspection
and its emphasis on present-day accomplishment and transcendence,
is part of a broader strategy to get beyond the Movement. For others,
however, a place on the map can serve to heighten the identification of
these cities with the Movement. For these activists, forging this link between the past and the future is the beginning of a thorough critique of
contemporary racism. That the same map can be used to further both of
these points is a reminder of the unsettled condition of memorial texts.

  Cognizant of the positive publicity generated by promotional literature such as *Alabama's Black Heritage* and *Alabama's Civil Rights Journey,*
states and private tour operators across the country have copied Alabama's efforts and produced heritage guides of their own (Yardley 1992;
Spritzer 1993; Mines 1998). In light of the considerable amount of
money involved in this sort of tourism—the Travel Industry Association
of America estimates that a tour bus of twenty-eight to thirty-two people
spends approximately five to seven thousand dollars per day on travel-
related goods and services (Travel Industry Association of America 1996;
Smiley 1998)—it is not surprising that both private and public tourist interests actively promote a heroic recounting of the Movement.
Interviews with state tourism officials and the widespread presence of
state-produced promotional literature testify to the desire on the part
of local and state governments to rectify their public image and attract
tourist dollars at the same time (Nabbefeld 1992; *PR News* 1993; Smiley
1998; Fuller 1999). These developments reflect the manner in which cities and states have become increasingly entrepreneurial in their pursuit
of capital investment and consumer spending (Harvey 1989b; Roberts
and Schein 1993; Hall and Hubbard 1996). Faced with reduced federal

support, declining tax bases, and increasingly fluid national and international markets, cities and states have taken an active role in promoting economic development. These efforts to attract investment and spending stand in contrast to the immediate post–Second World War managerial approach to urban development in which the city's primacy as a politico-economic growth pole was assumed. A hallmark of these more recent efforts has been the cultivation of public–private partnerships to leverage local history into attractions for investment and spending.

The goals of memorial entrepreneurialism and activism of the type described earlier at once complement and contradict each other. For instance, both the memorial sites that are the explicit focus of *Alabama's Civil Rights Journey* and the state's battered image presumably benefit from the positive exposure generated by the booklet. Relatedly, the promise of increased tourist revenues has been cited as a key moment in shoring up support for the development of Civil Rights tourism. In Birmingham, for instance, the desire to rectify the city's image—it was popularly known as "Bombingham" because of the impunity with which white supremacists carried out terror attacks on blacks—coupled with the promise of tourist revenues, consolidated the support of the local corporate community behind the project (Nabbefeld 1992; Cox 1995; Eskew 1998). Faced with criticism from grassroots activists that the process was not open to them, as well as complaints that revisiting the past would only produce further enmity, the public–private coalition that orchestrated the city's commemoration efforts hired a consulting firm to cultivate support for the project (*PR News* 1993). In an effort to reposition the city as a progressive member of the New South, the firm put forward the message, "Birmingham accepts its past, has begun the process of healing, celebrates its vital role in civil rights history, and continues to make progress toward improved race relations" (ibid., 5).

The campaign's theme of a sharp break between the violent past and the harmonious present is reflected in the comments of David Vann, an early supporter of Civil Rights tourism in the state and a former mayor of Birmingham. He succinctly expressed the overriding sentiment of many residents and business leaders to decouple the past and the present when he remarked, "I've always said the best way to put your bad images to rest is to declare them history and put them in a museum" (*Birmingham News* 1992). *Alabama's Civil Rights Journey*—with its emphasis on accomplishment and transcendence—confirms these sentiments. For David Vann and others, the map solidifies the Movement as something to travel along while journeying out of the past and into the present.

This dualism between past and present is not without its vulnerabilities, however. In contrast to the efforts of memorial entrepreneurs such as David Vann to segment the time and place of the Movement, other memorial activists, like the ones who organized the National Voting Rights Museum in Selma, strive to make connections between multiple temporal and spatial contexts. Described in *Alabama's Civil Rights Journey* as "the only museum in the United States exclusively dedicated to the voting rights struggle," the museum's volunteer staff works to overcome the partition between the past and the present by representing time and place in more shifting terms. For instance, visitors can read biographical sketches of local organizers from the past and the present. Importantly, the museum's docent, Joanne Bland, takes visitors on a tour of Selma that mixes the contemporary with the historical aspects of the Movement. Paramount among the concerns of the museum's volunteers is the desire to connect in the minds of young people the heroism of local Movement personalities with the contemporary struggle against racism. For these memorial activists, a place on the map, and other memorial texts more generally, reinforces their claims that the Movement is unfinished business.

Both David Vann of Birmingham and Joanne Bland of Selma presumably support the inclusion of their respective museums on the map in *Alabama's Civil Rights Journey*. Nevertheless, neither one can afford to ignore the essentially unsettled condition of memorial texts: *Alabama's Civil Rights Journey* is ambiguous as to whether its loyalties are to the past or to the present. As such, memorial activists and entrepreneurs alike must be prepared to contend with the multiple, sometimes contradictory, readings that might arise from memorial texts. The fact remains that the map, by further linking these cities with the Movement, can be interpreted as an endorsement or an indictment, an aid to remembering or to forgetting.

Heritage Tourism and the Preservation of Civil Rights History

The tensions over remembering and forgetting that animate *Alabama's Civil Rights Journey* are echoed in debates over preserving the Movement's sociospatial legacy. Although for many the Civil Rights Movement is epitomized by the sweeping grandeur of the 1963 March on Washington, an alternative defining characteristic is the manner it was planned and conducted among the mundane spaces of everyday life (Sandage 1993). Places deserving preservation by dint of their service in the Movement include churches, Masonic lodges, restaurants, hotels, and homes. Protest sites include places of public accommodation such as bus stations, lunch counters, and bowling alleys. Sites of marches and the places in which marchers were detained are also of interest.

Although calls have been made to preserve these local sites, the recency of the events and the vernacular character of the sites' architecture pose very real difficulties in the present preservation climate (Hayden 1995). Further, many of the places associated with the Movement have been decimated in the wake of desegregation and "urban renewal" (Davis 1998). For instance, no systematic efforts are currently being made by state and local preservation agencies to document the places associated with the Movement (Weyeneth 1995). The practices of local and state historic preservation boards are heavily influenced by the federal stipulation that places on the National Register be at least fifty years old. As a result, places associated with the Movement are recorded only incidentally when they happen to satisfy the age requirement. A nineteenth-century church where civil rights meetings were held might be recorded and preserved, but equally significant but more modern churches are overlooked.

Sites are also overlooked because of a lack of understanding of the complex networks that sustained the Movement. Although the formal leadership of the Movement came from churches, businesses, and national organizations, it was often private citizens who served as catalysts and organized for change (Morris 1984; Mueller 1990). For instance, black-owned beauty parlors were a key link in the Movement's organizing chain. They were often used for small meetings and as clearinghouses for information. Importantly, their owners were somewhat insulated from white economic retaliation because their clientele was largely, if not exclusively, black. As a result, beauty parlor owners were insulated from white retribution in ways that, for instance, black schoolteachers, who depended on white school boards for their salaries, were not. Activists encouraged beauticians to get involved. Nevertheless, this important role has not been acknowledged and no such salons have been preserved and memorialized (Weyeneth 1995)—an absence reflected in

Alabama's Civil Rights Journey. The rigorous simplicity of the map, the manner in which the text calls attention to a limited number of sites, and the unrepresentative selection of photographs work together to obscure the complex social geography of the Movement.

Within its major museums, the Movement is represented as having been won on the streets, from the pulpit, and in the courtroom. Little or no mention is made of the private and semipublic spaces of citizenship schools, neighborhoods, and homes where activists found food, shelter, and community. In this sense, there is a distinct privileging of the public over the private as the spaces generative of civil rights—a situation that maps closely onto the traditionally gendered division between public and private space. These mundane sites are perhaps the most important in understanding the mechanics of activism and the common valor of ordinary participants in the Movement. Further, looking at these places makes visible the role of women, who are often overlooked when the story is told as the Won Cause.

This gendered presence and absence is confirmed and reinscribed when considering the representational spaces of *Alabama's Civil Rights Journey.* Churches, parks, statuary, and museums are well represented, but more mundane sites are not. A case in point is the manner in which the booklet makes no mention of King's female advisers—an absence that stands in contrast to scholarship demonstrating the predominance of women in organizing and staffing the Movement (Payne 1990). Jo Anne Robinson's relative anonymity is a case in point. She was a central figure in organizing the Montgomery bus boycott and was part of the committee that invited a young Martin Luther King Jr., newly arrived in town and unknown in civil rights circles, to act as its spokesperson (Burns 1997), yet she is not mentioned in the booklet. Likewise, the site of civil rights worker Viola Liuzzo's murder by white supremacists in the wake of the Voting Rights March is marked by a monument along U.S. Highway 80 but is not included on the booklet's map, despite the fact that Highway 80 is the tour route suggested by the booklet and figures prominently on the map.

With regard to Civil Rights memorial texts overall, the role most often allocated to women and, more generally, the vast majority of Movement participants is that of allegory. Their representation as allegorical figures echoes the tradition within Western art of the female form embodying some idealized virtue or vice in order to confirm a man's character and destiny (Warner 1985; Monk 1992). In its treatment of the Movement, *Alabama's Civil Rights Journey* represents what might be described as the feminized mass. The booklet opens with portraits of King on its cover and second page, and the photos that follow are of unnamed marchers. The map, by deflecting attention away from the broader sociospatial context of the Movement toward a small number of sites identified with the public spaces of cities, confirms the limited scope of the text and photos. By virtue of their numbers, enthusiasm, and positioning (e.g., as a congregation vis-à-vis the pulpit or as marchers vis-à-vis the leader of the march), the feminized mass plays the allegorical role of confirming the masculinized leadership's righteousness. For their part, the vast majority of participants, though not invisible, are thoroughly localized and led. The result is a distinctly gendered scaling of participation: the Movement is cast as an isolated matter in which local marchers follow the leadership of national-scale actors. The conflation of scale and identity in *Alabama's Civil Rights Journey* yields the notion that an elite, male leadership won civil rights by transcending space to move between pulpit and street, courtroom and legislature.

Guides such as Alabama's play the role of gatekeeper, putting some sites before the public and screening others. For instance, the Illinois state tourism bureau removed any reference to the site of the police shootings of Chicago Black Panthers Mark Clark and Fred Hampton from its guide. Subsequently, the Pepperbird Foundation, a nonprofit organization that produces guides to sites associated with African-American history, included the site of the shooting in its guide to Chicago, alongside information regarding the 1960s urban riots and police conflicts (Weyeneth 1995). In the case of *Alabama's Civil Rights Journey,* the booklet makes no reference to Lowndes County. Located between Selma and Montgomery, Lowndes County was a hotbed of organizing by the Student Nonviolent Coordinating Committee (SNCC). Working with local activists, SNCC organized the original Black Panther Party and ran an independent slate of candidates for public office (Benn 1996). Its efforts laid the groundwork for the Voting Rights March and resulted in some of the first African Americans being elected to county offices since Reconstruction. Nevertheless, SNCC is not mentioned in *Alabama's Civil Rights Journey.* The marginalization of Clark's and Hampton's deaths and SNCC's organizing of Lowndes County suggests two distinct ways of producing the past: one that venerates it and the other that discloses it as a constructed field of power/knowledge, in the process opening it up for debate (Karp and Levine 1991). Representing the Movement as the Won Cause allows political actors to rhetorically position themselves as carrying forward a legacy of progress. In contrast to the Won Cause, these marginalized places raise the specter of state-sponsored assassinations and black militancy—topics that remain outside of traditional Civil Rights discourses of nonviolent, democratic change. As a result, *Alabama's Civil Rights Journey* foregrounds heroism, fortitude, and sacrifice as values that can be commemorated by all without explicitly identifying the effects of capitalism, nationalism, and racism.

Although sites associated with the history of local activists and women's participation are largely ignored or destroyed, some individual places are being added to the National Register of Historic Places. For example, in Charleston, West Virginia, the home of a local activist, Elizabeth Harden Gilmore, was placed on the National Register to celebrate her successful efforts to desegregate lunch counters. Sites such as this one hold out the potential for radically altering common notions of where history takes place and how it should be preserved. In the case of *Alabama's Civil Rights Journey,* the map identifies U.S. Highway 80 as the link between Selma and Montgomery. More significantly, however, it was along this route that the Voting Rights March delivered its petition to the Alabama state capitol in 1965. In 1996, the highway was designated a "National Historic Route." The National Park Service, local activists, and tourism interests are in the process of considering how the history associated with such a transitory site can best be memorialized. Suggestions include walking tours of the area, interviews with participants, and an interpretive center dedicated to the common marchers who gave the protest its gravity (Bland 1999). By encouraging tourists to travel this route, the booklet's producers have, perhaps inadvertently, introduced the possibility of transgressing the carefully scripted version of the Movement they otherwise reinforce.

Conclusion

According to Koonz, it is the "intrinsic instability of supposedly fixed and immortal landscapes that gives [monuments] their power" (Koonz 1994: 259). Similar observations have been made of maps, testifying to their shared qualities as memorial texts (Harley 1989; Wood 1992). The symmetrical authority of maps and monuments—in one case generated via claims to scientific accuracy, in the other by recourse to weighty materiality—stands in stark contrast to the inherent instability of the messages they bear. The connections among the cities that the map establishes with its stylized highways and short driving distances, in tandem with the pronounced absence of any other sites, reinforces the segmented, teleological overtones of the Won Cause suggesting that these cities were predestined to be the battlefields of the Movement. Nevertheless, the map's ambiguous treatment of time and its inclusion of Highway 80 offer fluid moments at which the booklet's narrative is open to contestation.

(This contrast between apparent fixity and radical impermanence accounts for the political value of maps and monuments as representational capital.) Although their manifest purpose is to summarize and synthesize into a coherent narrative the people, places, and events associated with the Movement, these texts serve to open new chapters of struggle associated with its memory. Far from neutral, consensual renderings of time and space, Civil Rights memorial texts are at once the product and the conveyance of contemporary politics associated with race, tourism development, and social memory.

3. Construction Sites and Showcases
Mapping "The New Berlin" through Tourism Practices

Karen E. Till

This summer, Schaustelle Berlin presents itself as the largest construction site in Europe. Nine weeks long the construction fences are open for the public and offer a foretaste of the Berlin of tomorrow. . . . And it [Schaustelle Berlin] is actually completely different each year. Whereas yesterday the excavations pulled one's view into the depths below, today one looks up to the high towers, above which orange-yellow cranes move. And some buildings already shine in new radiance. The Schaustelle Berlin changes its face from week to week, and with it, its program. (Partners für Berlin 1996: 44)

After German unification in 1990 and the relocation of the national capital, Berlin's material landscapes, economic activities, and symbolic functions changed dramatically. The Wall was removed, stretches of land once marginal were suddenly central and valuable, and historic sites were reconstructed and preserved. Since 1990, planners, architects, city boosters, and other urban experts began to emphasize Berlin's status as the world's largest urban renewal project. Their different visions for the future were communicated through maps, models of the city, virtual-reality simulations, newspaper articles, planning codes, architectural sketches, and even tourism practices (see Till, forthcoming). One representation of "The New Berlin" was "Schaustelle Berlin," or "Showcase

Berlin" (hereafter, Schaustelle), a summer-long series of city tours and cultural events launched in 1996 by a private public city marketing firm. Although city marketers have long "sold" and packaged the idea of a particular city, Schaustelle Berlin is unusual because it promotes a vision of a *future city* to *locals* through tourism practices. Schaustelle tours offer "behind the scenes" information about the city under construction and its projected future. Tourists are told they can "experience the rebuilding of the city" and visit sites "normally off limits" to the general public. They can explore ruins of historical buildings to be renovated along Unter den Linden, walk through half-built skyscrapers at the Daimler-Benz center at Potsdamer Platz (Figure 3.1), tour gentrification projects in the former East, and take bike rides along the path of the former Wall. "We have tours about the stones lining Unter den Linden, about the Spandauer suburb. For those who don't have time we offer the book *Berlin: Open City* for a walk through the city" (Partners for Berlin spokesperson, personal interview, Berlin, August 2000).

This summer program, according to one Schaustelle spokesperson, was not like "mass tourism" because it provided in-depth information to help city residents "understand what is happening in their city in the last ten years . . . and confront their city identity" (ibid.). Locals, according to this spokesperson, should not only learn how the city was changing through factual information, they should pass along this information to others. "What we want is that every Berliner becomes an ambassador for Berlin. So when he/she has a visitor, he/she can point out new things." Although Schaustelle may not be "mass tourism," the particular vision of the city being promoted is structured by tourism practices, including brochures, maps, and tours. In this chapter, I analyze how Schaustelle culturally maps "The New Berlin" through the tourism genre of frontstage/backstage and from the vantage point of the urban expert.[1] The city is represented as a series of continuously changing construction sites, or *Baustellen,* that are located in a new spatial-temporal frame as showcases, or *Schaustellen,* sites at which to look. The new focal point of the city is defined by recently built government and business and commercial centers, whereas Cold War historic divisions (of East/West) are erased and represented as tourist sites. The tours have been quite popular for a variety of reasons, including the thrill of watching and imagining oneself in a live construction display or feeling as though one can become an expert about a rapidly changing city. Before describing the tours, I provide some background information

Figure 3.1. Touring "The New Berlin": Going "behind the scenes" at the Daimler-Benz complex at Potsdamer Platz, Berlin, June 1997.

about city marketing, tourism, and the group responsible for Schaustelle, Partners for Berlin.

Partners for Berlin

City officials and elites have historically recognized the importance of creating a "look" for a city as a way to manage complex urban spaces and how a city will be understood by local and international audiences (see Philo and Kearns 1993). To frame an image of the city in the present often entails the power to define that city's past and future. By marketing a city, boosters sell a positive image of a place as unique by virtue of its special objects, peoples, and experiences. City marketing—a practice dating back to medieval Europe (Harvey 1989a in Goodwin 1993; see also Ward and Gold 1995)—has become more pronounced in recent years with the shift from industrial to service-based economies in many Western countries (Harvey 1989b; Zukin 1995). As local and national financial markets and structures have changed, cities increasingly compete with one another at the regional, national, and international levels for corporate and tourist dollars. City marketing is premised on a normative system of place-based classification that reduces the complexities of the urban experience. A strategy is developed to promote one city as standing out from, and as being better than, other cities elsewhere. New images of a place are created to replace images held by residents, investors, and visitors that are considered to be vague or negative by marketers (Holcomb 1993). At the same time, cities may be classified as belonging to an elite group of places, such as the global and cosmopolitan cities of London, Tokyo, and New York. Such classification systems can communicate an idea of where certain activities and peoples belong at multiple scales. If an image of the city becomes a dominant way of knowing about that place, that image becomes a status symbol that can also be purchased, sold, and consumed.

Although city marketers acknowledge their role in contributing to urban "symbolic economies" (Zukin 1995), they see their work as more than simply advertising or the selling of a place. They assert that place marketing enhances the image as well as the "reality" of a city (Holcomb 1993).[2] My research also indicates that city marketers claim that local residents can change their relationship to their home in positive ways through their marketing activities. One company that caters to local residents in this way is Partners for Berlin (hereafter, Partners), a private–

public partnership formed in 1994. The idea for Partners resulted from the former mayor of Berlin, Eberhard Diepgen, who, after the failed bid for the 2000 Olympics, wanted to promote a positive, postunification image of the city. Partners is contracted out by the city to promote Berlin at the international, domestic, and local levels through cultural events, outreach programs, public relations, advertisements, and other means. It is the first private–public partnership of its kind in Berlin, and perhaps Germany, and, though typical in structure for the United States, it is an unusual organizational form for city and place marketing in Europe (Partners spokesperson, personal interview, August 2000). The city subcontracts out Partners to develop and distribute city marketing images with a rough budget of eight million German Marks (in 2000). The real "Partners," however, are the corporate and other sponsors who have a vested interest in promoting Berlin domestically and abroad. Corporate Partners are the primary funders of the organization, contributing around fifteen million German Marks in 2000, part of which is given in material services. They also have a voice in the organization's decision-making processes. In 1994, there were twenty-eight founding companies and, by 2000, Partners had more than one hundred.

promotes one modern image of Berlin.

Since 1994, the main goal of Partners has been to organize cultural events, such as Schaustelle Berlin, for various target audiences, yet to promote a *single contemporary image* of Berlin. As one spokesperson explained:

> We want to bring the idea of Berlin into people's minds . . . also for investors. We want them to become interested in Berlin, maybe to start a company or business, and to create jobs. But we also address the Berliners because we don't want to ignore them in our marketing concept. They should feel comfortable in their city. . . . So we have different programs and different target groups. (Ibid.).

The overarching concept Partners developed for its programs and target groups is that Berlin is "new." As the 1999 Schaustelle brochure explained, "an original combination of living, life, and work . . . creates the urbanity, the modernity, the cosmopolitan attitude—which identifies the 'New Berlin'" (Eberhard Diepgen, former mayor of Berlin, English translation in brochure, p. 3). In the "Das neue Berlin" campaign, Berlin is represented as the capital city, a creative city, a cultural metropole, a livable city, and as an East–West metropolis or gateway city.[3] The themes of this campaign—an emphasis on the future, a good quality of life, and the centrality of the city—are typical for city "makeover" campaigns designed to attract and retain investments, consumers, businesses, tourists, and new residents (Holcomb 1993). Yet the use of city tours to promote these themes *to locals* appears to be unique. The Schaustelle Berlin summer program is advertised through local venues of information not normally accessed by nonresident tourists in their summer planning, such as local newspapers and radio stations, and is distributed through local mailings. Based on participant observation of the tours, informal conversations with tourists, and information provided by Partners, most of the people who participated in Schaustelle tours are city residents.[4] So why is Partners concerned with representing the city to locals through tourism practices?

In 1994, the fledgling Partners group conducted an "image poll" of the city, asking Berliners, German citizens, and managers in New York, Tokyo, and London about their image of Berlin and their wishes for the future. One Partners public-relations spokesperson explained that Berliners in particular felt good about their city, but they did not like three things: crime, graffiti, and construction sites (which were associated with traffic, noise, dirt, and dust). Similarly, informal conversations I have had with Berliners who lived in the city before unification (from both the former East and the former West) suggest that locals coped with the confusion and stress of the rapidly changing city by staying home, avoiding the center of the city, and moving within their local residential district *(Bezirk)*. For these individuals, it was difficult and exhausting to move around in the city when routes, networks, and individual buildings continuously changed for eight to ten years. The director of Partners wanted to "turn a negative aspect of the city into one of its strengths, make construction sites *[Baustellen]* into showcases or spectacles *[Schaustellen]*" (personal interview, August 2000).[5] Schaustelle Berlin was thus conceived and introduced in the summer of 1996. The tours (re)represent the city to individuals who have personal histories and memories of that city and live there. As one spokesperson explained, it is a cultural program designed to help Berliners—who already live in the city and are often referred to as "old Berliners"—discover "The New Berlin":

With the Schaustelle Berlin tours we want to provide evidence for those five themes [of "The New Berlin"]. Right now we are looking for tours that demonstrate and emphasize these strengths [of the city]. . . . I think that the Schaustelle is the best opportunity to inform oneself about Berlin. It's a propaganda battle, if I may use this word. One gets to know everything. (Personal interview, Berlin, August 2000)

Before I describe the tours, I should note that marketers, as well as some scholars, would not consider Schaustelle Berlin to be a form of tourism. City tourism research does not categorically include locals in their studies, but rather defines tourists as visitors to a place, individuals who travel to see unique places, events, and objects. In this view, residents of a place may only participate in tourism as workers, but not as consumers (see Crang 1997). Tourism from this paradigm is considered to be an "industry" and is defined largely by economic measures, such as dollars spent or hotel occupancy rates (Pearce 1995; Wöber 1997; for a critique see Rojek and Urry 1997a). In everyday practice, such definitions appear to be employed as well. The Berliners with whom I spoke who were participating in the tours did not see themselves as tourists. When I first conducted informal conversations with individuals on Schaustelle tours, I approached people with a general statement such as, "Hello, my name is Karen Till and I'm a professor at the University of Minnesota. I'm studying tourism and was wondering if you might answer a couple of questions about the Schaustelle tours." People were offended by my statement, stating, "But we're not tourists. We're Berliners." One woman pointed out that she gave city tours to tourists! Only when I defined myself as a visitor to the city were people more willing to discuss these tours. Similarly, Partners distinguishes between tourists and Berliners. A Partners' spokesperson explained:

(handwritten margin note: technically not actually tourism because they are locals taking the tour.)

> For tourists there are always tickets. We know that we have to give them a chance. But it is something special; people must have the feeling that it is not easy. It must not be mass tourism anymore. (Personal interview, August 2000)

This person's response indicates that because mostly locals go on Schaustelle tours, "ordinary" tourists (i.e., non-Berliners) probably would not be aware of the tours or have regular access to tickets. Unlike city tour companies that engage in "mass tourism" for profit, Partners limits access *to sites* but does not charge high prices for limited tours. Tickets range in price from two to fifteen German marks, which means that Partners subsidizes this program.

These examples suggest, then, that Berliners, as well as Partners' spokespersons, think of tourists as nonlocals and view Schaustelle as different from "ordinary" city tours. In recent years, however, a number of scholars have begun to define tourism as a set of cultural rather than primarily economic practices, a definition that also suggests a different understanding of the social category of "tourist" (Del Casino and Hanna 2000; Kirschenblatt-Gimblett 1998; Rojek and Urry 1997b). Drawing on Maxine Feifer's (1985) work, George Ritzer and Allan Liska (1997) use the concept "post-tourist" to discuss individuals who chose to engage in more eclectic forms of tourism, such as tourists who do not leave their home to travel but travel virtually to sites via the Internet. My research builds upon these discussions by calling attention to city tourism and marketing practices that cater to local residents. If tourists are individuals who leave behind their "normal" places of work, residence, and social life to go somewhere else for a short period of time (Urry 1990), certainly locals going on Schaustelle Berlin tours fit that characterization.

Yet even this understanding is somewhat limiting because of the bounded ways that "the city" is conceived of in tourism and marketing studies. I argue that the distinction between "normal" places and places "elsewhere" (be they places that reify mythologies of escapism or other imaginary "tourist" worlds) is (literally) misplaced. Cities are complex types of places. Political economies, everyday routines, perceptions of cities, cultural productions, group activities, networks, social memories, and representations inform and constitute what we think of as the urban and social spaces through which we move, live, work, and play. A significant part of the "reality" of cities, and of places more generally, includes dreams, desires, stories, and ghosts—those urban imaginaries—created by people who live and work in a place (Adams, Hoelscher, and Till 2001; Gordon 1997; Lefebvre 1991; Pile 1996; Till, forthcoming). Cities, in other words, are always "normal" and "somewhere else" for both residents and visitors.

As I describe in the following section, Schaustelle offers a structured way for locals to move out of their local networks and daily routines into "unfamiliar" parts of the city through tourism practices that represent "The New Berlin." Not only are new functions, networks, and landscapes described, but the physical experience of the tours is also framed by the genre backstage/frontstage. Representations of the (temporally limited) construction sites, or backstage, in other words, also define "The New Berlin" as a (future) global city (or frontstage).

"The New Berlin": From Construction Site to Global City

As the opening quote of this chapter suggests, Schaustelle's representations of the city must be situated within, as well as have contributed to, the cultural discourses and material realities of Berlin as a city under construction. In Schaustelle promotional materials, Berlin is described as a "forest of cranes" or *Kranstadt* (city of cranes): audiences are encouraged to watch the "symphony of cranes" build the city anew (Figures 3.1 and 3.2). A central image of a 1998 brochure cover, for example, is the blue iris of a circular eye. This eye reflects back images of the city's cultural landmarks and performances, including a cluster of cranes, to the viewing audience. It is an image that emphasizes a way of seeing (and hence understanding) the city. Of course, the very name of the program, Schaustelle Berlin, emphasizes the notion of that Berlin should be watched from a privileged viewing position as a spectacle, a kind of exotic vision that is different from everyday experiences because of its limited access in time.

This emphasis on looking, on the "gaze"—the unidirectional (and consuming) view of foreign worlds, scenes, and places from a privileged position—is, of course, one of the primary cultural practices of tourism (Urry 1990). Tourism sites are considered spectacles because they are defined as places and experiences not located in the realm of the "everyday." According to John Urry (1990), tourists leave their established routines to stimulate their senses. The sense of departure from the everyday is pleasurable, even exciting. But tourists are also interested in experiencing and witnessing the mundane details that go into creating those spectacular performances. Schaustelle Berlin tours also represent a sneak preview of "The New Berlin" through the structure of the backstage, that is, through a physical experience of going "behind the scenes" of the city being built. Dean MacCannell's classic 1976 work describes this idea of the working region, or backstage (MacCannell 1989). Because backstage regions are considered "off limits" to the viewing audience, the audience (tourists) wants to see and experience those backstage places, peoples, and activities. The more elusive and the more difficult it is to

Figure 3.2. Staging the "Symphony of Cranes": representing "The New Berlin" in 1996. Schaustelle Berlin program cover, Partners für Berlin, 1996.

gain access to the backstage, the more authentic that world appears to tourists. Of course, the irony is that such "backstages" have themselves become a tourist genre, a genre that Schaustelle Berlin employs to gain legitimacy for its representations of the city.

Although MacCannell's main argument—that tourism is about the search for authenticity—has been challenged in recent years (e.g., Crang 1997; Ritzer and Liska 1997), his work is significant because he points to a central paradox of tourism as cultural practice. Drawing from Erving Goffman's (1959) work, MacCannell argues that every backstage is necessarily defined by a frontstage, or performance space of tourism. Thus, just as Schaustelle tours provide limited "backstage" access to the Berlin represented as construction site, the tours must simultaneously represent a frontstage to the construction site, namely, Berlin as a world-class city. Berlin is not only represented as a site of urban renewal, as a "city in transition." Schaustelle tours, by bringing visitors to see "the capital city as it will evolve," also reveal a frontstage that was already unveiled by 2000 (Figure 3.3):

> In the fifth year of the Schaustelle, a change is apparent in the program. While in the previous years the visitor was led behind the construction fences, in this year [2000] you will be shown numerous finished buildings. The curtain lifts, the future has begun. (Partners für Berlin 2000: 10)

As the tourism genre of backstage/frontstage suggests, producers of tourism sites and symbols employ a series of ever-shifting dichotomies, including backstage–stage, artificial–authentic, present–future, exotic–everyday, real self–tourist self, and tourist–worker. These dichotomies are staged and performed in the spaces between the material trace and the symbol, between the fleeting moment and the seemingly permanent site. To understand tourism as cultural practice, then, is to explore how tourism sites are represented as clearly delineated types of places, yet are, at the same time, always in motion because of the cultural performances of tourism. As Rob Shields (1991b) has argued, tourism practices fluctuate between representational, interpretive, and experiential spaces located somewhere between the tourist gaze, material landscapes of tourism, and sites and symbols of tourism. For scholars, this means that tourism cannot be simply understood through a "reading" of symbols, such as maps, because these symbols cannot be separated out from the material spaces of tourism (Del Casino and Hanna 2000). Both represent and constitute place as tourist site. Further, because tourist sites are also created by the bodily presence of tourists, workers, and locals (who have varied interpretations and experiences and whose social roles are also in flux at these sites) (see Crang 1997; Del Casino and

Figure 3.3. The "frontstage" unveiled: representing "The New Berlin" in 2000. Schaustelle Berlin program cover, Partners für Berlin, 2000.

Hanna 2000), tourist sites and their representations are always both imaginary and "real."

In the next section, I explore how the spaces of "The New Berlin" are represented through Schaustelle brochures, maps, and tours. I argue that these representational practices detach buildings, ruins, and sites from their dense, multiple historical urban contexts and relocate them as showcases, or objects of tourist fascination to be viewed in particular ways. The process of detaching places from historical contexts and relocating them in a new spatial frame ("The New Berlin") occurs through textual descriptions, images (especially the photographs and maps), and tours, representations that, in different ways, provide a kind of "reality effect" for these new mappings of the city.

A City in Transition: Schaustelle Berlin Programs and Maps

A new Schaustelle Berlin program is printed every year that offers a guide to the upcoming events and tours for that summer.[6] In 1996, for example, the theme was "Summer in Berlin: Theater, Construction, Boulevards" (Figure 3.2). In 1999, the program cover announced: "Tickets, Tours, and Schedules: Potsdamer Platz, Federal Ministry Buildings, and much more." By 2000, however, rather than proclaim a theme, numerous city offerings were listed: "Summer in Berlin: Expo 2000 in Berlin: Berlin: Open City: Culture Summer 2000: The highlights: Inner City Plan." Brochure imagery similarly communicated a change in emphasis from the city under construction to a well-established city that offered an array of summer activities. In the first three years, program covers represented the city as a construction site with cranes looming overhead; people watched cultural events and the city being built (Figure 3.2). By 1999, the cover presented a blurred image of the new Sony-Daimler-Benz business centers at Potsdamer Platz, as though the buildings themselves were in motion. In 2000, the movement stopped; the cover depicted a crisp picture of "The New Berlin" standing elegantly—and completed—at dusk (Figure 3.3).

The program covers indicate a shift in what Partners hoped Schaustelle would achieve. Already in its second year, when construction sites were still the most prominent and popular tours, the program began to offer tours of *completed buildings.* For example, when asked what was different in 1997 compared to 1996, Volker Hassemer, the former Berlin minster of cultural affairs and now Partners director, said "Schaustelle is

[margin note: image of "New Berlin" loses the history and content of a place.]

no longer a festival of construction sites, but rather a festival of finished buildings. A good example is the Philip-Johnson-House at Checkpoint Charlie" (*Der Tagesspiegel,* 1997). People attending the tours in 2000, however, associated Schaustelle with construction site tours. One Partners spokesperson explained that they would need to change that image because so many buildings were already completed:

> Schaustelle should not mean construction sites anymore. . . . We will always offer tours, but we will only point out what happens where. We do not organize the events, but we collect data about it. We help tourists and Berliners to organize their summer. . . . And there is always the option to use Schaustelle as an opportunity to learn more about the development of the city. But, overall, Berlin is itself a Schaustelle all summer long. Our new concept is: in Berlin *is* the Schaustelle. (Partners spokesperson, personal interview, August 2000)

This shift in concept and representational strategies—from showcasing particular construction sites in the city to showcasing the city itself—was also reflected in program maps (Figure 3.4). More generally, the city is represented by a complex design of footprints for existing buildings and buildings under construction. The aerial extent of the city represented in the maps expanded through time. In 1996, the design of building footprints covered only the central part of the map; in 1997, it covered the entire layout (Figure 3.4). By 2000, this layout was expanded to include one-third more area. Nonetheless, with the exception of the 2000 map, Schaustelle program maps were probably not used by individuals to find the location of a tour. Rather, Schaustelle maps, much like the other representations of Berlin in the programs, provided the reader/tourist with conceptual information about how the city was changing from year to year.

The different "realities" projected in the maps from 1996 to 2000 communicated the sense that the city was in rapid transition and that by 2000 the new city had arrived. The 1996 and 1997 map title is "Inner City Map," whereas the 2000 map states, "The New Center: Between the River Spree and the Landwehr Canal" and features "The New Berlin" logo in bright red in the right-hand corner. The maps indicate the categories of the tours and highlight specific buildings accessible by the tours. For example, individual buildings were listed numerically under categories such as "Information," "Showcases," "Construction

Innenstadtplan

Information
- Schaustellen-Counter an der INFO BOX
- Schaustellen-Counter im Kontorhaus Mitte
- Schaustellen VVK Fullhouse Service, Budapester Straße (nicht im Plan)

Baustellen- und Objektbesichtigungen
- Daimler Benz Areal
- Neue Hackesche Höfe
- Checkpoint Charlie
- Kulturkaufhaus Friedrichstraße
- Ökologisches Bürohochhaus
- Dresdner Bank / Pariser Platz
- Quartier 205 der FriedrichstadtPassagen
- Quartier 206 der FriedrichstadtPassagen
- Quartier 207 der FriedrichstadtPassagen
- Innenstadtmodell der Senatsverwaltung für Bauen, Wohnen und Verkehr, Behrenstraße 42
- Mit-Machbaustelle
- Tiergartentunnel
- Informationszentrum der Bundesregierung für die Hauptstadtplanung (Hauptstadt-Modell)
- Reichstag
- Gemäldegalerie

Ministerienstandorte/Objektbesichtigungen
- Presse- und Informationsamt der Bundesregierung
- Bundesministerium für Wirtschaft
- Bundesministerium der Justiz
- Bundesministerium der Finanzen
- Bundesministerium für Verkehr
- Auswärtiges Amt
- Bundesrat
- Bundesministerium der Verteidigung
- Bundesministerium für Arbeit und Sozialordnung
- Museumsinsel
- Bundespräsidialamt (nicht im Plan)

Bestand   Planung

- Adlershof
- Rummelsburger Bucht
- Karow Nord
- Hellersdorf
- Marzahn
- Nordkreuz
- Wilhelminenhof
- Technologie- & Gründerzentrum
- Spreeinsel
- Landsberger Tor
- Lichtenberg
- Deutsches Technikmuseum
- Berlin Museum
- Ludwig Erhart Haus
- Abwasserpumpwerk Wilmersdorf
- "Plohn" am Bonsigturm
- Oberbaum City
- Siedlungsverdichtung Bellastraße
- Treptowers

Figure 3.4. Mapping "The New Berlin": 1997 inner-city map of construction sites and showcases. Schaustelle Berlin Program, Partners für Berlin, 1997.

Sites and Objects of Interest," and "Federal Ministry Buildings and Objects of Interest." These categories were represented by bold colors, such as bright red, kelly green, royal blue, and dark purple—colors that seemed to jump out from the page because they were mapped on top of muted colors such as white, skin-tone, and apricot (in 1996), and gray and taupe (in 1997). In contrast, the 2000 map was more typical of a general-use map. It noted transportation stops (for the metro, streetcar, and train) and was more user-friendly and prominent in the program, located in the inside back jacket and flap. It had an English and German legend and a different page format, one similar to a magazine (A4 format). Longer pages resulted in larger font sizes for the names of streets, nodes, and networks; this map was much easier to read as a result. The colors used in the 2000 map were more typical for standard European maps (Mark Lindberg, personal communication, 2001), including periwinkle blue, tangerine orange, tan, and grass green to represent the building categories of "New Buildings by Private Investors," "Cultural Institutions," "Buildings of the Federal Government, the State of Berlin, Embassies," and "State Representations, Party Headquarters, Foundations, and Associations," respectively. Unlike the earlier maps, these colors were not dramatically different from the muted background colors of pale yellow, taupe gray, lime green, and white, nor did any one color category dominate.[7]

The differences between the maps communicated to the reader/tourist that Berlin was undergoing rapid change but had "settled" by 2000, a temporal sequence that was significant for locals who had gone on Schaustelle tours in previous years. The new spatial-temporal frame of the city was emphasized not only through the sequence of programs and maps, but also through the ways Schaustelle classified sites of interest into new functional regions.

The Frontstage: New Urban Centers

In the brochures, Berlin was defined by new centers, in particular the government district and business centers. Descriptive texts (with short English summaries) and imagery (color photographs, sketches, advertisements, maps, and page designs) represented the location of a showcase site, listed the architects and/or firms involved with the construction/reconstruction, and highlighted new buildings and districts. Schaustelle brochures instilled in the reader a sense of excitement of what was to come in Berlin and expectations about the tours (and future city). These symbols represented space functionally through the relative locations of individual buildings (in relationship to other buildings and districts) and through networks connecting new functional urban regions (such as the government district, commercial centers, residential areas, and cultural centers).

In all the brochures, the new buildings of the government district were highlighted, such as the renovated Reichstag building and the new buildings of the "federal belt." The government precinct of the new capital was described as being located in the heart of the city near the River Spree, yet also decentralized because many government ministries were to occupy already-existing buildings. Many tours to individual ministries and government offices were offered; these buildings were also included as part of popular city tours, such as "Hauptstadt im Werden" (The capital as it is becoming), "Berlin—wie es wird" (Berlin as it will become), or "Die Zunkunft hat begonnen" (The future has begun). New and renovated buildings defined the edges of the 1997 map; set off in red, the buildings symbolically represented a central government frame that was connected to commercial centers through transportation networks. In the 2000 brochure, these buildings were located in explicitly named districts, including the "Parliament and Government Quarter" and the "Ministries and Regional Representatives" area. The brochure also described the number of new jobs created in the new capital city through the multimedia, information, service, education, and science and technology sectors that were described as significant economic activities of "The New Berlin." Tours that year also showcased the working spaces of the completed government district, going behind the scenes of the new federal ministries, news media stations, and the suburban "scientific city" of Adlershof.

"The New Berlin" was also defined by new business centers. Schaustelle depicts Berlin as an emerging global city through representations of corporate and consumer spaces, especially around Potsdamer Platz, Pariser Platz, Friedrichstrasse, Checkpoint Charlie, and the Hackesche Höfe— all places in the former East. The 1996 guide, for example, described "Baustelle Potsdamer Platz" and emphasized the Weinhaus Huth building, the highlight of the most popular walking tours of Potsdamer Platz that year. The map accented new business regions along Friedrichstrasse. Similarly, in 1997, "A walk through the center of Berlin" described a tour of "Berlin, Friedrichstrasse: Yesterday, Today, Tomorrow." And, of course, the 1999 and 2000 brochures, while emphasizing the move of the federal government to Berlin, depicted the new Sony-Daimler-Benz high-rise business complex at Potsdamer Platz on their covers (Figure 3.3). This historic, now corporate, commercial city center has become the most popular destination for Schaustelle "tourists" every year.

In brochures, new transportation networks were mapped that linked the government district and business centers to situate Berlin as a European regional train center. In the 1997 Schaustelle map, burgundy depicted transportation networks of new road layouts (especially around Potsdamer Platz and Checkpoint Charlie) and transportation links (particularly the north–south link between the government district and Potsdamer Platz). Also present in brochures was the new link connecting the government district in the West to Hackesche Höfe and Alexanderplatz in the East, two areas being renovated through private investment. These networks, as a showcase, were also on display. One of the most popular tours of 2000 was the underground tour of the Lehrter Regional Train Station, the new transportation hub for Berlin, its surrounding region, and Europe (Figure 3.6). This tour also emphasized the new transportation connections between government districts and business centers. The movements and flows of the city, in other words, were represented as fundamentally changed in Berlin. Cold War divisions and even immediate post-Wall divides do not appear here.

Touring East and West: A New Spatial Framework

Schaustelle representations of "The New Berlin" map a new set of relative, functional, and experiential locations on top of those that formerly existed. Barbara Kirschenblatt-Gimblett (1998) argues that fragments become objects of display by virtue of the manner in which they are detached. Through Schaustelle tourism practices, when places are represented as construction sites they are detached from existing spatial and temporal contexts to become objects at which to look. New urban centers are created through the erasure and commodification of Cold War divisions, in particular of the former East and West. A different "sense of place" is also communicated for districts *(Bezirke)* and their functions than existed before and immediately following unification.

Although the base map for all programs covered the former Eastern district of *Mitte* and parts of the former Western district of *Tiergarten,* there were only subtle clues to indicate the former Cold War division of the city or the changing landscapes immediately following unification. In addition to the representations of changing buildings from year to year, a couple of street names changed from the 1996 map to the 1997 map, such as Clara-Zetkin Street (the name of a communist resistance fighter), which was changed to Dorotheen Street. In none of these maps, however, was the former path of the Berlin Wall(s) indicated, even though Schaustelle regularly offers bike and bus tours along the path of the Wall. Partners wanted to promote an image of Berlin as being "open" and cosmopolitan, and to distance this new image from earlier associations of Berlin as a walled and divided city, as an "island" (Partners spokesperson, personal interview, August 2000). Thus, in brochures, Schaustelle represented the Wall as a kind of reality that was not "visible" in the material landscape of new construction (and hence not mapped), but was nonetheless important as a tourist site. For example, on a bus tour I took in 2000, individuals wanted to know where the Wall stood when we crossed between East and West Berlin. Although many Berliners may remember where the Wall once stood, they also tried to live their lives ignoring that division. Certainly, few people would know its exact path throughout the entire city. In "The New Berlin," however, locals can now employ an expert guide to show them how and where to "look" at the landscape to find evidence of the Wall's (unseen) presence. This information can then be relayed to guests who came to visit. Another obvious symbol of the formerly divided city is Checkpoint Charlie, which was listed as a construction site in Schaustelle maps for 1996 and 1997. Tours that went to or included Checkpoint Charlie showcased the new American Business Center construction site. On one of the few English-speaking bus tours that Schaustelle offered in 1997, people were more interested in knowing why so little of the Wall and the control gate were left standing than in hearing details about the new business center.[8] Although this tour was unusual because it specifically catered to non-locals and non-German speakers, similar discussions may have taken place on other tours, but were perhaps motivated by a German, as opposed to an American or foreign, variant of Cold War tourism.

Another subtle clue of former East and West division was apparent in the 2000 map. In that map, alternative art and social locales that spontaneously grew immediately following unification in the former East were mapped as "cultural institutions." Tacheles, for example, grew as an

exhibition, bar, dance, performance, and social space as a result of a protest occupation of the building by artists, activists, and other squatters.
This large, five-story building and its back courtyard and garden area
are located between Friedrichstrasse and Oranienburgerstrasse. Shortly
after unification, the building was condemned because there is no back
wall on the entire building. Because of the squatter movement, this social and creative space spontaneously became an icon of the alternative
Berlin scene. Years later, as the neighboring streets became increasingly
gentrified (into an art and cultural district) so too did Tacheles. It is now
viewed as a trendy place, attracting people who want to enjoy and watch
(rather than politically engage in) alternative art scenes. Other places
mapped as cultural institutions include the Hackesche Höfe, private
developments that capitalize on youth to middle-aged retro nostalgia
for urban "courtyard culture" *(Hofkultur)*. Once considered run-down,
dreary housing, these turn-of-the-twentieth-century tenement buildings
in the former East were renovated and are now full of hip urbanites who
go shopping, watch movies, go to exhibitions, eat, people-watch, and get
their hair cut in the series of connected courtyards.

Former divisions of the city are, in Schaustelle logic, represented
as tourist sites that contribute to economic relations only. Places like
Checkpoint Charlie, Tacheles, and Hackesche Höfe, when located as
tourist sites in "The New Berlin," have become museums of themselves.
To paraphrase Kirschenblatt-Gimblett (1998) when sites, buildings, objects, or even ways of life can no longer sustain themselves economically,
"they 'survive' . . . as representations of themselves" (151). Although the
material landscapes of these places are a result of different and overlapping historical, social, political, and economic relations that have contributed to the formation of the contemporary city, in "The New Berlin"
they exist as showcases to be mapped and sites at which to look.

Going "behind the Scenes": Schaustelle Tours

> Berliners and their guests have an unusual chance to participate in this
> exciting process of planning and construction. (Former Berlin mayor
> Eberhard Diepgen, quoted in Partners für Berlin 1996, English summary
> in program, p. 3)

Schaustelle tours represent Berlin's "backstage" through physical access
to particular buildings, engineering feats, districts, and networks (Figure
3.5). Moreover, the tours of construction sites are given by the very city

experts who are building the new city, such as architects, planners, corporate managers, transportation engineers, and historic preservationists. I interpret the tours as live exhibitions, or staged performances of "The New Berlin" that represent a particular topography of the city as well as a privileged viewing position from which to experience the city. In the process of staging "The New Berlin" as "real" (through expert, detailed information), the tours may also have (re)represented an individual's relationship to what he or she considered to be "real" in the city. In other words, through the representational spaces of the tours, Schaustelle simultaneously produced certain kinds of imaginative geographies from and in which locals/tourists might have situated themselves and redefined their everyday experiences and perceptions of the city.

The spectacle of construction was in itself enough of a reason to want to go on these tours (Figure 3.5). The sublime of construction anticipates the finished product. Further, Berlin's backstage of construction is appealing because of its limited access in time. For locals, going "behind stage" was defined by the knowledge that each tour was different from hour to hour, that the tour, in fact, might not be available next year or even for the next person. On tours I took of the Isozaki building

Figure 3.5. The "backstage": the spectacle of construction atop the Isozaki building, Potsdamer Platz, June 1997.

at Potsdamer Platz, the Neues Museum in the historic district, or the Lehrter Regional Train Station, part of the thrill was knowing that these were sites in process, that tomorrow, maybe even the very next minute, these buildings would become less rough, more polished. Tourists were asked to be careful, to step over this rubble or that wire, to gently walk on planks over holes. Many tour guides allowed individuals to leave if they did not want to take the risk of getting injured during the tour; some offered construction helmets. Thus the very bodies of the locals moving through the spaces of construction (i.e., the representational spaces of the tours) became part of the backstage of construction and the frontstage of "The New Berlin" (Figure 3.6).

Not only did going backstage offer the allure of imagining what the "finished" object might look like, it encouraged the local/tourist to indulge in the pleasure of pretending to be someone else, such as a conceptual architect, engineer, or even construction worker. As the tourists watched construction workers build skyscrapers or took a bus tour with a city planner or asked questions while walking through the ruins of old museums with historic preservationists, they participated in the live display and staging of "The New Berlin." Again, to quote Kirschenblatt-Gimblett (1998), live exhibitions

Figure 3.6. Locals embodying "The New Berlin": touring the Lehrter Regional Train Station with experts and residents. August 2000.

create the illusion that the activities you watch are being done rather than represented, a practice that creates the effect of authenticity or realness. Semiotically live displays make the status of the performer problematic, for people become signs of themselves. We experience a representation even when the representers are the people themselves. (55)

The tourist, in other words, could participate in the construction and representation of the capital city through the imaginary and material spaces of the tours (Figure 3.6). But these spaces of representation were always defined by the (safe and controlled) vantage point of an "urban expert" from above. Tourists were told about the goals of the designers as well as the technical difficulties they faced. For example, in a 1997 tour of the Jewish museum designed by Daniel Libeskind, after hearing about the conceptual design, locals/tourists discussed what kind of exhibition space could be created given the unusual sculptural nature of the building's interior spaces. Of course, locals/tourists were also interested in wondering what it would be like to be the workers on the construction sites, especially on tours of partly completed buildings (Figure 3.5). Through the representational spaces of the tours, workers as well as locals/tourists become signs of the "real" construction site of Berlin. For example, at the Isosaki building tour at Potsdamer Platz, people wanted to know: How many cranes are here? How long do the workers work? How many people were injured or died at the work site? How often do crane drivers go to the bathroom (which was then related to local jokes about how much beer a crane driver can drink before having to go to the bathroom)? However, on these tours specific information about the workers was not provided, such as where they came from (Ireland?), what were they paid, what their benefits were, and so on. Rather, locals/tourists positioned themselves in a pleasurable imaginary setting, as a construction worker, high above the ground located somewhere in the urban jungle of cranes (Figure 3.5) or underground creating new tunnels (Figure 3.6), settings that for tourists do not include social conflict or inequity.

[margin annotation: picturesque image of construction]

Concluding Notes: Living in "The New Berlin"

We are different than those construction site tours. We give a lot of facts and info.

Other cities are completed, you know where everything is. Berlin is not a complete city yet. In ten years probably I could show the finished product. We want to say that Berlin is a large architectural exhibition.

Each and every year things change. Normal tours might show you similar things, but they do not go into depth. We tell you who is constructing what and what lies behind it. Other sightseeing tours in cities are
always superficial. I don't have to do a tour a second time in Munich,
but in Berlin I have to do it again and again because things change so
fast. (Partners spokesperson, personal interview, August 2000)

Schaustelle Berlin is a unique marketing-tourism program because local
residents are the target audience of city promotion. A new image of the
city is represented through the structure of the "backstage," a temporary space in which Berlin is depicted as a construction site continuously changing and in motion. "The New Berlin," or frontstage of the
construction site, is "a large architectural exhibition." As such, it is not
defined by historical divisions but emphasizes movement across former
Cold War divisions and highlights new government and business centers from the vantage point of urban experts.

Schaustelle representations and cultural practices have had an influence on economic activities, images of the city, and material landscapes.
Schaustelle thus far has been a success and its impact has been felt on
the local city tourism industry. Tours have been popular; many sold
out quickly, and most needed advance purchase. By 1999 and 2000,
Partners began to charge (minimally) for its programs instead of offering them for free, and the 2000 brochure became a general magazine
for city events and tourism in which a "Berlin Cultural Calendar"
with listings of other city tours and the year's highlights for the "Berlin
Cultural Summer" was included. Ads were placed for other city tours in
Schaustelle programs, including those that claimed to offer alternatives,
such as the "Schaustelle from below: Critical tours of the construction
site Berlin" offered by the environmental organization BUND (Bund
für Umwelt und Naturschutz Deutschland) (BUND advertisement, in
Partners für Berlin 1997a: 31). These tours offered different "behind the
scenes" tours of what was "really" happening at the construction sites
and thus also used the Schaustelle tourism genre of frontstage/backstage.
However, unlike Schaustelle, on these tours guides challenged locals/
tourists to look at the city from nonofficial, yet expert, perspectives.
They questioned the transportation and building designs of the new
business and government centers (BUND spokespersons, personal interview, September 2000; participant observation of Potsdamer Platz tour,

August 2000). Although alternative city tours have always existed in Berlin, their presence in the Schaustelle catalog, either working in conjunction with Partners (such as StattReisen) or by claiming to provide alternatives (such as BUND), suggest that Schaustelle as a concept influenced the dominant ways of "seeing" and representing Berlin, or at least had a large influence on city tourism iconographies.

As I have suggested, the representational spaces of Schaustelle included the bodily performances of locals who also became symbols of "The New Berlin." Vincent Del Casino and Stephen Hanna (2000) have argued that tourism maps, symbols, sites, and material landscapes always reproduce and simultaneously destabilize structured tourism spaces and categories of identity, such as tourist and worker. Did Schaustelle influence the ways that locals talk about, think of, and experience their home city and themselves? Although I do not have the data to answer that question here (a topic that warrants future research), I would like to conclude by mentioning some preliminary local/tourist responses.

Based on informal conversations I had with Berliners on five different kinds of tours in 2000, I had a strong sense that these individuals liked Schaustelle Berlin tours. Of course, each person who went on the tours is situated in a variety of social spaces simultaneously and has multiple identities, so each individual probably had distinct experiences and interpretations of the tours. But still, these individuals mentioned that Schaustelle was informative and "a good way to see the city in a different way." They also considered it to be different from other city tours because it offered in-depth information. A couple of people also mentioned that they liked the small groups. "It is far better than the special 'Open Door Days' [for new federal buildings, such as the Reichstag]; on those days it is crowded and you don't get much information." A couple of people mentioned that they liked seeing how the city was changing; through the tours one could experience "a before and after effect." Only one person mentioned that she was unhappy with a tour she had had, but said she would like to see the building again with a different guide.

Overall, very few young people went on the tours; most were middle-aged to elderly, and almost all were from the former West. Many had gone on tours in previous years, and within a single summer, I recognized some repeat visitors. The individuals chose specific tours for various reasons, such as being interested in a theme (for example, the move from Bonn to Berlin), or wanting to know more about the history or technical aspects of a particular building. Some individuals from the former West said they were curious to learn more about the eastern part of the city. One East Berlin couple associated Schaustelle with information about urban renewal in Berlin, comparing it to the "Info Box," a bright red temporary building that housed information about the future city located at Potsdamer Platz. Others were on a tour because their first choice was sold out. An elderly couple said they like going on city tours during the summer. Two people went because they were part of a singles group; the group had purchased the tickets and offered it to these individuals. On two tours, parents brought their children along. So, Schaustelle has also become a social space for some locals (Till, forthcoming).

Most people expressed curiosity about the city and desired to learn about particular places. Other people seemed to enjoy the entertainment value of the tours; they may have wanted to do something fun in the city or try something new during the summer holiday months.

A typical part of the tours, for example, was the individuals (who, on the numerous tours I observed, were always men) who asked challenging questions to the tour guides or offered the group answers to questions that the tour guides could not provide. In a sense, they liked knowing information about their city (being tour guides of "The New Berlin"?) and being more expert than the experts. Going on these tours may have reaffirmed their sense of being male, of being Berliners. The experience may have given them a sense of control over the rapidly changing political, economic, social, and material contexts of Berlin. Other people on the tours clearly got a kick out of these "hecklers."

There were perhaps other reasons why Schaustelle tours were popular among locals. I have suggested that the tours, as live displays, represented the everyday lives of others building the city. When we encounter such live performances as representations, we are forced to make comparisons of ourselves to the people we are watching. Thus, Schaustelle offered residents the possibility of playing with their understandings of the city from the fluid position of local/expert/tourist. When we compare ourselves to others we can, however briefly, pierce the membrane of our own quotidian world, allowing us for a brief moment to be spectators of ourselves, an effect that is also experienced by those on display (Kirschenblatt-Gimblett 1998: 48). This is perhaps the appeal of visiting places that are out of the realm of the "ordinary" yet are simultaneously part of the everyday. Rather than "escape" one's life-worlds through tourism, those very cultural practices offer us the unusual chance to become spectators of ourselves. By performing our identities as momentarily local, momentarily tourist, momentarily worker, momentarily expert, or some other social role, we construct as well as confront the multiple spaces, both "real" and imagined, that constitute the cities in which we live.

Notes

A McKnight Humanities Summer Fellowship, an Office of the Vice President for Research, Dean of the Graduate School University of Minnesota Summer Fellowship, a VP Research/Graduate School Grant in Aid generously funded the research for this project. All translations from the German were done by Gundolf Graml and myself, unless otherwise noted. I wish to thank Gundolf Graml and Beth Muellner for their assistance with this project, and Mark Lindberg for his assistance with the maps for this study. My deepest thanks are extended to the staff of Partners for Berlin for generously sharing their office space, time, and support.

1. This article is based on ethnographic and semiotic documentary research about Schaustelle Berlin conducted from 1997 to 2000. In 1997, I conducted participant observation of a sample of different categories of these tours alone and with my colleague Rhodri Williams; in 1999 and 2000, I again conducted participant observation of tours by myself. I also went on one "alternative tour" offered by BUND in 2000 (see the section titled "Concluding Notes"). From 1997 to 2000, I informally spoke with individuals on the tours, and, in 2000, I asked a series of semistructured questions to individuals who wished to answer these questions on five different types of tours. I conducted a series of in-depth interviews with Partners for Berlin directors and public-relations managers, and spokespersons for BUND in 2000. I also conducted a semiotic analysis of Schaustelle tour brochures from 1996 to 2000, the Partners for Berlin Web page (www.berlin.de/schaustelle), Partners' newsletters, newspaper articles about the tours (as collected in the Partners public-relations archives), and surveys and analyses about the tours conducted by a marketing agency hired by Partners to evaluate the program.

2. Such a statement might be interpreted to mean that marketing activities result in improvements in the economy, political status, and material landscapes of a place. Who defines that reality, and for whom a place improves, however, are not usually discussed by marketers.

3. For a discussion of "The New Berlin" concept, see Till, forthcoming.

4. Although Partners does not have exact numbers distinguishing locals from nonlocals on the tours, it did acknowledge that Berliners were the main

audience. In 1998, it hired a tourism marketing company to conduct a survey of "tourists"—that is, non-Berliners—to see how the program could be expanded. Only one person in the entire survey was not from Germany.

5. Although the Berlin Senate had already initiated a similar concept in previous years under the title "Betreten Erbeten" (roughly translated as "You're welcome to come in"), Schaustelle Berlin was conceived of at a different scale, that is, in terms of the entire city (Partners for Berlin spokesperson, personal interview, August 2000).

6. In 1998, a version of the program was made available in *Der Tagesspiegel*, a national newspaper with local distribution. In 1997 and 1999, there were two editions of the Schaustelle program (one for each half of the summer). The 2000 brochure was sold for five German Marks.

7. The 2000 map was more flexible; another category could be added without having to dramatically change the color scheme, layout, production costs, and quality. This was a more expensive map to make than the earlier maps and, most likely, someone had to make a special case to expand the size, legend, and enhance the colors used (Mark Lindberg, personal communication, 2001).

8. The expert guide mentioned that the city was considering painting a red stripe on the street or imprinting a brass line running the height of the Wall (in adjacent buildings) to designate this past in the landscape.

4. "A Walk through Old Bodie"
Presenting a Ghost Town in a Tourism Map

Dydia DeLyser

From the outset, from the first documents describing the acquisition of the ghost town of Bodie and planning its new future as a California State Historic Park, the primary interpretive tool was meant to be a map-based, self-guided tour brochure. Today, just as had been planned in the mid-1950s, the vast majority of the roughly two hundred thousand estimated annual visitors to the park purchase the current sixteen-page map-based brochure. With the best intentions, plans for the map and brochure coverage included Bodie's minority populations and a broad interpretive period focusing not on the town's gold-mining boom period in the 1870s and 1880s, but rather on the period of the town's decline, the period represented by its current, much-reduced state as a ghost town. But the exigencies of brochure production, the challenges imposed by the often limited availability of detailed historical knowledge about the town, and the realities of Bodie's remains (thought to represent just 5 percent of its boom-period extent), have left the different editions of the brochure to disproportionately emphasize not only the 1880s, but also certain of the town's inhabitants, while leaving out others. The resulting landscape text, interpreted map/brochure in hand, seems to bear a striking resemblance to the contemporary suburban realities of the Anglo-American family groups that make up the majority of Bodie's visitors. Just the same, Bodie's visitors do not interpret the park only through the map/brochure: they bring both other knowledges and their own lives to the text, interpreting the town's landscape intertextually and constructing links to Bodie's past in their own present-day lives (see Harley 1989; and Wood 1992). Connecting Bodie's artifacts to objects having personal meaning in their own lives, visitors thereby link themselves to the mythic American West presented to them both in Bodie's map/brochure and in the town's landscape.

In this chapter, I explore such connections, detailing the presentation of the park through its map/brochure as well as its reception and interpretation by visitors. In so doing, I attempt to take a cue from Denis Wood and John Fels, who, in 1986, declared the "anthropology of cartography . . . an urgent project," asking "what *are* those maps actually used for?" (Wood and Fells 1986: 72).

Not to draw too strong a connection with Wood and Fels, but it was in that same year that I made my first visit to Bodie. By 1988 I had a seasonal job there as a carpenter on the maintenance crew, a job I held for ten summers. In the early 1990s, as a graduate student, I began a participant-observation study of Bodie as part of my dissertation research. Immersed in the community, I interviewed staff members and visitors both formally and informally, observed thousands of visitors, and answered their questions on a daily basis. This chapter is based in

Figure 4.1. Contemporary Bodie.

those years of observation and interviewing, life and interaction, conversations and smashed thumbs. Altogether I hope that my experiences, as well as the experiences of others in which I shared, both as a researcher and as a staff member, will help to further the project Wood and Fels called for, as well as to contribute to our broader understanding of what Mike Crang has called the "spatial stories" that tourists engage in: the "[c]onscious tellings of lives through particular spaces" (Crang 1999: 252).

Planning and Presenting a Ghost Town

Although the users of tourism maps may not always question a map's origins, it is important to understand that each such map has not only a present but also a past (see Wood 1992). Behind each tourism map lies a history of its development and production, a history linked to the landscape the map claims to represent. It is to this history and landscape that I first turn.

What visitors to Bodie State Historic Park find today is not unlike what appeared before the eyes of the Division of Beaches and Parks's first representatives, sent to investigate the acquisition of the townsite in the mid-1950s.[1] Located in the remote, high-desert mountains east of Yosemite National Park, the town of Bodie lies nestled in a treeless valley at more than eight thousand feet. Thirteen miles from the main highway, and reached by road, including three miles of dirt, the remains of Bodie, some 125 buildings and their contents, astonish most visitors. Writing to Chief Newton B. Drury in 1956 to forward Bodie's acquisition by the Division, Division Historian Aubrey Neasham described the scene:

> [The remaining buildings] show the effects of their battle against time and the elements. Yellowed with age, all are stamped with the seal of authenticity. Private houses, stores, a church, school and mine offices, in various degrees of picturesque dilapidation, are represented. Foundations of buildings, crumbling walls, the old cemeteries, mine dumps, shafts and roads and streets give added evidence of what was once here.
>
> Perhaps one of the greatest assets of Bodie is the fact that so much of the original furnishings exist in the buildings that do remain. To compile a list of these materials would take months of time. Suffice it to say that even some of the original groceries remain in boxes unopened on the shelves of stores. A veritable treasure house of materials thus remains

to interpret the life of another day. (Neasham to Drury, office memo, February 27, 1956, p. 2, Bodie State Historic Park Unit History Files)

From the earliest, the Division's intentions were not to restore the town, but rather to arrest the decay, to preserve Bodie just as they had found it. As District Superintendent Clyde L. Newlin put it to Chief Drury in September of 1955, "stabilization of the existing scene should be followed instead of a development or restoration program. . . . retain all exterior appearance and charm of the authentic ghost town, ie.: curved walls, sagging roofs, broken windows, etc." (Clyde L. Newlin to Newton B. Drury, September 29, 1955, "Town of Bodie, Recommendations—Master Plan and Operations" p. 1, Bodie State Historic Park Unit History Files). And from the beginning, planners for the proposed park advised that no directional or interpretive signs be used within the townsite, but rather, as Superintendent Newlin proposed in 1955, that Bodie be presented to visitors by means of a "leaflet with an orientation map to designate locations and sites" (ibid., 2). In 1956, Neasham's proposal expanded somewhat upon Newlin's, suggesting "a published leaflet telling of Bodie's history . . . [and] indicating a tour route for visitors to follow to important sites" (Neasham to Drury, office memo, February 27, 1956, p. 3, Bodie State Historic Park Unit History Files). This emphasis on the history of the town, to be accessed through its ruins, is critical for it has led to the current map/brochure's perceived emphasis on Bodie's boom period in the 1870s and 1880s, at the expense of any other period in the town's past or present.

Thus, although early planning documents advise a historically oriented, map-based, self-guided tour brochure, the plans themselves were at first rather vague. By September 1979, when Bodie's Resource Management Plan, General Development Plan, and Environmental Impact Statement were published, those plans had been much more clearly delineated. The General Development Plan called for a focus away from the time of Bodie's boisterous boom, setting an interpretive period for the townsite "after Bodie ceased to be an operating mining town." Just the same, the plan continued both Newlin's and Neasham's specific recommendations:

Exploration of the ghost town is the most exciting visitor activity at Bodie. Important to visitors' enjoyment are the self-guided tour brochures. A brief history of Bodie, an orientation map, identification of structures or sites, information on their historic uses, and how they reflect life in Bodie should be contained in the brochures. This information should be keyed to buildings and sites by numbered wood posts. (California Department of Parks and Recreation 1979: 49)

Indeed, this is a precise description of the current map/brochure and its use in contemporary Bodie State Historic Park. But what that simple description elides are the vagaries of the available historical record, as well as the complex issues and problems related to interpreting "life in Bodie" in the past based on the ruins remaining in the present.

The current brochure, titled *Bodie State Historic Park* (California Department of Parks and Recreation 1988; hereafter, Map/Brochure), includes sixty-nine numbered buildings and sites, whereas the first brochure, titled *A Walk in Old Bodie,* included only thirty-six (California Division of Beaches and Parks n.d.). Although the first brochure was simply produced and printed in black-and-white with no photographs, the current three-color brochure features many photographs, both historic and contemporary. And although the numbers of people who used, or still remember, the original brochure (published sometime after 1963, and replaced in 1973) are small compared to those who use the current brochure (published in 1988 with visitation at the park steadily rising), the original brochure is critical because much of its information and description has passed, largely unaltered, into the brochure's later incarnations.

Today the museum/bookstore in Bodie sells more than ten different books about Bodie, but when the original brochure was produced there was only one: Ella M. Cain's *The Story of Bodie,* published in 1956, just as Division staff was working to acquire Bodie. Thus, at the time of the brochure's original publication, little about Bodie's past had been published, and none of it was scholarly. Testifying to the importance of Cain's book, the original brochure includes a bibliography (omitted from the current edition) that references Cain's book as the only published source directly about Bodie. Because of this one book's importance, it is worth exploring both the book and its presentation of Bodie's past before returning to the map/brochure.

Although Cain's book has been incredibly influential (both for its heavy use in the brochure and for its easy accessibility to readers); although its tales of "the lawless days of the old camp" are engaging; although Cain herself testifies in the Introduction, "This much I can tell you in truth: This history is authentic. These stories are true" (Cain 1956: vii, vi); and although the stories she presents are certainly true to the prevailing social memories of Bodie and its boom period, there is no reason to believe that they are all based in historical fact. This is not to attempt to undercut Cain's own claim about the veracity of her work, but rather to attempt to position her book, the most important book about Bodie's past yet written, in a broader discourse about Bodie and its past.

Ella M. (Cody) Cain was born in Bodie in 1882, soon after the town's gold-mining boom had quieted. Although she spent parts of her childhood and early adult life elsewhere, she later returned to Bodie, working as a schoolteacher until she married David Victor Cain, a member of one of the town's latter-day prominent families (ibid., vi; and O'Rourke 1978: 27). Cain remained in Bodie for much of the rest of her life, and by the 1950s it was she who had established Bodie's museum in the former Miner's Union Hall. Thus, by birth, by marriage, and by interest, Ella Cain was well positioned to write tales of the town's past.

Following a tradition of writing about Bodie established by other former residents (e.g., Smith 1925), Cain describes a Bodie bifurcated between polite society and the lawless element (which included prostitutes and gamblers among its cast of lawbreakers). Blending personal experience with exaggerated tales of violence and bravado, she seamlessly melds fact with fiction to create a romanticized saga of her town's past (see Rickard 1932; and DeLyser, forthcoming). But Cain's book not only lapses back and forth between her own reminiscences and other stories she cannot have personally remembered, between events from Bodie's boom period and those that happened many years after the town's decline, and between readily established historical details and colorful tales that cannot be documented; it also includes an exaggerated and glamorized saga of Cain's own family (particularly that of her in-laws), projecting for them a broad and sweeping influence on the town. Importantly, each of these elements has been retained in the various versions of the Bodie brochure (see DeLyser 1998). The result (both in Cain's book and in the map/brochure) is that while some sections, like that on the growth of Bodie's mines, are grounded in the town's boom period and dates are clearly stated, others focus on characters and events from much more recent times, though dates identifying the period are nowhere mentioned. But because the book (and the brochure) are anchored in

Bodie's boom period, readers leap readily to the conclusion that *all* the events and characters portrayed date from this time—there is no reason to assume otherwise.

Although Ella Cain's book is easy to criticize by picking its tales apart for their myriad factual inaccuracies (see ibid.), perhaps her text could better be viewed in a different light, for Cain makes no attempt at writing a scholarly history, nor does she claim to be accurately reporting the factual minutiae of Bodie's past. Rather, she openly acknowledges the subjective and anecdotal nature of her account: not old enough to remember the boom herself, she writes in her introduction: "I have tried to give you a true picture of the Bodie I knew," a town where "[t]here was never a gathering of old timers, never a fireside group, that stories of the lawless days of the old camp were not told"—stories she herself informally collected. Thus it is clear enough for close readers that Cain's is an effort at presenting Bodie as it lived in the minds and stories of its residents at the very end of its existence as a gold-mining town, and as seen by members of the town's latter-day most prominent family. Hers is a work not of history but of social memory, a work that serves not to document the past as it actually was, but rather to describe the past as it was kept alive, and continuously relived, by some of Bodie's citizens (see, for example, Russell 1927; Glassock 1937, who both spoke with Cain's father-in-law when they visited the town). For her, then, including certain *fictitious* tales of the town's past is as important as documenting actual events.

But because Cain's was the only book about Bodie available when the Division of Beaches and Parks published the first Bodie map/brochure, the Division lacked the resources needed to question Cain's tales, the tools needed to deconstruct her text—and so it did not; many of the detailed stories of Bodie's colorful past passed from Cain's book of reminiscences into the park's self-guided tour brochure. The map/brochure too became an instrument of at times undocumentable tales of Bodie's past, seemingly grounded in the boom period, but actually layered over a much longer span of time—except that, in the brochure, they are introduced (in the official state of California guide, and without Cain's anchoring in personal reminiscences) unproblematically as fact.

"A Walk through Old Bodie"

Opening the current Bodie brochure, readers are immediately greeted by the map that will guide them on their tour. Meticulous in every detail, streets are laid out and named, each building is accurately footprinted, and most are also numbered and named. The bulk of the text follows these names and numbers, in numerical order, through the town, closely linking the subsequent text to this map on the first page. Further linking text to map, subsections of the map (including the names and numbers of the buildings and sites described on that page) are reproduced on later pages. Sixteen pages long in total, the brochure includes descriptions of many buildings and sites, as well as both historic and contemporary photographs. Thus, the map that this chapter treats is more than a series of symbols for buildings and streets: it can scarcely be divorced from its accompanying multiple-page text. As Brian Harley has argued in the context of seventeenth-century European maps, "[r]ather than being inconsequential marginalia, the emblems in cartouches and decorative title pages can be regarded as *basic* to the way [maps] convey their cultural meaning" (Harley 1989: 9; see also Harley and Zandvliet 1992; Wood and Fels 1986). I wish to extend that argument here to the realm of tourism maps and to the often lengthy texts that accompany such maps. To me, such maps must be understood together with their complete texts. In this section, I explore how such a map/text "makes present" a *partial view* of the past, enabling it to become part of our present, for, as Denis Wood writes, "[t]he map's *effectiveness* is a consequence of the *selectivity* with which it brings this past to bear on the present" (Wood 1992: 1).

Clearly, as the primary interpretive tool, Bodie State Historic Park's map/brochure is critical in conveying a sense of this ghost town to visitors, but what it conveys may not be what it at first seems. Because the map serves to anchor the self-guided tour of the town as it is now visible to visitors, it describes the buildings in present-day Bodie, not those in the Bodie of the nineteenth century. But the text of the brochure transfers the emphasis to Bodie's boom period. Although some of the entries in the brochure's text mention later dates, the map appears without further context or comment. Although the map shows only a small portion of the buildings that once stood in Bodie (and the brochure does mention that only 5 percent of the town now remains [p. 3]), the buildings shown on the map stand in for the whole—they stand in for all that Bodie is thought to have been in the 1880s. Thus, by representing the remains of the town with great accuracy, but giving little or no indication of what else was once there, the map acts as a synecdoche: a

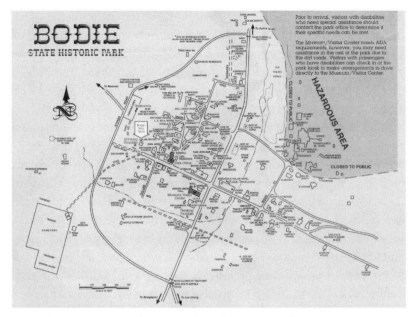

Figure 4.2. Brochure map. Courtesy of California State Parks.

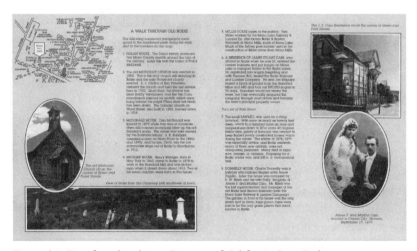

Figure 4.3. Page from brochure. Courtesy of California State Parks.

part (contemporary Bodie State Historic Park) stands in for the whole (the whole town that once existed). But not only that, for as Michel de Certeau has proposed, in landscape, synecdoche "enlarges one element of space"; it replaces the whole with a fragment, and therefore amplifies detail (de Certeau 1985: 137). The remains, as the new whole, take on greater meaning.

This is, of course, something for which the unnamed and uncredited authors of Bodie's brochure cannot, in fairness, be taken to task. As an orientation map to Bodie State Historic Park, designed not for experts on Bodie's history but for visitors who most often know nothing about the town they are walking through, the map is an efficient guide. And, in fact, even now, nearly four decades after Bodie's first map/brochure appeared, there is still no agreement among historians on how many buildings existed in boom-period Bodie, on where precisely they stood, or on which businesses or persons occupied them.[2] Further, the map itself nowhere claims to be a map of the town in the 1880s; rather, it is titled simply "Bodie State Historic Park," implying a contemporary orientation. Clearly, then, no underhanded cartographer or manipulative graphic designer set out to deliberately mislead the public in creating this map (see Monmonier 1996). But the map may be misleading just the same—misleading because of its use in the context of the brochure's text and Bodie's evocative landscape. The jump from what can be seen (in the meticulously accurate footprints of the remaining buildings) to what cannot be seen (boom-period Bodie) occurs in conjunction with the texts of the brochure and the landscape, with the map (and the portions of it reproduced throughout the brochure) acting as springboard for the visitors' own interpretations.

Opposite the map, underneath the heading "Welcome to Bodie" a dramatic stage is set for the interpretation of the rest of Bodie's ruins. Although the brochure is at pains to mention that what is seen today are the "remains of Bodie. . . . just as time, fire, and the elements have left it" (3), it also leads into a description reminiscent of the glamorized mythic West Americans know from film, fiction, and television, rather than a declining mining town for decades barely clinging to survival. The first paragraph begins with a picturesque portrayal of Bodie's decay; the next paragraphs extend that decay from the physical shell of the town to the social makeup of the town during the boom period. Setting the stage first with the discovery of gold in 1859 and then rapidly moving to the height of the boom in 1879, the brochure reads:

> By 1879 Bodie boasted a population of about ten thousand and was second to none for wickedness, badmen, and "the worst climate out of doors." One little girl, whose family was taking her to the remote and infamous town, wrote in her diary: "Goodbye God, I'm going to Bodie." The phrase came to be known throughout the west.
>
> Killings occurred with monotonous regularity, sometimes becoming almost daily events. The fire bell, which tolled the ages of the deceased when they were buried, rang often and long. Robberies, stage holdups, and street fights provided variety, and the town's 65 saloons offered many opportunities for relaxation after hard days of work in the mines. The Reverend F. M. Warrington saw it in 1881 as "a sea of sin, lashed by the tempests of lust and passion." (Ibid.)

It is worth examining this passage in more detail. Although any description of boom-period Bodie notes that it was a "shooter's town," historian Roger McGrath, meticulously examining court and newspaper records for Bodie's boom period, documented only some seventy shootings (and but thirty-five deaths) (McGrath 1984). Over the five boom years, the result is an average of one shooting nearly every two months, a large number to be sure, but not an "almost daily event." Similarly, McGrath found eleven stage robberies, only ten reported "garrotings" (muggings), and fewer than one hundred property crimes, and concluded that "the total amount of robbery, burglary and theft was really very small" particularly when compared to urban areas today, but also when compared to eastern cities at the time of Bodie's boom (ibid., 182, 248–50). This is not to say that boom-period Bodie was a peaceful and quiet place, for, even if the number sixty-five cannot be confirmed, Bodie certainly had numerous saloons, dance halls, and related establishments, and most likely sixty-five is an accurate estimate.[3]

The Reverend Warrington's tone is perhaps not surprising for a man of the cloth living in a mining town where saloons were so numerous, where the Sunday-closing law for saloons could not be enforced, and where not one church graced the streets.[4] Of course, a Victorian minister could not by any means be considered a neutral authority in commenting on a mining town, but the Reverend was not the only one to offer so dire a description of Bodie.

In the brochure, the reference to the little girl's diary appears to confirm the Reverend's opinion. This diary quote has been reprinted in many histories of Bodie, but, interestingly enough, has never been (to my knowledge) traced back to its original source. Despite its lack of confirmation, this tale has emerged as an important part of Bodie lore.[5] Regardless of whether or not the tale is true, the brochure prints it as fact, claiming also that it "came to be known throughout the west." The tale helps to confirm Bodie's wicked reputation, and also, along with the rest of the introduction, to anchor the interpretive period of the brochure, and therefore of the park in general, in Bodie's boom period (see DeLyser, forthcoming).

Indeed, except for the reassurance that "Bodie's badmen are all in their graves," the brochure's introduction never moves beyond 1881. The introduction draws readers to thinking about Bodie's boom period, setting the stage in their minds for what is to follow. The false-fronted buildings of Bodie's Main Street connect visitors to images of the 1880s familiar to them from film and television. The unpainted, ramshackle cabins and their dusty interiors express the decay of a long period of time, further confirming the late-nineteenth-century interpretive period. Thus Bodie's landscape and the brochure's text work together to encourage visitors to the park to see the 1880s and not some other time period.

These suggestions are so strong that objects in the landscape that are very clearly *not* that old often do not disturb the impression of an 1880s town. Visitors, for example, gather with glee in front of the town's two gravity-feed gasoline pumps where a 1927 Graham stake-bed truck is parked. They often climb on the running boards, or simply stand before the front bumper to pose for a family photograph. A wooden sign wired to the bumper tells visitors the make and model year of the truck, but the knowledge that the truck is *not* from the 1880s does not dismay them, nor does it dissuade them from asking questions related to life in Bodie in the 1880s (rather than in the 1920s). Annually, when maintenance workers lean under the hood to service it, visitors eagerly circle around them, asking, before returning to other questions centered on Bodie's boom period, not "Are you going to move it out of here?" but "Are you going to get it running?"[6]

If Bodie's landscape does little to dissuade visitors from seeing the 1880s, the map/brochure does even less. The brochure describes sixty-nine numbered buildings and sites, as well as a dozen other buildings and sites that do not have numbers. The printed descriptions vary in length, from two words to three paragraphs, and although some of the descriptions are explicit about the time period they describe, most are not (see, for example, "Miller Rooming House" on p. 12 for a reference to a latter-day resident for whom no dates are provided). Of the buildings and sites described in the brochure for which I was able to identify the time period(s), less than one-third described boom-period people, places, and events, while more than half described those of a later period.[7] Thus, the brochure leads visitors to draw connections to Bodie's boom period that are often spurious.

But the brochure does more than simply set Bodie in a specific time period, whether that period is accurately described or not. The map, brochure, and Bodie's contemporary landscape give the impression of a town made up largely of single-family homes. If Bodie once had such a housing shortage that men slept on billiard tables and saloon floors (McGrath 1984), and if men bunked together crowded into small houses, there is now no sign of it for Bodie's houses, even its rooming houses, feature only one bed per room, and sometimes only one bed per house.[8] This creates the impression of a far more family-oriented town than boom-period Bodie ever was: Bodie's boom-period population was 90 percent male (McGrath 1984), but in Bodie's map/brochure, explicit references to family situations (mentioning a wife, or a son, for example) are made for more than three-quarters of all the residences described—an implied family context that is made real to visitors by presences in the landscape as well. Bodie's school—itself converted from a lodging house, the Bon Ton—for example, stands prominently and readily recognizable on Green Street, one of only eight two-story buildings remaining. Whether boom-period Bodie was a family town or not, contemporary Bodie certainly *is*, for most of the park's visitors experience Bodie in the context of their own families. Because meaning is generated in social context, this likely leads them to project their own family contexts onto the past as well, further influencing an impression that Bodie was a family place (see Bruner 1994).

If Bodie is presented as a family town, the Cain family is often the focus of this narrative. Influenced by Ella Cain's book, the brochure's text mentions the Cain family at ten different locations. Led by progenitor J. S. Cain, who "arrived in Bodie when he was 25, entered the lumber business, put [lumber] barges on Mono Lake . . . [,] expanded into wagon freighting, leased the Bodie Railroad and Lumber Company . . . [,] leased a [mining claim,] . . . took out $90,000 in 90 days . . . [,] and became the town's principal property owner" (Map/Brochure: 3), this one family dominates the text. That Cain was a minor figure in most of the activities described, that nearly all of them took place long after Bodie's boom had quieted, and that some of them are reported only in Ella Cain's book of reminiscences is nowhere mentioned (see Billeb 1986; DeLyser 1998; Loose 1979; McGrath 1984; Wedertz 1969). But readers of Bodie's brochure would have no reason to doubt the text's accuracy (just as the writers of the original brochure had no resources to verify the accuracy of Cain's text). The Cain story, then, is assumed by readers to be true. And, read as truth, the story unfolds as one of pioneer heroism, projected back into Bodie's boom period.

If the Cain family's story presents one of American pioneer success, so too do most of Bodie's other family narratives. In the map/brochure it is implied that Bodie was a full-employment town: nearly every building is described by the occupation of its inhabitants. Bodieites' struggles with unemployment, a prominent feature even during the boom (McGrath 1984: 123), is never mentioned as the narrative proceeds from career to career. Further, most of the careers mentioned are managerial and white-collar—"HOME OF STUART KIRKWOOD, owner of the stables (site no. 23). This house was also occupied by E. L. Benedict, former manager of the Bodie Bank (site no. 25)" (Map/Brochure: 6)—rather than the blue-collar careers of miners and mill workers one might expect in a gold-mining town. In fact, nearly half the people described are small businessmen or entrepreneurs, with fewer than one-quarter of the people described as working for anyone other than themselves. With a nearly equal number of homes and businesses described, the implication is that Bodie was a middle-class town full of independent small businessmen, rather than a mining town where many, working in mines and mills, struggled to make ends meet.

Despite the map/brochure's evocations of Bodie's wild and violent past (in its introduction and other sections offering general descriptions), in the landscape these elements too take second stage to the narrative of entrepreneurial work and middle-class family values, for sites of violence and crime are just that: sites, not buildings. Bodie's most serious crimes are reported as happening offstage and off-map: not only are they not numbered buildings or numbered sites, but they occurred out of the range of the walking tour in the map/brochure: the lynching of Joseph DeRoche occurred in what is now an empty field, effectively south of the tour's reach (p. 14), and "several" stage robberies occurred north of the townsite (p. 10). Visitors and staff are widely aware of the safeness of Bodie's current environment and often joke about it, like the couple who compared my life in Bodie in the 1990s to the lives of Bodie's boom-period inhabitants, noting with a laugh that the difference was that I "won't get shot." Through Bodie's map/brochure and contemporary landscape, visitors and staff experience the dangerous past at a safe distance.

But if the story Bodie tells, through its landscape and its brochure, is safe, middle-class, and family oriented, it is also almost entirely white. In a sense, this should not be surprising because Bodie's boom-period population was overwhelmingly Anglo (McGrath 1984: 110). But in the brochure Bodie's minority populations are scarcely mentioned, a vexing problem that can be illustrated through Bodie's most prominent minority group, the Chinese.

The only non-Anglo person or population of Bodie identified by a numbered site in the brochure is "Chinatown," at the extreme northwestern end of the tour. Once one of the largest Chinatowns in California, crowded with shops that served both Chinese and whites (McGrath 1984), it is now an empty field. Thus, like Bodie's dangerous past, Bodie's ethnic Other is experienced in the landscape through the non-artifactual. The map/brochure mentions the onetime presence of "general stores, laundries, gambling halls, saloons, boarding houses, and even a Taoist temple" (p. 7), but, unlike Bodie's other sites (such as the Wells Fargo Express Office or the Occidental Hotel), none of the businesses in Chinatown is mentioned by name, and none of the businesses is described by its owner. Unlike Bodie's white businessmen, Bodie's Chinese are not described as entrepreneurs but as a faceless mass confined to a virtually featureless part of town.

And here Bodie's presentation of minority groups is not unlike the presentations of such groups at other historic sites. With long histories of poverty and marginalization in American society and culture, the homes and businesses of minority groups, like those in Bodie's Chinatown, have seldom been as well preserved as those of the white middle and upper classes. For example, at Colonial Williamsburg, the interpretation of black history is a more recent addition to the museum's agenda, and must be carried out despite a relative paucity of material artifacts relating to African-American life in the town. What this leads to in Williamsburg, as Eric Gable, Richard Handler, and Anna Lawson have noted, is the reification of white history through buildings and artifacts, but the much more conjectural presentation of black history. Thus, despite their attempts to portray black history, because of the power of the artifactual presentations of white history, black history necessarily appears less formidable (Gable, Handler, and Lawson 1992). In Bodie, with no Chinese businesses still standing, no windows left to peer into, the once-significant Chinese population is further marginalized.[9]

But whereas in Colonial Williamsburg, buildings can be (and have been) reproduced, Bodie's preservation policy prohibits such new construction, so areas like Chinatown (where the buildings were lost long before Bodie became a park) will never be rebuilt. This presents a challenge for interpretation, but it is not one the brochure takes up: although the "Sam Leon Bar" is described by name, it is nowhere made clear that Leon was Chinese, and, indeed, one of latter-day Bodie's most prominent businesspeople (Johnson and Johnson 1967).[10]

Bodie's boom-period population was not only overwhelmingly Anglo, it was also overwhelmingly male: only 10 percent of those listed in the 1880 census were women (McGrath 1984: 110). Just the same, more than three-quarters of Bodie's residences as described in the map/brochure are those of families, reflecting the brochure's actual emphasis (unstated) on Bodie's later history, when Bodie was a much more family-oriented town. Despite their acknowledgment, these women generally remain nameless and are known primarily through the accomplishments of their men: "METZGER HOUSE. Henry Metzger, born in New York in 1860, came to Bodie in 1878 to work in the Standard Mill and was its foreman when it closed down about 1916. Two of his seven children were born in this house" (Map/Brochure: 4). Those women who are named are often prostitutes (such as Lottie Johl, the only woman for whom a building is clearly named), or members of the Cain family (pp. 3, 10). Although Annie Miller operated one of Bodie's largest hotels and was one of the town's last businesspeople (Sprague, forthcoming), accomplishments like hers are nowhere mentioned because women's lives are marginalized along with Bodie's minority populations.

What is important here is what the stories presented in Bodie's map/brochure and landscape represent about Bodie—how they portray Bodie in social memory, how they represent the American past as seen and felt in this ghost town. Bodie is no longer the town it once was; instead, it is a remnant that features some of the more prominent homes and businesses, those that have best weathered time, fire, and the elements. Confirmed by the landscape, the map/brochure presents a town of hardworking pioneers, and portrays a series of Anglo-American small businessmen living, many with families, in single-family homes, and with women playing often-unacknowledged secondary roles. The only minorities described are virtually written out of the landscape, confined to an empty field and off-map locations. Similarly, Bodie's lavishly described violent past is nowhere visible in the contemporary landscape, for scenes of past violence are similarly located off-map or in empty fields. In Bodie's landscape and map/brochure, the middle-class values of patriarchal Anglo-American society appear to have triumphed.

What Is this Map Actually Used For?

From the remote distance of an academic office or classroom, taking apart the text of a brochure that was written with limited resource materials to describe a remnant landscape to a very different audience may seem a simple task. But the importance of the brochure's text in this case lies not just in any factual inaccuracies or missed chances to represent a multicultural past. As is surely the case with other tourism maps, what is more interesting is how visitors actually *use* this text, and what it comes to mean to them through their use of it.

Selling for just one dollar and available at different locations in the park, the brochure is used by almost all visitors to Bodie, but not everyone who reads the brochure reads it in its entirety, and not every visitor purchases his or her own brochure. As with exhibit captions in a library or museum, probably only a few people read every bit of the text, and, in the extreme environment of Bodie (often beset by hot sun or sudden rain, hail, or snow, even in summer), very few of the park's visitors actually make it to every single one of the brochure's sixty-nine numbered sites.[11]

Most often, a party arriving together will buy one brochure and then share it.[12] As at other popular tourist sites, visitors to Bodie often arrive in nuclear-family groups, and young children will take turns reading the brochure's text aloud to the rest of the family. These kids can frequently be heard either straining or showing off their reading skills, so that something as simple as reading the brochure becomes an educational experience. Thus, Bodie's map/brochure is shared and the landscape is experienced in a family context, one heightened by the readings of children.

It would take several hours to complete the entire tour the brochure describes, but most visitors spend far less time in the town. Staff members working at the entrance station often recognize people on their way out who came in only an hour earlier. And staff members walking through the townsite are frequently asked questions like "What do you recommend we see if we only have an hour?" Although many visitors find Bodie compelling and would like to stay longer, the restrictions of long travel distances and tightly planned vacations (with hotel reservations already made, or children getting hungry for lunch or dinner) cannot be ignored. Some come well prepared with a picnic lunch and spend a full day; others who bring no food with them do not have this luxury.[13] Because most ghost towns, as one visitor put it, contain "only rusted cans," many who arrive in Bodie for the first time are often unprepared for Bodie's relative wealth of artifacts and buildings, and did not plan much time for their visits in their itineraries. As a result, in Bodie, as at so many other popular tourist attractions, many visitors find themselves rushed.

For these hurried people the park's brochure may become even more important: the brochure is printed in attractive sepia-toned colors and filled with both historic and contemporary photographs, and many visitors keep it to look at again later, or as a souvenir of their trip.[14] In fact, some keep their brochure long enough to bring it on their next visit. In the early 1990s, for example, it was not uncommon to see visitors using the *old* (second) version of the brochure (distinctly different from the current [third] one and immediately recognizable) as their guide—a brochure that had not been sold since 1988. These people saved their copies for several years and thought to bring them back to Bodie on this subsequent visit. Tourism maps as apparently mundane as the Bodie map/brochure do have lives outside of the place they were designed to describe.

Further, tourism maps also have lives beyond their own texts, for, as with other texts, readers clearly bring their own lives, knowledges, and stories to the readings of such maps (Harley 1989; Wood 1992). Observing and interacting with visitors to Bodie, this becomes clear often in

Figure 4.4. Couple sharing brochure.

small details of visitors' conversations. Standing with her family before the building identified as the "Wheaton and Hollis Hotel and Bodie Store," a girl of about ten proudly bore the responsibility for reading the brochure aloud, but here she departed from the printed text, making up her own: "This was the mall," she declared, linking this large building with a place that was relevant in her own life, rather than engaging with the brochure's description of the building as a former U.S. Land Office, or looking in the windows to describe the bar or the billiard table visible inside. Across the street, standing before the "Boone Store and Warehouse" where the shelves are still stocked with merchandise, a woman in her late thirties ignored the brochure's description of Daniel Boone, descendant Harvey Boone, as well as its description of the clever use of empty tin cans for siding material, announcing instead, "This was the country store," evoking images of shops selling quaint kitchen souvenirs rather than the blasting powder, laudanum, or gear oil found on the shelves inside Boone's store.

While some visitors depart from the brochure's text to create descriptions meaningful to their own lives, others draw intertextual connections that are more broadly held, linking life in Bodie to the American mythic West. Visitors entering the townsite from the parking lot generally pass an interpretive sign that, like the opening of the brochure, describes gunfights and debauchery in Bodie's saloons. With this (or

Figure 4.5. Visitors peer into Boone Store.

the similar description at the beginning of the brochure) still in mind, moments later they come to the first building marked on the tour, the Dolan House. But although Dolan itself is a simple and relatively common name, one man in his mid-forties misread the name in his brochure and thereby created a link to a more notable western family: "The Dalton House," he read, thus making a connection between Bodie and that notorious family of American outlaws.[15] What these three examples convey is that although visitors clearly use the map/brochure to access Bodie's past, they also bring other knowledge to their readings; the text acts as a springboard for their interpretations.

Despite the brochure's help, and despite the map's meticulously accurate representation of the buildings of contemporary Bodie, a number of visitors still get lost. Even with their maps in hand, once in the townsite some are unable to tell the direction of the parking lot (hidden from view) and cannot find their way back to their cars without directions from a staff member. Others complain that the small sections of the map reprinted on relevant pages confuse them: "We can't tell where we are on this map." Still others miss the directions the brochure provides (for example, "Return to Main Street and turn left" [p. 13]) and find themselves confronted with number posts out of the chronological sequence presented by the brochure—and for some this can be frustrating. What this points to is that some readers take both the map and the text very seriously, desiring to follow the tour that the map/brochure lays out with precision.

But not all seek to follow the numbered tour quite so exactly. Many visitors to Bodie wander where they wish, often allowing excited children to determine where next to turn, or which buildings to peer inside of. For them, the brochure is a loose guide that they can use to obtain information when they want it, rather than a fixed way of exploring the park; they use the number posts in front of buildings to look those buildings up in the brochure regardless of whether they come across those posts in numerical order. Thus, though the brochure appears to present one dominant narrative, in practice it is used in individual ways by different visitors, so that even though a particular narrative is perceptible in the text overall, that narrative may be subverted or ignored in the spatial practices of visitors as they explore the townsite.

Still other visitors, even when they are not lost, have priorities in mind that the brochure may not address directly enough, causing them

Figure 4.6. A child and her mother gaze into Bodie's schoolhouse.

to come to staff members with their questions. Because so many visitors are hurried, they are often concerned about missing certain highlights of the town, so some of the questions most frequently asked by visitors (often while gesturing to their maps or asking that the sites be pointed out to them on the map) relate specifically to map items: Where was the saloon? Where was the jail? Where was the whorehouse? Of these three, only the jail is identified as such directly on the map (as well as in the text of the brochure). Because Bodie had not one "whorehouse" but rather an entire red-light district, that part of the park is identified on the map by the name of a street: "Site of Bonanza Street. Also known as 'Virgin Alley' and 'Maiden Lane,'" all euphemisms for what went on there. Although attentive readers quickly recognize this, the brochure's further description never uses the term "red-light district," "whorehouse," or "prostitute" and many visitors still ask staff for directions. And though no building is directly identified in the brochure by the word *saloon,* three buildings on Main Street have bars in them and generally confirm visitors' expectations of what a saloon *should* look like. Once they come across these buildings, visitors are satisfied at having seen a saloon, but, because the text does not label them saloons, visitors who have not yet seen the buildings themselves often ask staff directions to "the saloon."

Such specific questions imply that visitors need help beyond what the map provides to navigate the townsite, but what is more important is what the content of such questions implies; visitors, already familiar with mythic portrayals of the American West, arrive in Bodie expecting to find it such a place (DeLyser 1999). In the mythic "Wild West" familiar from film and television, these three features are among the most prominent, to the point that, in a town associated with the mythic West, all three features are expected or even demanded.

Thus, although the map/brochure was designed to offer a tour route through the park, perhaps the majority of visitors end up using it instead as a reference tool for much more impromptu (if often hurried) explorations, guided in part by prominent cultural narratives (like that of the American mythic West) and in part by visitors' own personal predilections. Such tourism maps can become, in the hands of their users, flexible texts with multiple uses.

And if the text of the map/brochure is one that is flexibly adapted to the needs and interests of individual visitors, so is Bodie's landscape text itself. Visitors often come to Bodie in order to "see what life was like back then," something that could lead them to reflect on a life far different from their own. And certainly, for those who engage in Bodie's mythologized raucous and violent past, that past is very different from their lives in the present. But in addition to the tales of a glamorized mythic West, what many visitors end up perceiving is a life actually quite similar to their own (ibid.).

Because of the vagaries of fire, harsh winds, and heavy snow loads, many of Bodie's original buildings have not survived. But that is not the only reason; as the town's population declined, those remaining gradually moved into the nicer and larger homes, leaving the smaller and more poorly built homes abandoned. Thus, what remains in Bodie's landscape today disproportionately reflects the lives of Bodie's middle classes: of the tent cabins that lodged eager miners during the boom none has survived, and of the dozens of small shacks that sheltered others, only a few examples remain. Entire working-class neighborhoods are now missing from Bodie's landscape, but a cluster of solid middle-class homes near the town's Methodist church still stands.[16]

Inside, visitors find furniture, wood stoves, and common household items—many of them familiar from their own lives. Although most of these artifacts were left behind by Bodie's latter-day inhabitants, many visitors are not so discerning, and generally assume most of the abandoned possessions to be from Bodie's boom period. But what they *are* discerning about is recognizing artifacts of personal interest to them. One young woman, wearing skillfully handmade clothing, marveled at the sewing machines. A young man recognized cans of Campbell's soup. Both connected their lives to the lives of Bodieites of the past through these everyday artifacts. What appeared to these people was not just the violent side of mythic West, but also the lives of "ordinary people," people like themselves.

Through these everyday artifacts scattered inside the middle-class homes and interpreted together with the map/brochure, visitors perceive a community not that unlike the suburban realities shared by most of them: if the population presented in the brochure's text appears to be mainly white and middle class, so too are the majority of Bodie's contemporary visitors. Ultimately, then, what many visitors see in these two texts (the landscape and the printed) is a reflection of a life in many ways quite similar to their own.

Conclusion

The question of how people connect themselves to important narratives of the nation and the nation's past is an intriguing one, though it can be difficult to trace, let alone to answer. We can, however, use insight from cases where the events are current, for which the linking to narratives of the nation can be relatively easy to understand, to shed some light on the process. Marita Sturken has written about the experiences of Americans with the 1986 explosion of the space shuttle *Challenger*; although most of us were in no way directly connected to this tragedy, according to Sturken, we remember this catastrophic event by positioning ourselves in relation to it, by reciting where we were when it happened, and explaining the circumstances under which we first heard of the disaster (Sturken 1997). In cases where the events to which we seek to connect ourselves have long since passed from the reaches of our personal memories, or even recent family memories, so that no "real" or direct connection can any longer be made, it becomes more difficult.

But this, I argue, is precisely what visitors to Bodie State Historic Park do every day. By reading the map/brochure's tales of violence and bravado familiar to them from decades of exposure through film and fiction to America's mythic West; by reading also the snippets of stories of the lives of people who seem both so ordinary and so like them (people with families and middle-class jobs, for example); by gazing at the artifacts left behind in the houses and buildings, objects often so mundane but therefore also so immediately recognizable and *placeable* in the everyday lives of the visitors, visitors to Bodie are able to link themselves to the dramatic narratives of the mythic West, and the importance of its pioneering spirit in American culture.

Bodie, as presented by the map/brochure, is, from the outset, clearly and directly identified with America's mythic West. But what remains in the landscape is a series of leaning homes and tumbledown businesses, glimpses of the lives of apparently *average* citizens. And it is to these citizens of the past that many of Bodie's visitors can relate. Map/brochure in hand, looking at and into Bodie's buildings, the park's visitors see lives like their own projected into the past, and thus Bodie's past, and, by extension, America's heroic and mythic western past, become meaningful to them in their present.

That most of the past presented in the landscape and the map/brochure is actually much closer (in time) to contemporary visitors than Bodie's boom period, and that the realities of Bodie's boom period were actually much more multicultural and working-class than the text of the brochure presents, is perhaps not the most important thing we can learn from this analysis of these two texts (the landscape and the printed). Although New Western Historians and other scholars have labored to make America's western past rightfully more inclusive, the Wild West in landscape and in other texts like Bodie's map/brochure may remain one of the last white places in an increasingly diverse western United States (see Limerick 1988; Limerick, Milner, and Rankin 1991; White 1991; and DeLyser 1999). Disturbing as this is, it is something that can be changed, and is, in fact, changing. In recent years, not only have Bodie's visitors themselves become a more diverse group, but more and more information has been learned and published about Bodie's past, information that could be used to revise the current well-intentioned but flawed map/brochure so that it more accurately represents both the citizens of Bodie's past and the visitors of its present.[17] But important though such revisions would be, there is something else that can be learned from this, something that extends beyond the possible flaws of the map/brochure, and possibly beyond the bounds of Bodie, to help us understand how sociospatial identities (Shields 1991b) are constructed and reenacted in part through texts such as tourism maps.

Tourism maps have long been overlooked both by cultural geographers and by critical cartographers, though they are often looked at and used uncritically by members of the public (Del Casino and Hanna 2000). And yet, as this chapter has demonstrated, each tourism map has a present as well as a past, and a lived as well as a textual reality. Tourism maps are key texts through which tourist landscapes at historic sites are interpreted by visitors, often helping them to make the past meaningful in the present. At times leading visitors' interpretations with compelling narratives, these maps and their narratives may also be either subverted or ignored by tourists in practice. By excavating the history behind Bodie's map/brochure, by closely examining its text, and by exploring the ways that visitors to Bodie State Historic Park actually engage this text in Bodie's landscape, I have attempted to show how the map/brochure itself presents sociospatial identities, and how visitors interact with the map/brochure to make the space their own, to make the past meaningful in their present. Surely the close examination, both documentary and ethnographic, of other such tourism maps can lead us even further.

Notes

To the staff and visitors at Bodie State Historic Park I owe a great debt of gratitude: they not only made this work possible through their permission and participation, but also enriched it (and my life) with their insights, friendship, and support. The work was further supported by funding from the Geography

Department and the Graduate School of Syracuse University. Mark Monmonier helped me to think critically about maps, and to write with some degree of fluidity. Vincent Del Casino and Stephen Hanna honored me with their invitation and then encouraged me patiently but persistently. Helen Regis listened and offered critique. Paul Greenstein first traveled with me to Bodie, helped nurture my love for this place, and has provided valuable criticism on this work. Portions of this work appeared as chapter 5, "Presenting a Ghost Town: Bodie State Historic Park" in DeLyser, "Good, by God, We're Going to Bodie! Landscape and Social Memory in a California Ghost Town," Ph.D. dissertation, Syracuse University, 1998.

1. The Division later became known simply as the California Department of Parks and Recreation, now California State Parks.

2. As Larry Poag notes, "I have come to believe that a completely accurate rendition [of Main Street in 1880] may be impossible" (Anonymous [Larry Poag], n.d.). See also the differences between Poag's map and Brownell Merrell's map of Bodie's businesses in 1880: the two do not even agree on the street layout or names, let alone the disposition of the actual businesses. Neither attempts, as the brochure does, to label Bodie's homes by the names of their occupants.

3. In December 1878, before Bodie's boom had reached its zenith, the Grass Valley (California) *Union* reported that Bodie had forty-seven saloons (quoted in Johnson and Johnson 1967: 26). The first article to describe Bodie as a ghost town, without citing its source, claimed that Bodie had sixty-five saloons (Van Loan 1915).

4. The Reverend's letter is dated January 25, 1881; Warrington did not acquire the property on which Bodie's Methodist church now stands until July of the following year (McGrath 1984; Wedertz 1969; the letter is reproduced in full in Johnson and Johnson 1967: 101).

5. See for example, Cain 1956; Glassock 1937; Loose 1979; Russell 1927; Smith 1925; and Wedertz, 1969. For commentary on the quote, see DeLyser, forthcoming. The brochure does not differ from other written accounts except that in the brochure it is a written diary entry and not a spoken prayer as it is in other accounts, and that other accounts sometimes substitute *I* for *we* in the little girl's quote.

6. The truck is used as part of the Park's float in the 4th of July parade in the neighboring town of Bridgeport. Through most of the 1990s its maintenance was largely my responsibility.

7. As I have tried to make clear, this is not for lack of interest, or for lack of trying, but rather mainly from lack of information: Bodie's boom-period population was remarkably mobile and there is no agreement among Bodie scholars on who lived in which house or who operated which business during the boom. Although much is indeed known about Bodie's businesses (information

obtained largely from newspaper records), far less is known about the residences. As a result, much of the residential information has come from the extensive oral histories that park staff people have meticulously collected over the years—information that, because of its grounding in the living memory of individuals interviewed, necessarily relates to post-boom periods. In fact, however, although this post-boom focus is not what the brochure appears to present to readers, it is explicitly what is called for in the Park's General Development Plan (California Department of Parks and Recreation 1979).

8. One notable exception to this is some of the seasonal housing lived in by park staff—the room I often slept in, for example.

9. Even the location of Chinatown relative to Bodie's other ruins contributes to the marginalization of this group. Originally situated just north of the center of boom-period Bodie, after the devastating fire of 1932 the center of town shifted to the south so that today's visitors perceive Chinatown to be in a remote location, far from the main homes and businesses.

10. Similar elisions have been made in the cases of Bodie's Native American, Mexican, and African-American populations (see DeLyser 1998). The brochure mentions no African Americans, for example, but *could* tell of William O'Hara, a prominent businessman and mine owner in Bodie's pre-boom days; it was after a cave-in in his Empire Mine that the rush to Bodie began (Loose 1979; Wedertz 1969).

11. Evidence of this can be found in the fact that the upper reaches of the townsite are often completely devoid of visitors, even on days when the lower part of town is crowded. Because the more remote buildings also have fewer artifacts in them, many visitors at first intent on seeing everything change their minds as their level of exertion rises and the number of artifacts declines. "Let's turn around" and "Let's go back down" are not uncommon sentiments in the remote parts of Bodie.

12. Some buy more, and some of those do it because they plan to subdivide their group and send one brochure with each part of their party. This often happens along gender lines, with women and small children exploring as one group while men, and often older male children, roam in a second group.

13. The park provides only water; no food or drink is for sale, and the nearest services are twenty miles away.

14. Only extremely seldom does the park staff find brochures in Bodie's trash cans. What this suggests, though, is merely that the brochures leave the park, not that they are all necessarily treasured: some may end up in a trash can farther down the road.

15. In the 1880s and 1890s, three brothers of the large Dalton family—Robert, Grattan, and Emmett—became the notorious Dalton Gang who, despite their affiliations with law enforcement, stole horses, held up trains, and robbed banks in the trans-Mississippi West (see Lamar 1998: 284–85).

16. In Bodie, whether during boom years or later, there simply were no upper-class residences, the town's upper class being an absentee population living in "civilized" places such as San Francisco and New York. And, in fact, judging by the remaining homes, what qualified as middle class in Bodie was in fact displaced downward from middle-class standards in the nation as a whole. My thanks for their insights in this regard to Marguerite Sprague and Paul Greenstein.

17. This is a project in which I, for one, would eagerly participate.

5. Representing Culloden

Social Memory, Battlefield Heritage, and Landscapes of Regret

John R. Gold and Margaret M. Gold

Only men's minds could ever have unmapped into abstraction such a territory.

Norman MacCaig, *The Celtic Cross*

Former battlefields are often unprepossessing places. Unless an army has been trapped in a confined space by enemy ambush, fields of combat tend to lack imposing topography. Flat ground allows infantry commanders to deploy their forces in optimal formation and artillery commanders to establish uninterrupted lines of fire, at best looking for slight undulations or ridges to give themselves points of tactical advantage. Whatever their appearance during the heat of battle, most battlefields scarcely merit a second glance for their inherent landscape qualities once the debris of war has been cleared away. Despite that, battlefields and other sites associated with war and violent conflict have a profound significance. Names such as Crécy and Agincourt, Passchendaele and Ypres, Bull Run and Gettysburg, Rorke's Drift and Mafeking serve as the mnemonics of political, social, and cultural history. Scholars employ them as events to delimit recognizable periods within which to construct historical narratives. Reenactment societies use them to present living history to modern audiences. Tourist agencies incorporate them into themed packages for consumption by visitors.

The battlefield that is the subject of this chapter characterizes this genre. The view across the site shown in Figure 5.1 reveals a largely featureless section of the area known as Drummossie Moor at a spot approximately five miles east of Inverness, the largest town in northern Scotland. Scenically, it is wholly unremarkable other than affording some distant views north over the Moray Firth toward the mountains of Ross and Cromarty. Located on a slowly rising ridge at around five hundred feet above sea level, it primarily consists of tussocky grassland, interspersed with small streams and waterlogged hollows. Until recently it was bisected by the B9006 Inverness–Nairn road and largely covered by trees planted in the late nineteenth and early twentieth centuries. Forestry plantations still fringe its northeastern and southwestern boundaries. There are no impressive earthworks and no hauntingly evocative redundant military structures. Yet, notwithstanding this unpromising description, Figure 5.1 also depicts a place that is comfortably the most visited tourist attraction in the north of Scotland. Each year thousands of tourists arrive from all over the world to wander round, read the interpretive notices, call in at the visitor center, and stare at a handful of small memorials.

Description of Battlefield.

To find the reason, one need do no more than mention the site's other, more familiar, name—Culloden. Even those without Highland

Figure 5.1. View north across Culloden Moor.

ancestry find that Culloden has a resonance that makes it more than just the point where, in 1746, the army of the Hanoverian King George II defeated the forces of Charles Edward Stuart in the last formal battle fought on British soil. Culloden represents a key moment in the development of both the Scottish nation and the Union of British states. The decisive government victory effectively extinguished the remaining Stuart claim to the British throne and set in train processes of socioeconomic, demographic, and political change that irrevocably altered the relationship of Scotland, especially Highland Scotland, to the wider British state. Military and political triumph, however, do not necessarily destroy cultural aspiration. In the quarter-millennium since the event, the significance of Culloden has been mapped and remapped on many occasions, as different generations contest its cultural meaning.

[margin note: Culloden was major turning point in Scotland's history.]

This chapter examines the nature of this remapping process over time as reflected in representations of Culloden intended for consumption by the visitor, as mediated both by interpretive materials at the battlefield itself and in literature designed for the tourist. At the outset, it is important to recognize that the process of representation has a dual character. Broadly speaking, *representations* are images or likenesses that stand for something, but inevitably the act of *representation* is selective. Choosing to show or emphasize a particular element or set of attributes may well mean downplaying or ignoring others. This is compounded by the fact that "representation" can also mean to speak for something else. In this way, the act of representation can involve not just illustrating an object, person, idea, or scene, but also speaking on its behalf. Representation, therefore, is both a cultural and a political process.

In light of that understanding, this chapter is divided into five main sections. The first briefly introduces the subject of battlefield tourism, drawing attention to the broader cultural contexts and narratives that have underpinned interpretive strategies. The next section provides background on the battle of Culloden, its immediate aftermath, and the factors underpinning early representations of the battlefield in travelers' accounts and guidebooks. The third analyzes the remapping of Culloden in response to the agenda of romantic Jacobitism and the growth of Scottish tourism. The fourth section examines the literal and figurative remapping of the site as sacred space under the aegis of its current owner, the National Trust for Scotland. The Conclusion considers the multiple and contested meanings of Culloden that have emerged over time and suggests that the remapping process may yet remain incomplete.

Battlefield Tourism

Battlefield tourism is not a new phenomenon. The battle of Waterloo in 1815 attracted spectators while the fighting still raged and the scene of the battle remained one of Belgium's most popular tourist attractions throughout the nineteenth and twentieth centuries (Seaton 1999a; Semmel 2000). Thomas Cook started tours to South Africa to visit battlefield sites before the Boer War's conclusion in 1902; indeed, so many tourists were arriving that the High Commissioner, Sir Alfred Milner, called on them to stop, as they were interfering with the war effort (Lloyd 1998: 20). The numbers visiting these locations were, in turn, eclipsed from the 1920s on by those traveling to visit the battlefields and military cemeteries associated with the First World War (Seaton 2000). More recently, visits to theaters of war in Southeast Asia (Peleggi 1996; Henderson 1997, 2000), Balkan Europe (O'Reilly 1996), and the Middle East (Azaryahu 1993; Smith 1998: 206) have widened the scope of what is now a booming sector of the international tourist market, increasingly serviced by specialist tour operators (e.g., Fletcher 2000; TWE 2001).

The increasing popularity of battlefields with visitors, particularly in the nineteenth century, reflected a variety of factors, including improvements in personal mobility, antiquarianism, and greater sensitivity toward conserving the past. The practices of battlefield interpretation changed accordingly. Custom-written maps and guidebooks started to circulate that not only informed visitors where to go and what to see, but also suggested how they should tour the site once they had arrived. Visitors were encouraged to follow routes that picked out significant points and locations. The maps and markers helped to mediate their movements, enjoining them to pause at *this* point, gaze in *that* direction, and reflect in particular ways on the events that had occurred. "Markers" in the form of plaques, statues, commemorative stones, memorials, and site maps were commonly added to make the otherwise undifferentiated terrain of battlefields come to life. As Diller and Scofidio (1994: 47) remarked:

> The battlefield . . . becomes an ideologically encoded landscape through the commemorative function of the "marker". As a marker inscribes war

onto material soil, *it* becomes the sight. Without the marker, a battlefield might be indistinguishable from a golf course or a beach. Guided by a system of markers and maps, the tourist/strategist reenacts the battle by tracing the tragic space of conflict by foot or by car.

The key point here concerns *narratives,* defined as structured accounts of actions and events. Narratives help clothe the world of the past with meaning, making sense of sequences of events, resolving ambiguity, and, not infrequently, identifying heroes and villains. At the same time, they are sources of power. The support that historians give to particular values and the extent of their attachment to the cause that they are studying both impact on the act of narration. Through the resulting narratives, historians can propagate accounts that justify their own positions or those of the order they represent. The construction of narratives therefore can, and frequently does, serve a powerful ideological function.

For the most part, the ideological message encoded in the interpretation of battlefields conformed to the traditional "drum and trumpet" style of military history (Samuel 1994: 440), which warmly praises military achievement in its own right and for its role in fulfilling national destiny. From the late nineteenth century onward, this message became interlaced with notions of sacred space. Sacred space at its simplest refers to the interconnection of the sacred and the secular, the spiritual and the material, the eternal and the temporal (Gold 2000). Battlefields became increasingly regarded as places sanctified by the blood of those who had died for a just cause. This outlook marked a profound change from previous practice concerning the treatment of the dead, which, before this time, had been resolutely unsentimental. At Waterloo, for example, the authorities buried the dead in unmarked mass graves that were then largely forgotten (Laqueur 2000: 7). The living, however, now accepted the spiritual responsibility of caring for the sites where they fell and were interred.

This change in attitude was illustrated by practices adopted during the American Civil War, when the descriptions of cemeteries drew heavily on the language of the sacred (Lloyd 1998: 21). President Lincoln's Gettysburg Address in November 1863, for example, pointed to the sanctification of the battlefield by the blood of the fallen (Linenthal 1991; Wills 1992). Growing acceptance of the idea that the living should commemorate the sacrifice of those who perished became further evident during the Anglo-Boer War and became a matter of British national priority after the First World War (Winter 1995; Saunders 2001). As Heffernan (1995: 294) states:

> Before 1914, the construction of official burial sites and memorials to the casualties of war was rare. In Britain, warfare was generally recalled in poetic or literary form, or in shrines devoted to national heroes like Nelson or Wellington. The anonymous masses who fought and died were usually ignored. Since 1918, official war commemoration has focused more directly on the fate of the ordinary soldier, symbolized by the interment of the Unknown Warrior in Westminster Abbey and the unveiling of the Cenotaph (meaning 'empty tomb') in Whitehall on Armistice Day 1920.

These forms of remembrance and their associated interpretations remain the staple fare at many battlefield tourist sites, but several qualifications must be made. First, only the most important sites are normally treated as sacred space. Battlefield archaeologists interested in First World War sites in France and Belgium, for example, note that, with limited exceptions, "the Belgian and French national boards of antiquities have not yet really regarded them as sites worth preserving, not due to their cultural heritage value anyway" (Fabiansson 2001). Second, greater plurality of interpretive narratives is now apparent. In some cases, comprehensive counterhistories are now offered that stress defeat or disinheritance instead of national pride in righteous victory. Minority groups, especially aboriginal or other "conquered" peoples, recognize and resent their exclusion from the established history of conflicts (e.g., Healy 1997).[1] Acceptance of their case by the custodians of sites initiates a process of adjustment by which the vanquished or excluded gain a stake in interpretation. In other cases, the defeated party becomes the dominant partner in weaving the narrative of interpretation, finding ways of presenting an unpalatable past that are acceptable to the needs of the present.

The treatment of *landscapes of regret* provides a case in point. These are places that are deeply etched in social memory as scenes of defeat and loss, sometimes tinged with anger or disgrace. At the same time, landscapes of regret are not solely places for lament and despair. Their uncomfortable history is ameliorated by compensating factors, such as pride in gallantry, demands for redress of perceived brutality, and hopes for renewal. Moreover, they can play a vital role in transmitting the agreed representations of the past that are the basis of social memory (Fentress and Wickham 1992). By supplying a recognizable focus, battle-fields give tangible expression to alternative readings of the past, allow-ing visitors to assume the mantle of pilgrims paying their respects to the sacrifice of forebears and perhaps also express their allegiance to a com-mon cause. The next sections show how such an interpretation gradu-ally emerged for Culloden and the ways in which it was expressed.

In Search of Culloden

The events of 1745–46 were part of a protracted struggle for succession to the English, Scottish, and, subsequently, British thrones. From the 1688 "Glorious Revolution" that expelled the King James II until the death of the last credible Stuart claimant in 1788, the ruling Establishment lived in periodic fear of French-backed intervention to restore the Stuart dynasty and Roman Catholicism to Protestant Britain. This came to a head on two major occasions, with the Jacobite risings of 1715 and 1745, respectively known as the "Fifteen" and the "Forty-Five."[2] In each case, the Stuart Pretenders landed and raised their forces in Scotland, but the resulting campaigns were essentially dynastic, religious, and per-haps social-systemic rather than a battle between nations.[3] The Forty-Five specifically was fought on behalf of rival claimants to the British throne, with armies drawn up from complex sets of alliances. There were Scottish clansmen lining up with the Hanoverians and English supporters of the Stuarts: indeed, more Scots fought under the Duke of Cumberland than for the Jacobite cause. Hence, notwithstanding the pervasive mythology that permeates so much tourist literature, neither the Fifteen nor the Forty-Five amounted to a contest between England and Scotland per se.

Culloden marked the end of a yearlong campaign. This saw Prince Charles Edward Stuart, or "Bonnie Prince Charlie," first land on the Outer Hebridean island of Eriskay (July 23, 1745) and sail on to Glen-finnan, where the royal standard was raised (August 19, 1745). After a se-ries of victories, the Jacobite armies advanced south through Scotland and into England heading for London (Figure 5.2). They eventually reached Derby in the English East Midlands. Lacking promised reinforcements from France and failing to recruit many English recruits, the Jacobites made the tactical decision to retreat north on December 6, 1745, on hearing that Hanoverian forces were returning from Continental Europe to face them. After a series of battles and skirmishes in the early part of 1746, the two armies converged on Culloden for a battle that the Jacobite command was keen to fight for tactical and logistic reasons (Reid 1994: 49–57).

Culloden Moor, however, marked the denouement for the Stuart cause.

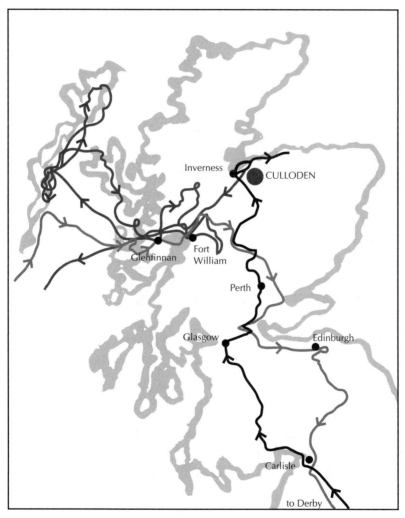

Figure 5.2. Charles Edward Stuart's campaign, 1745–46.

By April 1746, the Jacobites were poorly provisioned and outnumbered, with their chances of victory further hampered by their commanders' strategic mistakes—not the least of which was selecting a site for battle that greatly favored their opponents. When the opposing forces gathered on April 16, 1746, the open ground suited the cavalry and artillery that the Hanoverian forces possessed and the Jacobites lacked. The gentle slope and marshy ground, drenched after recent rain, reduced the effectiveness of the Highlanders' traditional broadsword charge. Less a battle than a rout, the fighting was over in under an hour, with around twelve hundred Jacobites slain against 310 Hanoverian losses.[4]

The immediate aftermath of the battle saw the Hanoverian forces under the Duke of Cumberland pursuing the tattered remnants of the Jacobite forces, including Charles Edward Stuart, through the Highlands. After five months in hiding, the prince finally escaped back to France on the privateer *L'Heureux* on September 20, 1746. Sufficient peace had returned by October 1746 for the issue of a royal proclamation commanding "a General Thanksgiving to Almighty God, throughout England, Wales and Berwick-upon-Tweed," for his help

> in suppressing the late unnatural REBELLION raised within this Kingdom by wicked and desperate men, supported by our enemies abroad, and formed to depose and murder us, subvert the Religion, laws and Liberties of our Kingdoms, and set on the throne thereof a POPISH PRE-TENDER, bred up and instructed in ROMISH superstition, and arbitrary principles; whereby we and our Kingdom are delivered from the calamities of an intestine war, and the public peace is restored.

The British government then turned to the problem of how to avoid further "rebellions" of the type experienced twice in the previous thirty years. Initial reprisals against rebel clans and disarmament measures were quickly followed by a conscious longer-term policy that sought to remove the conditions that helped foment revolt. Strategies adopted for this purpose included confiscations of estates, attempts to destroy the cultural identity of rebel clans, and dismantlement of the system of land tenure and ownership. Above all, official policy sought to remove the area's quasi independence by integrating it into the wider British economy.

The battlefield itself, however, quickly faded from public consciousness. Under the supervision of government troops, local people gathered the bodies of the dead soldiers, sorted them into groups, and buried them in collective graves. No memorial markers were built. Any erected for the dead of the Stuart forces would have fallen foul of the proscription of Jacobitism. The British government, for its part, showed no interest in memorializing the contribution of its own soldiers who fell at Culloden. Its victory celebrations centered on the Duke of Cumberland's triumphant entry into London rather than seeking any Scottish focus for commemoration.

Silence then descended on Culloden. The few travelers who visited the battlefield primarily commented on the beneficial consequences of the government's victory for the British people (Gold and Gold 1995). On August 16, 1769, for example, Thomas Pennant wrote that he had passed over Culloden Moor, "the place that North Britain owes its present prosperity to, by the victory of April 16, 1746" (Pennant 1771: 144). A generation later, John Lettice echoed his sentiments. His letters record that "it was not possible to pass the scene where it was fought, without some feeling of triumph," with comments about the necessity of the event for "the civilization of the Highlands," although tempering his remarks somewhat by adding regret that the victors "should not have been contented with conquest" (Lettice 1794: 258). Generally, however, Culloden did not feature in the accounts of visitors to the Scottish Highlands in the late eighteenth century. Those venturing as far north as Inverness and Loch Ness normally traveled close to the site, but the nearby Culloden House aroused more interest than the battlefield. For instance, despite their considerable interest in other aspects of the Forty-Five, the redoubtable Dr. Samuel Johnson and his companion James Boswell failed to mention Culloden Moor in their copious journals, despite passing it on their 1773 Scottish tour (Chapman 1924: 60).

Part of the problem was that for a century after the battle, the site was hard to locate. Although a road had been put through the battlefield in the 1740s and upgraded to a carriage road in 1835, there was nothing to indicate that the visitors had arrived. Visitors relied on the often unreliable accounts of previous travelers and on local guides whose English, in this Gaelic-speaking area, might be poor or nonexistent. There were few guidebooks or maps. As one traveler noted: "I am convinced the interior parts of this country are very inadequately laid down in the maps of Scotland, and the names of places are often either altogether wanting, or at an amazing distance from where they ought to be" (Cordiner 1780:

115–16). Although the first Ordnance Survey one-inch (1:63360) series of maps began to appear for England and Wales in 1801, their Scottish equivalents were not published until the second half of the nineteenth century (Table 5.1). The relevant sheet covering the Culloden area only appeared in 1876.

Table 5.1. Editions of the Ordnance Survey one-inch (1:63360) map series for Scotland

Edition	Surveyed	Published
1st	1845–78	1856–87
2d	1894–95	1896–97
3d	1901–10	1902–13

Source: Based on information from Harley (1964: 42–43)

The earliest commercial guidebooks that covered the Inverness region appeared in the early nineteenth century, but the battlefield did not always figure on the accompanying maps. To take an example, a pioneering guidebook by the father-and-son team of George and Peter Anderson (1834) contained just one folded map covering the whole of Scotland produced by James Arrowsmith, a London-based cartographer. The map located Culloden House and the nearby stone circle at Clava but omitted reference to the battle of Culloden, even though the mapmaker commemorated other battlefields associated with the Forty-Five with the date and the familiar crossed-swords emblem. Recognizing the difficulty of finding the site, the authors supplied directions that would have required visitors to exhibit skills approaching those of a surveyor. To locate the battlefield, visitors were advised to watch a succession of landmarks appear and disappear as they progressed along the road. Once a distant hill known as Dun Daviot came in sight, they were given the following instructions:

> when a considerable portion of the road before the passenger (about a quarter of a mile in length) leads the eye directly to the top of a tabular rocky hill bearing south-east, at a distance of five or six miles, it will be found that a straight line, drawn from Dun Daviot, just mentioned, to Fort George, which will be seen rising at the termination of a long

peninsula jutting out into the Moray Firth, will cut across the public road just at the collection of graves sought for. They consist of two or three grass-covered mounds, rising slightly above the adjoining heath, at the distance of about 200 or 300 yards from a small patch of corn land and a cluster of cottages, between which and them a marshy hollow also intervenes. On all sides the prospect is here bleak and dreary. (Anderson and Anderson 1834: 107)

It would be some decades before the appearance of field markers at the battlefield made the traveler's task easier. Precedent had been set by the construction in 1815 of a monument at Glenfinnan to record the prince's landing in mainland Scotland. Certainly during the 1830s, there were plans to raise funds by public subscription to erect "a tumulus or obelisk" at Culloden "to mark the spot where the contest took place" (ibid.). Yet these and several subsequent appeals came to nothing and, meanwhile, the graves themselves remained unprotected. With what now seems astonishing insensitivity, the 1835 road improvements had cut directly through the graves, with the workmen reinterring the disturbed remains wherever they felt convenient. Visitors also had no qualms about pillaging the site for souvenirs to take home. When William Howitt visited in 1836, he noted that parties of tourists would dig in any likely place to find some fragments of bones or artifacts to take away as a memento, an easy task given that in many places the bodies lay within a foot of the surface (Howitt 1840). The neglect was symptomatic of the general picture; Culloden remained a somewhat forgotten site on the fringes of British, or even Scottish, consciousness.

Romantic Jacobitism

Impetus for change, when it occurred, came from two interrelated sources. At one level, new attitudes toward Culloden and what it represented drew inspiration from fresh readings of Scottish history. Although it is not possible to present the historiographic issues fully here, it can be broadly argued that a new ideological construction of Scottish history formed in the salons and journals of Victorian Britain during the nineteenth century.[5] It centered on Anglo-British constitutional history. Historians argued that English constitutionalism had brought civilization and advancement to Scotland. Pre-Union Scottish history was redundant

as a pointer toward progress (Finlay 1994: 127) and therefore became recast as a mythic cultural history, centering on the legends and myths of
the Celtic regions of Highland Scotland.

At another level, changing attitudes toward Culloden were rooted in
romantic Jacobitism. The story of Bonnie Prince Charlie fitted seamlessly in a style of history that traded in heroic leaders, ancient chivalry,
and myths of the golden age. The eighteenth-century pan-European
Romantic movement had already created great interest in the scenery,
myths, and legends of Highland Scotland (Gold and Gold 1995: 77–79).
Jacobite balladeers, poets such as Lady Carolina Nairne, and novelists
such as Sir Walter Scott helped to portray the prince as the heroic but
ill-fated warrior. His quest was the equivalent of the Odyssey of antiq-
uity, with the added advantage that Charles Edward's travels could be
readily related to known locations. His defeat at Culloden, in particular,
was recast as a modern equivalent of the battle of Thermopylae in the
classical Persian Wars: a comprehensive defeat with sufficient redeeming
factors to allow historians to find something to celebrate.[6]

In keeping with the new mood, the campaign for monuments at
Culloden continued. A foundation stone for a "giant" memorial cairn was
laid in 1849 and a large heap of stones was accumulated ready for its construction, but lack of funds caused the project's abandonment by 1852.
An enthusiastic Jacobite, Edward Power, commissioned another cairn in
1858. This too was never completed, but a dedication stone prepared for
that monument was retained and used in the subsequent twenty-foot-
high cairn that the landowner Duncan Forbes built in 1881 (Figure 5.3).
The inscription of the dedication stone tells an important story (Figure
5.4). After the name of the battle and the date, the stone states that here
are "the graves of the gallant Highlanders who fought for Scotland &
Prince Charlie" and they "are marked by the names of their clans."

This, as may be recognized, placed a particular slant on history.
The Stuart dead were now appropriated for the cause of Scotland and
Scottish national identity (McArthur 1994). Around 1880, Forbes also
commissioned headstones for the clan graves, carefully differentiating
the graves of individual clans or simply labeling the remains as belonging
to mixed clans if there was doubt. In 1963, the Military History Society
of Ireland sponsored another memorial for the Irish forces ("the Wild
Geese") that fought for the Jacobites. They also had a tangible identity
conferred upon them, with the memorial's Irish Gaelic dedication hail-

Figure 5.3. The Memorial Cairn.

ing them as "the breed of Kings" and "as eager warriors and heroes." Yet if a process of commemoration had begun that drew heavily upon the language of the heroic, it did not extend to the opposition. The cultivated field where the government soldiers lay gained a small stone. Placed in position in 1880, its inscription merely read: "Field of the English. They were buried here." No tales of gallantry and valor, but by that stage it was unlikely that any other message would have been conveyed. Although the extent of the atrocities committed after Culloden is now challenged, the powerful social memory of the injustice perpetrated by the dead soldiers' colleagues, and the regime that they represented, did not then permit other readings of the past.

Those promoting tourism in the Scottish Highlands avidly embraced this theme. Culloden, together with the other sites associated with the prince, was adopted as an attraction by newly established tour operators such as Thomas Cook (Brendon 1991: 38–56) and by the railway companies, which were actively developing their Scottish networks. The Inverness and Nairn Railway, for example, issued a booklet describing scenes close to the route of the railway and supplying details for access to Culloden Moor (Anderson and Anderson 1856; see also Anderson and Anderson 1865). Peter Anderson went on to produce the

Figure 5.4. Inscription from the Memorial Cairn.

first comprehensive guidebook to assist tourists visiting the battlefield (Anderson 1867). Designed particularly for sale at station bookshops owned by its publishers John Menzies, its preface linked this project with Anderson's previous work on the railway guide:

> HAVING been for some years resident in the neighborhood of the Culloden Railway Station, the Author's attention has been a good deal engaged with the scene and incidents of the expiring struggle of the Stuart dynasty, and the last battle fought on British ground. (Ibid., 5)

He then specified his aim:

> though the battle of Culloden has been repeatedly described in the course of works of more general history and disquisition, the circumstances are becoming unfamiliar to the public at large; and it has been thought that a separate account, embracing a survey of what has been said on various controverted points by different writers, with the addition of more minute topographical details, and the aid of received local tradition, might be acceptable, more especially to strangers visiting the field of battle. (Ibid.)

[handwritten margin note: want for a tourist text]

Part travel guide and part primer on the history of the Forty-Five, the guidebook then presented the history of the encounter at Culloden in chronological sequence. For each phase, it supplied topographic information, itineraries, and detailed instructions as to how to reach the battlefield on foot. Maps drawn by a local surveyor, James Fraser, indicated the general disposition of the forces (Figure 5.5). The accuracy with which they depict the battle lines is questionable, given that, as a later source noted with some exasperation,

> Seldom can so many differing maps have been drawn of one battlefield. Maps have obviously been done from hearsay and without the map-maker having any personal knowledge of the ground. However attractively executed some of them are, they can be needlessly confusing. (NTS 1965: 30)

[handwritten margin note: confusion w/ the many different maps drawn.]

Nevertheless, the marking of the positions of the opposing forces was vital. Few of the previous maps were in the tourist domain. Anderson's map now inscribed the outline of the hostilities fought in 1746 back on to the field at Culloden. From this point forward, visitors were enjoined to see Culloden Moor as a battlefield rather than just a war cemetery.

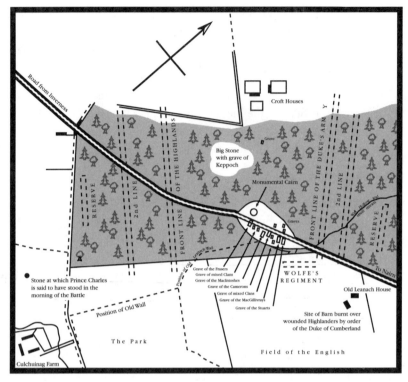

Figure 5.5. The battlefield at Culloden from 1867 Plan.

The guidebook enveloped its account of the battle and its aftermath in a narrative steeped in sentimental Jacobitism. The prince is represented as a farsighted individual let down by mediocre, frequently "foreign" advisers—an ironic notion given his background. The "romantic enterprise" (Anderson 1867: 5) of his advance on London had been thwarted, even though its boldness "might have achieved at least the temporary reinstatement of the Stuarts on the throne of Britain." Culloden itself was a tale of mistakes and poor advice by others, but the role of the prince and his foot soldiers in the battle was beyond reproach—a tale of heroic struggle in the face of overwhelming odds. The actions of the Stuart side are discussed in detail and placed in context throughout. By contrast, the government forces are primarily the opposition who turn up for battle. Their leaders are coldly efficient and seemingly resented for their ungentlemanly act of having superior numbers of forces. Their actions are seldom scrutinized unless they can be linked to atrocities and scant effort is made to place them in the context of the military or political history of mid-eighteenth-century Britain.

The production of this guidebook also coincided with the growth of a themed approach to visiting the Scottish Highlands. From the 1870s onward, it became common practice for guidebooks to print maps of Prince Charles Edward's advance, retreat, and final wanderings in the Highlands as reference points for Scottish tours. The map itself gained iconic status. Difficulties of the terrain and lack of effective communications meant that only the most hardy felt inclined to travel as pilgrims on the route that it inscribed, but tourists flocked to key sites such as Culloden, Glenfinnan, and the Isle of Skye to savor the grandeur and pathos of the Forty-Five. Their number even included the British monarch, Queen Victoria, who wrote the following in her journal for 1874:

> Yes and I feel a sort of reverence in going over these scenes in this beautiful country, which I am proud to call my own, where there was such devoted loyalty to the family of my ancestors—for Stuart blood is in my veins, and I am now their representative, and the people are as devoted and loyal to me as they were to that unhappy race. (Victoria 1968: 173)

Yet despite the enthusiastic embrace of the romanticized Stuart cause, there remained a contradiction in the prevailing treatment of Culloden. Construction of the Forbes monuments had provided a core attraction for the visitor. By contrast, the moorland, which Anderson had remapped as a battlefield, was still far from being sacred space. The site was planted with conifers and larches in the 1890s. Although described as a "green open space in the midst of plantations" in 1890 (Anonymous 1890), the situation changed dramatically in the next two decades. The third edition of the Ordnance Survey's one-inch series, published in 1911, shows the battlefield covered by woodland—apart from the Field of the English, which had always remained under cultivation. By 1920, the visitor could see very little of the battlefield because only a space around the Forbes memorials was left free from tree planting (see Figure 5.5). The view north across to the Firth to the mountains was obscured. Isolated monuments like the Keppoch Stone became difficult to find, with one visitor noting that "Small weather-worn stones rise from the heath and stand among the slim trees" (Morton 1929: 175). An intentional policy of obliterating Culloden from the map could scarcely have been more effective.

Further indignities were to follow. A line of telephone poles and wires was placed directly across the battlefield. A bungalow was built in 1937 between the Old Leanach cottage and the memorials. Increasing tourism, promoted particularly by Inverness-based coach proprietors, led to vehicles arriving throughout the day and being parked in a chaotic manner on the grass verges next to the memorials. The cairn itself, according to a 1947 guidebook, was "threatened by cafes and tea-houses" (Anonymous 1947: 48). Most observers were agreed that the site lacked atmosphere, was overcrowded in summer, and needed more protection from damage.

Only gradually was that protection afforded. In 1902 a fence was placed round the cairn to protect it from the unwelcome attentions of visitors, variously accused of clambering on it, carving their initials, or using it for target practice. In 1925 the Culloden Memorials were officially scheduled as Ancient Monuments, prompted by a campaign by the Gaelic Society of Inverness, which had assumed responsibility for maintaining them. More important perhaps was the gradual transfer of the land in piecemeal parcels to the National Trust for Scotland (NTS), an independent charitable body established in 1931 with wide legal powers to hold lands and properties of national significance in perpetuity. Virtually all the battlefield came into the hands of the NTS, through gift or purchase, between 1937 and 1989. Consolidation brought new possibilities for management and interpretation of a site widely regarded as important but severely neglected. Literally, as well as figuratively, it was time to remap Culloden.

Sacred Space

In the late 1950s, the decision was made to "recreate the eighteenth-century scene" (Prentice 1976: 153). This immediately raised questions of authenticity. "Authenticity," of course, is not a quality of objects in their own right but is something ascribed to them by someone with the responsibility to say they are authentic (Fees 1996: 122). The site had changed beyond recognition in more than two centuries. To return it to an appropriate state for visitors to appreciate the battle fought here rather than simply inspect some memorials meant decisions about removal of features regarded as inauthentic. The extensive work necessary proceeded slowly given the need to cooperate with a disparate range of landowners, public authorities, and funding bodies. The cluster of ramshackle cafés and teahouses near the cairn was removed. In 1960, the General Post Office—then responsible for providing telephone services—dismantled the line of poles that crossed the battlefield and buried the wires underground. The bungalow built in 1937 was purchased by the NTS and demolished in 1972. In 1980, the trees were felled after the plantations were purchased from the Forestry Commission with financial assistance from the Countryside Commission for Scotland (now Scottish Natural Heritage). In 1985, cooperation with the Highland Regional Council and traffic agencies allowed the rerouting of the road to the north away from the graves. The old road was subsequently dug up and landscaped. The Old Leanach Cottage, an important site from the battle that since 1959 had been used as a visitor center, was supplanted by a custom-built replacement in 1970. As well as allowing restoration of the cottage, the new visitor center (enlarged in 1984) and its car park create a point of arrival for visitors and a means of channeling access to the site. Gradually, as a result of this lengthy process, Culloden was returned to open moorland on which it was possible again to see the heath in its entirety. The physical reconstruction of the battlefield was complete.

The new map of Culloden presented to visitors expressed not just the changed features of the moorland but also the spirit of this reconstruction (Figure 5.6). Although the memorials and the stones are still clearly marked, it is the initial formations of the opposing forces that catch the eye. Largely stripped of physical features and references to topography, the map turns Culloden Moor into a tabula rasa on which is written the battle lines as they formed at 11 A.M. on April 16, 1746. How the forces came to be there and what then happened is left to the associated process of interpretation.

What is impressive about that interpretation is the extent to which it offers both a seamless official history and a frame for directing the gaze of the visitor to the battlefield. It is conveyed through guidebooks for those who take self-guided tours, through the narratives purveyed by audiovisual displays and battlefield reconstructions at the visitor center, by the student guides who escort parties around the site, and through the field interpretive materials. Broadly, it consolidates the lachrymose account offered by romantic Jacobitism with the notion of sacred space. The key theme is that Culloden was an important watershed. Static and audiovisual exhibits at the visitor center describe the traditional way of life of Highland Scotland and the place of a noble militarism in the

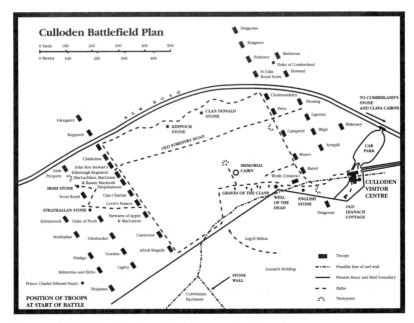

Figure 5.6. Culloden Moor as currently represented.

functioning of its society. They hint at a golden age in which people lived close to the land in their ancestral domains. This land of tranquillity was irrevocably destroyed in the aftermath of Culloden by enemy forces that were alien, colonizing, and Other. To some extent, then, it is not just a political cause that was at stake, but also the cultural and economic future of Gaelic Highland Scotland. The details of the military campaign are told in standard partial fashion that Peter Anderson, from a century earlier, would have instantly recognized. Mistakes by commanders are acknowledged, but it is the noble sacrifice of what are represented as Scotland's finest rather than errors or foolhardiness of leaders that is emphasized.

At the same time, it must be stressed that this style of narrative is not immutable, a point that can be appreciated by comparing the 1965 guidebook (NTS 1965) with the latest available edition (Sked 1997). According to the 1965 guide (NTS 1965: 5), Culloden was now

a place of pilgrimage for many, from home and overseas, not to mourn forlornly for the "lost cause" of the Stuarts, but to pay their homage to the memory of the heroes and brave deeds of that long past day.

After a description of the topography of the site and the role of the Forbes family—themselves the recipients of "harsh treatment" from the Hanoverian government after Culloden (ibid., 7)—the guide provides a walking tour of the memorials in nine clusters. Each is allotted its own note of poignancy, often linked to the overworked phrase "mortally wounded." Tales of brutality by the Hanoverians and gallant comradeship by the doomed Jacobites lend color to the solemn text.

By time of the 1997 edition, the author at least feels the need to add historical context, downplaying the Scotland versus England theme of earlier accounts and stressing that "Culloden was a battle in a civil war" (Sked 1997: 2). There are cautious comments about the phrasing of inscriptions on memorials and lack of sympathy in Lowland Scotland for the Jacobite cause. Nevertheless, there are striking resemblances to past narratives. The events of Culloden are explained from the Stuart position and the battlefield tour remains much the same. Visitors are offered a powerful narrative, a story of tragic defeat coupled with a sense that this is the place where traditional Scotland, the real and authentic Scotland, came to an end. The caveats and reservations are pushed to the margins. Landscapes of regret are difficult places in which to accommodate dissonance. → a tension or clash.

Conclusion

Writing about the process of mapping, Denis Cosgrove (1999: 2) noted that its "measure . . . is not restricted to the mathematical; it may equally be spiritual, political or moral." It is an apt characterization of the broad scope of the processes at work in representing Culloden. In the course of this chapter, we have shown the wealth of meaning that lurks behind the apparently straightforward task of representing the battlefield to the tourist. The detail shown on maps, the messages inscribed in field markers, and the topographic description found in travel literature testify to changing narratives. In part, those narratives conformed to trends generally seen in the development of battlefield tourism, but their content and timing were different from experiences elsewhere. The chronological sequence identified in this chapter illustrates how a battlefield that was neglected for more than a century and lingered at the fringes of social memory was progressively transformed. New readings of Scottish history and the spread of the sentimental tenets of romantic Jacobitism then led to reappraisal. Travel writers helped to remap Culloden as a battlefield rather than a war cemetery, but it was still many years before the site was represented as a place of pilgrimage, endowed with the properties of sacred space. That development awaited the physical reconstruction of Culloden as open moorland and the development of an integrated approach to site interpretation.

It is safe to say that the powerful narrative propagated at Culloden will persist because it is also an important ingredient in the way that the heritage industry sells Scotland (Gold and Gold 1995). Yet it is also a restrictive narrative that circumscribes the range of lessons that can be drawn from this place. Some of those lessons concern the understanding provided of the way the battle was conducted. Failure to resituate the Hanoverians in the account, for example, removes the broader context of military history. The one-sided approach provides no clear picture of why British forces were involved elsewhere in Europe at the time of the Jacobite rising (the War of Austrian Succession), or the tactical lessons recently learned from battles such as Dettingen (1743) or Fontenoy (1745) that were carried forward to Culloden. Other lessons concern the misrepresentation of Scotland and the Scottish people. The equation of Highland Scotland with Scotland in general distorts the state of a nascent, modernizing nation in which economic prosperity, generated by the union with England and Wales, had eroded the extent of support for the Stuart cause. Moreover, the understated acknowledgment of the embarrassing fact that many "clansmen" actually fought and died for the Hanoverian side distorts the nature of Scottish, and indeed *English,* identity in the mid-eighteenth century.

However, narratives do change. Post-devolution Scotland has perhaps less reason to tie the lessons of Culloden to a mist-strewn and melancholic Jacobite past. Landscapes of regret are certainly places inscribed in social memory as sites for solemnity and mourning, but they also have the capacity to symbolize pride in achievement and hopes for renewal. Those who map the physical, cultural, political, and moral meaning of Culloden for the tourist have the opportunity to point to alternative narratives, narratives that link the events of the Forty-Five to debate about the contemporary and even future identity of Scotland. The legacy of Culloden, therefore, can embrace a dynamic plurality: one that celebrates as well as mourns, one that looks forward as well as back. It is a plurality that cries out to be expressed.

Notes

We would like to thank Matt Stimpson for his assistance in drawing the maps that accompany this chapter and Brian Brown for his ability to turn slides into JPEGS, a task that transcends our understanding.

1. In passing, it is worth drawing attention to a growing body of scholarship that highlights a kindred, but somewhat different phenomenon to that discussed here, namely, the increasing attraction of tourists to places identified with death and atrocity (Rojek 1993; Seaton 1999b; Tunbridge and Ashworth 1996; Lennon and Foley 1999, 2000).

2. There were also other smaller uprisings in 1698 ("Dundee's Revolt"), 1708 (the "Franco-Jacobite Invasion"), and 1719 (the "Hispano-Scottish Invasion").

3. A note on terminology. The word *Jacobite* comes from the Latin word for James *(Jacobus)*. It had originally been applied to anything pertaining to the reign of James I (James VI of Scotland), but was readily available to apply to the cause of the deposed James II and his son. *Pretender* comes from the French word *prétendant* meaning "claimant" (see Lenman 1995).

4. Estimates vary greatly depending on the source and whether the author is counting only the brief battle itself or adding in the losses from continuing skirmishes in the period immediately after Culloden. Jacobite losses are sometimes placed as high as two thousand and Hanoverian losses are now thought to have been higher.

5. For more information, see Donnachie and Whatley (1992), Kidd (1993), and Finlay (1994).

6. The battle occurred in 480 B.C. Greek historians could find enough merit in a rearguard action by the hopelessly outnumbered Spartan king Leonidas and his three hundred soldiers to allow them something to commemorate. As a result of the Spartans' perceived valor, Thermopylae was one of the first battlefields to see the appearance of commemorative markers, in the shape of memorial columns.

7. A cairn is a traditional Scottish marker built from piled stones.

6. Dialogues of Difference

Contested Mappings of Tourism and Environmental Protection in Butte, Montana

Mary Curran

> resistance does not just act on topographies imposed through the spatial technologies of domination, it moves across them under the noses of the enemy, seeking to create new meanings out of imposed meanings to re-work and divert space to other ends. (Pile 1997: 16)

In this chapter, I explore the ways in which Butte, Montana, has been constructed through tourism and environmental discourses, both of which marginalize the voices of the city's working class. To ground this exploration of Butte's contested identity politics I examine two maps of Butte. The first is a tourism map produced by the Butte-Silver Bow County Chamber of Commerce; the second, a map of mining-related contamination in Butte produced by Butte-Silver Bow Planning Department for the federal Environmental Protection Agency (EPA). In the context of the first map, the Butte Chamber of Commerce is working to reproduce a historical image of a locale constructed by a diligent, hardworking, and colorful group of miners and their families by valorizing them and their contributions to building Butte's industrial landscape. This image is complicit with the operations of local capital that, as we will see, is uninterested in the struggles of Butte's workers. The Superfund map of the EPA, on the other hand, is intended to represent Butte as a site of environmental degradation. The EPA, however, has no interest in or intention of exploring the role of individual workers or capital in the production of the polluted landscape of Butte. The scientific discourse that constructs Butte as a contaminated site in the EPA map, like the tourism map, does not challenge the processes that produced this landscape in the first place.

Even a superficial reading of these maps demonstrates that they have a common base of experience: Butte's mining past takes center stage in both representations. I want to argue, however, that these maps tell us even more about the complex social and spatial relations that work to erase the everyday struggles of the people who produced Butte's current (and past) landscape. Put quite simply, I want to create a dialogue between the maps to uncover the power relations that produced these representational regimes. By dialogue, I mean to consider how these maps "fit into one another, interpenetrate one another, support one another, reinforce one another, auto-engender and engender one another" (Wittig 1988: 431). The dialogue is valuable because each map is attempting to fix Butte within a narrowly defined representational regime (Hall 1997). Moreover, the dialogue exposes the intertextual linkages that constitute each map not simply as a piece of paper but as a broader space that includes not just the map but its margins and the social context in which the map is produced and interpreted (Del Casino and Hanna 2000).

It is not enough, however, to deconstruct the historical narratives that inform these maps. Instead, the intention of this chapter is to destabilize the maps' representational regimes by indicating how these texts try to subvert "the multiplicity and possibility of alternative voices" (Massey 1999: 281) in Butte. Reading the maps against each other, we begin to disentangle the complex webs of social and spatial relations that have produced these images for popular consumption. And yet, that is not enough, for the voices of Butte's working class are themselves still marginalized by such a reading. To address this lacuna, I turn to the voices of Butte's citizens and their stories about Butte as a place.[1] The dialogue becomes further complicated because I am not simply looking at mapped representations. I am, instead, creating dialogue between the maps and the people whose lives those maps claim to represent. The interviews allow investigation of the ways in which residents have interpreted the politics that created both maps. Working with local people's representations of place, it is possible to locate residents' "buried, subjugated knowledges" (Foucault 1980a: 83) and demonstrate how both maps operate as a form of "bourgeois colonization" (Philo and Kearns 1993: 28). This is not an assertion that there is an "authentic" Butte possessed by a particular class; it is a search for a more inclusive account than that afforded by both maps. In sum, I am interested in investigating how the power relations that produced both maps erase the past and present struggles of Butte's citizenry to create a livable city.

To accomplish my goals, it is necessary to step back and examine what each map is trying to say, while at the same time analyzing the maps for what they are also trying to hide. To do this, I augment my critical interrogation of both maps with the narratives of Butte's working class. This constitutes the first level of a dialogic analysis of each map's representational regime. But, as I have noted, this is not enough, because if we keep the maps separate we fail to fully understand the degree to which they are mutually constitutive (i.e., they both try to produce Butte and its citizens in ways that are complicit with hegemonic readings of local—and global—social and spatial relations). Thus, there is a need to extend this dialogic approach to examine the intertextual relationships between these maps. Such an analysis, I argue, exposes the power relations that both maps deploy in their productions of Butte's mining landscapes. I begin my analysis with the tourism map.

The Tourism Map

The tourism map (Figure 6.1) was produced by the Butte Chamber of Commerce and is available at the Butte Visitor Center in two forms—as an 8½ by 14-inch sheet that also features black-and-white photographs and as part of a forty-eight-page *Visitors' Guide*. Both maps are printed in black ink on white paper. The tourism map asserts the primacy of Butte's mining identity through the mine head frame in the upper right-hand corner and the inclusion of street names—Quartz, Mercury, Platinum—that signal the resources that brought miners to Butte. Little text appears on the map, other than a list of tourist sites and the names of the streets on or near which the sites are located. Streets without sites deemed attractive to tourists are not printed on the map, which was produced with funds raised from a hotel tax.

Although the map naturalizes mining, it does not prepare a newcomer for Butte's landscape. Hundred-foot-high metal head frames strewn across Butte Hill pierce the thin mountain air. The mining landscape—a conglomeration of vast excavated areas, towering piles of debris, up-

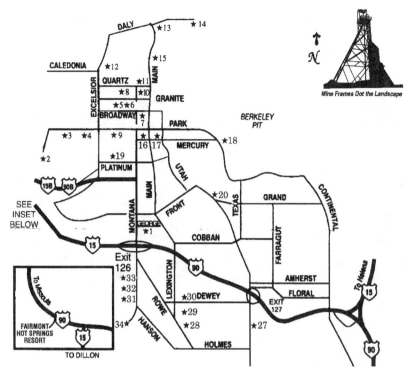

Figure 6.1. Chamber of Commerce tourism map, Butte, Montana. Reproduced with permission from Butte–Silver Bow Chamber of Commerce.

rooted boulders, and barren earth—is startling. Turquoise banners proudly proclaim the historic uptown district that clings to the steep incline of Butte Hill. They flutter from streetlights that illuminate rows of rundown brick and stone buildings that evoke a gritty urbanity that belies Butte's location in a state known for "rural" settlements scattered across vast open spaces (Figure 6.2).[2] Vacant lots interspersed with eclectic architecture recall a punch-drunk prizefighter's rebellious gap-toothed grin.

Other newcomers, who arrived while mining was ongoing, said they were also stunned by the physical landscape. Butte-Silver Bow Historical Preservation Officer Mark Reavis (1995) said his first response was to ask himself, "What the hell happened here? The stunted junipers, the environment, the dryness." Another nonnative (Waring 1995) described Butte's landscape as a factory:

Figure 6.2. Photograph showing effects of mining. Photograph by author.

> One night someone took me to see them working on the Berkeley
> Pit. . . . There was always noise—in the day it was background, at night
> it seemed much louder. It came to me that Butte was really an outdoor
> factory. You can go from one machine to another, but there's no roof.
> All the debris is scattered everywhere. We were living in an outdoor
> factory—slag heaps, discarded machinery, minidumps. It was never
> picked up at that time.

Because mining operations were scattered throughout the town, there
never was a clear boundary between work and other community activities; the city itself was a mining operation and other activities were
secondary.

To some residents, however, this city amid mine waste is beautiful.
For example, while delivering a lecture at the University of Montana in
1995, former state representative Fritz Daily said:

> I'm from Butte. I love Butte. I don't know a better place to live . . . I
> don't think the [Berkeley] Pit's ugly. When I look at mine dumps and
> mine waste, I don't think it's ugly. But when I drive through Kellogg,
> Idaho [another mining town], I think it's ugly.

During my interviews, I noted that people who grew up in Butte described the place as a social network and, more often than not, located that network within mining activities. Only those who had lived away from Butte for some time or had come to Butte from somewhere else mentioned the physical landscape.

Similarly, with the exception of the Berkeley Pit, which I will discuss later, the tourism map does not dwell on the physical landscape. Instead, it directs tourists to colorful mining locales that will fulfill their preconceptions (Urry 1990). For example, the number 1 on the map locates the beginning of tours on the Old No. 1 trolley tours and then directs people to the World Museum of Mining Orphan Girl Express Railroad (number 2 on Figure 6.1), the Mineral Museum (4), and the Anselmo Mine Yard (12). The city streets that the trolley traverses and the map's references to Helena, Billings, and Missoula, other major cities in Montana, constructs an urban/rural binary that reinscribes a history in which, although Montana is commonly represented as a rural state, rural areas have been considered primarily as background to activities in the few urban areas (Toole 1959, 1972). The map's valorization of urbanity also evokes past residents' celebration of their differences from the rest of the state, which was expressed in their descriptions of their home as "Butte, America" (Emmons 1990), removing Butte from the rest of the state.

The map's reference to Helena, the state capital, recalls the Anaconda Copper Mining Company, which, from its base in Butte, dominated the state's economic, representational, and political systems. By 1900, Anaconda, known simply as "the Company" to Montanans (Toole 1972), employed 75 percent of the state's wage earners (Malone, Roeder, and Lang 1993; Toole 1972) and owned all but one of the state's daily newspapers and many of the weeklies (Toole 1972). The company used its employer status and newspaper ownership to manipulate the state legislature to win tax laws favorable to mining (Malone, Roeder, and Lang, 1993) and to garner sufficient political clout to call out state and federal troops to occupy Butte against striking miners seven times between September 1914 and April 1920 (ibid.; Toole 1972). Montanans expressed their suspicion of Anaconda's dominance by referring to Butte as "the black heart of Montana" (Emmons 1990).

Mining itself was also suspect to some. One of the characters created by Montana writer Ivan Doig says:

It may have been that parts of Montana like ours were apprehensive, actually a little scared of Butte. There seemed to be something spooky about a place that lived by eating its own guts. (Quoted in ibid., 62)

Butte's identity as rural Montana's "other" has had long-lasting impacts. Mark Reavis (1995) said that people in Washington State, where he grew up, advised him against moving to Butte to take his current position. Sara Weinstock (1995), the EPA's project director, a Butte native who had lived in Helena, Montana, for ten years with her son before returning to Butte, said that her son's friends in his Helena school "told him he'd be beat up" when he moved to Butte. Because Anaconda controlled so many newspapers throughout Montana, most people outside of Butte's borders were not aware of the dangerous and hostile environment (in terms of both the physical environment and relations with Anaconda) that necessitated the performances of toughness that were often seen as threatening by outsiders.

The dangers of hard-rock mining are manifest in the map's reference to the Granite Mountain Mine Memorial (14), which is dedicated to the 165 miners (Emmons 1990) who died in what has been represented as the worst hard-rock mining disaster in the United States.[3] Their deaths can be directly related to Anaconda's ability to exert influence at the state level. Although Montana law mandated metal bulkheads that could be opened between mine shafts, because state officials did not enforce the law, mining companies continued to use concrete bulkheads that could not be opened. The trapped miners died because they were unable to open a concrete bulkhead.

Butte miners were uncomfortably aware that each year underground increased the possibility of developing a fatal respiratory illness— silicosis—which resulted from exposure to silicate particles in poorly or nonventilated mine tunnels. Caught, quite literally, between a rock and a hard place, in their quest for economic security, miners routinely accepted the risks of their occupation. Finn (1998) recounts an incident when the head of the Butte Miners' Union successfully challenged Anaconda's decision to X-ray the lungs of senior miners. Because a report had indicated that older workers would likely fail the exam, the union boycotted the X rays to assure that miners whose lungs showed black spots would not be fired. "The union won the right for men to risk their lives in unsafe conditions so that they might get a full pension should they live long enough to retire" (Finn 1998: 182). Given that miners who reached the age of forty were considered old and that they had on average a fifteen-year working life in the mines (Emmons 1900), few miners likely collected pensions. Health dangers extended aboveground, threatening the health of the women who washed miners' clothes and children who, despite warnings, played on abandoned mine shafts (Finn 1998).

Other health dangers resulted from resistance to Anaconda. The *Visitors' Guide* refers to the 1917 lynching of Frank Little, an organizer for the Industrial Workers of the World (IWW) and notes that Dashiel Hammett fictionalized the event in his novel *Red Harvest*. The *Guide* does not mention that Hammett, who had worked for Anaconda as a Pinkerton agent (known in Butte as "Company goons"), called his fictionalized Butte Poisonville. Nor does it direct tourists to Little's gravestone, purchased by Butte residents, which states in chiseled letters that Little was "Slain by capitalistic interests for organizing and inspiring his fellow men." The Anaconda Road, where striking miners were shot down by Anaconda's guards (Ross 1995), is also not included in the *Visitors' Guide*.

Because the risk of illness and/or death was a constant, residents adapted by valorizing their abilities to survive Butte's dangerous environment, in some ways performing the identities the tourism map is based on (Butler 1988; Del Casino and Hanna 2000). For many residents, the risk made life in Butte more exciting than life outside of the town limits and Butte residents tougher than outsiders. The combination of "fear and bravado" created a climate of "danger and defiance" (Finn 1998: 185). It is not a coincidence that Evel Knievel, America's celebrated risk taker, grew up in Butte.

The terror experienced in people's relations with Anaconda permeates stories of Butte. In 1947, writer John Gunther reported residents' panicky attempts to monitor Anaconda's actions:

> Anaconda has a number of large black automobiles, with low-numbered license plates; bystanders say "The Company's out!" much as they might say "The elephants are loose!" when these leave the Hennessey Building [the home of Anaconda's operations] for unknown destinations. (Gunther 1947: 169)

The effects of that panic were long-lived. At a 1996 conference on Women, Labor, and Community at the University of Montana, Butte resident and AFL-CIO employee Marilyn Maney told the story of a woman in Butte whose picture was taken when, as a child, she marched in Frank Little's funeral cortege. Until the day the woman died at the age of eighty-two, Maney said, the woman lived in fear that Anaconda would discover that she was the little girl in the photo and exact retribution on "her, her family, and her union."

The tourism map directs visitors to a safer and more comfortable Butte than that experienced by a large number of residents. Tourists are directed up the Park Street hill where they pass the Mother Lode Theater (9), the Mineral Museum (4), and end up at the World Museum of Mining (2). Along the way, tourists pass the gracious homes of former mine owners and managers (Figure 6.3).

The map's references to the Arts Chateau (5) and the Copper King Mansion (8) represent Butte's mining past through tropes of wealth and comfort, which signal the working-class neighborhoods to which tourists are not directed. The contrast between the large homes on the west side of Butte and the tiny miners' homes on the east side illustrates dramatically how space was deployed to maintain and naturalize class relations (Figure 6.4).

It is significant that the tourism map assigns only two spaces to women—Our Lady of the Rockies (27) and the Dumas Brothel Museum (17). These spaces both reinscribe the binary of women as saints or sinners that was stressed in Butte's Christian churches (Finn 1998) and naturalize heterosexuality. Our Lady of the Rockies also evokes the dark time when the Atlantic Richfield Corporation (ARCO), which had purchased Anaconda's Butte properties in 1977, closed the mines in 1982. As the town struggled with the loss of its economic base, mining identity, and population as workers left in search of jobs, laid-off male workers began to construct the ninety-foot white-painted steel statue that now hovers over Butte from her Rocky Mountains site.[4] Reavis (1995), who was a newcomer when Our Lady was constructed, said the project reinvigorated the town.

> The town had a real problem in 1982. It had to make a decision whether to live or die. There was a certain community acknowledgment that we had to build something new. . . . The statue was a sign that we were still here despite all these community controversies. I saw a real change. The town stopped and took a look at themselves.

Figure 6.3. Home of an Anaconda company manager. Photograph by author.

Figure 6.4. Working-class neighborhood in Butte, Montana. Photograph by author.

The reference to women also recalls the women's union activities that do not appear in the male-produced histories of Butte (Emmons 1990; Malone 1995; Malone, Roeder, and Lang 1993; Toole 1959, 1972). In 1890, women formed the Women's Protective Union (WPU), organizing as a class of workers rather than by craft (Maney 1996). While the men's union focused almost solely on wages, worker safety, and job security, the WPU established a library, assisted members with housing, child care, medical and legal services, and gave classes on such topics as job-skill training, economics and politics, personal hygiene, and the care of sick children. It also campaigned for equal civil and political rights for men and women, national health, unemployment insurance, and a retirement plan for all workers.

The map's reference to the Mai Wah (16), located in the heart of the former Chinatown, points to a social history punctuated by moments of racial and ethnic tension as successive waves of immigrant groups followed the Irish and Welsh and settled into ethnic enclaves in Butte (Emmons 1990). Although, in statements to the press, Anaconda always represented Butte as exceptional and miners as a homogeneous group (Finn 1998), union members often split along ethnic lines. This was the case in the conflict between the more conservative Irish-dominated

Butte Miners' Union and the more radical Finns at the turn of the last century (Emmons 1990).

Like Anaconda, the tourism map represents Butte as exceptional. The map also asserts a vibrant, colorful, prosperous, homogeneous, and male place. The constitutive others—the social histories of struggle about class, gender, and ethnicity—can only be found in the broader map space (Del Casino and Hanna 2000): the intertextual space that makes present other (often oppositional) representational practices on which the map relies to sustain its meaning.

The EPA Map

The map of contaminants (Figure 6.5) is printed by the Butte-Silver Bow County Planning department and is available through the EPA, which began to investigate environmental conditions in Butte as ARCO was shutting down mining operations. The results of the investigation, which was conducted by an influx of primarily middle-class professionals, indicated that Butte's soil was laced with three million cubic yards of old mine tailings, arsenic, lead, cadmium, and mercury. Silver Bow Creek, which had been contaminated by runoff from Butte's soils, carried the pollutants from Butte into the Clark Fork River, where arsenic-laced soil is piled up at a dam in Missoula, some 120 miles west of Butte. The entire Superfund site includes twenty square miles of tailings ponds, 175 square miles of soil and plants contaminated by smelting operations, thirty square miles of unusable agricultural land, and 150 miles of contaminated riverbed along Silver Bow Creek and the Clark Fork River.[5] Because the area of contamination was so vast, the EPA divided it into "operable units," based on geography and type of contamination (USEPA 1991).

The EPA's map represents uptown Butte and much of the area in the southern part of town as contaminated. Although this map is oriented to soil contamination, it indicates other operable units—Lower Area One, Colorado Tailings, Montana Pole, Clark Tailings, and the Berkeley Pit. The labeling of the Anselmo Mine Yard, tailings sites, and mine pits signals the mining operations that produced the contamination. The mining operations in turn reference Anaconda and the social inequalities that shaped identities in Butte.

The map's shading, which delineates reclaimed and unreclaimed areas, illustrates the relationship between space and class in Butte. The lighter area along Park Street, where mine owners and executives lived, had less

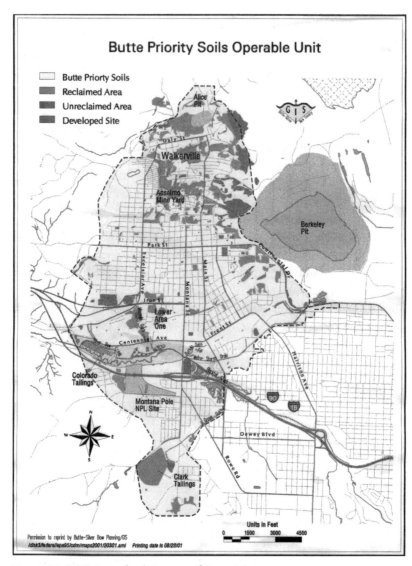

Figure 6.5. EPA's Superfund site map of Butte, Montana.

dangerous levels of contaminants than Walkerville, the Anselmo Mine Yard, and the miners' neighborhoods on the west side. One resident (Ray 1995) said he was not unduly concerned about exposures to contaminants because his "house was built by the Anaconda Company. There's no lead, no arsenic. They knew where to build for their executives."

The pervasiveness of contamination indicated by the map references provisions in federal mining law that give mining companies rights to land beneath the surface; property owners hold title to surface rights only. Following underground veins of ore, mining companies regularly relocated people. This property relationship has had a profound and long-lived effect, one resident explained:

> There's a psychological factor. The Company owns the whole town. It really is a factory. You can live here in your little house but can be kicked out at any time. You're living on borrowed time. My property's defined as part of the Old Plymouth Lode. It's described in mining terms.
>
> There's no idea of res publica. Everything is private property owned by an absentee landlord. Not only isn't this your property; it's the enemy's property. (Waring 1995)

The map also implies the federal law that grants the EPA the authority to enter a locality, investigate, define a problem, and craft a solution. Under the agency's public participation procedures, it held public hearings to elicit comments on proposed cleanup plans. Although ARCO, which, as owner of the site, had been cited by the EPA as the potentially responsible party that would be held liable for cleanup costs, and environmentalists from across the state participated in the hearings, few Butte residents became involved. Weinstock (1995) attributed residents' failure to participate in the hearings as a lack of concern about the contamination, resulting from their familiarity with the mining landscape and their discomfort that they had unwittingly exposed their children to pollution:

> our first meeting was in Walkerville. We were closing Alice Baseball Field. People in their eighties said they played on that field—and so did I. I think it's the grieving cycle—denial.

Weinstock said the denial surfaced when, "for the majority, even with lead, there was denial with the children's health. But if you got a new fence, okay." The EPA's engineering orientation creates problems in situations like Butte's, she said:

> You can't send in male engineers to deal with an emotional issue. The engineers say, "I'm not a psychologist." That's where we make our mistake. I've been at several conferences pushing the EPA on this. Explain

to them [the people of Butte] that it's not their fault that their kid was put in this situation and then they can go on.

Although the EPA was puzzled about the lack of participation, it did not conduct a health study despite a published investigation of federal statistics (Moore and Luoma 1990) that indicated that, relative to the 480 largest U.S. cities, Butte's men and women suffered from an unusual and statistically significant prevalence of heart and kidney disease and cancers (especially of the pancreas, Hodgkin's disease, and trachea, bronchus, and lung). Weinstock (1995) explained that the agency determined that it would be more effective to spend limited funds cleaning up the contaminants to reduce exposures than to study their effects.[6]

Although familiarity and discomfort are plausible explanations for lack of participation, neither considers the working-class subject position formed during the near century of Anaconda's domination. Some residents' awareness of continued power imbalances (Maney 1995; Reavis 1995; Waring 1995) may have led to individual decisions to boycott the process. When discussing the difficulties of dealing with the EPA, Reavis (1995) said that although the local government had some influence, there was "nothing in the track record that would show that any public participation would have changed the course." Waring (1995) argued that Anaconda's dominance over the state's political system did not inculcate a sense of participatory democracy or a desire on the part of citizens to cooperate with government. Government, he said, "was seen as belonging to 'the Company' and the laws were a foreign language of those occupying Butte."

Some residents' economic concerns overrode health worries. When asked about illness, Maney (1995) replied, "I tend to worry more about what happens if I lose this job and I don't have health insurance." Similarly, a member of ARCO's retirees' club (Shea 1995) said that he and other retirees feared that ARCO's assessed liability might result in a corporate decision to reduce or eliminate their pensions.

The EPA's map also evokes the influx of both environmental professionals who provided the data on which the map is based and the environmentalists who have been embroiled in the cleanup process. Some see their presence as an intrusion. This resentment is often expressed along the axis of class. Reavis (1995) referred to environmentalists as "trustfarians," indicating that they had never had to pay the price for

their beliefs. In response to a question about the effect of the contaminants on the quality of life in Butte, Maney (1995) replied, "Whose
quality of life?" There are different kinds of contamination, and some
are more dangerous than others, she argued. The "vitality and quality
of life" in Butte comes from its working-class culture, which she sees as
threatened by the values of middle-class professionals:

> This is a working-class culture that takes care of each other. This is a
> quality of life I don't believe I would have had somewhere else. . . . The
> quality of my life, quite frankly, is much higher than those I know from
> other places—a lot better than the physical.

Not all residents view the newcomers as threatening, however. Chief
Executive Jack Lynch (1995) maintained that Butte has benefited from
their presence:

> they have been a real economic boon. . . . The number of engineering,
> environmental, investigation, and remedial firms currently doing busi-
> ness here, as well as the major expenditures on cleanup, have proved in
> many ways beneficial.

Like the profits from the mines, the economic benefits of cleanup
have also been distributed unevenly. One resident (Shea 1995) noted
wryly, "Superfund's doing some good. It's making millionaires out of
two contractors." Butte's employment and unemployment rates confirm
his assessment. According to the 1990 census, Butte-Silver Bow County
had a higher percentage of managerial and/or professional support per-
sonnel (25.6 and 32.1 percent, respectively) compared to the state's per-
centages of 24.1 and 28.2. The same census showed county unemployment at 9.7 percent, compared to a state rate of 7 percent. The cleanup
created professional job opportunities but did not produce the types of
jobs needed by laid-off miners.

During the planning process, Mary Kay Craig, a Butte native who
had recently returned to Butte after living out of state for years, was
hired by the Clark Fork-Pend Oreille Coalition, comprised of Montana
and Idaho citizens who wanted to organize Butte residents to press for
a more stringent cleanup. Craig, who also became a member of the
Citizens' Technical Education Committee (CTEC), a group funded by
an EPA grant to explain the agency's findings and plans to residents,
worked tirelessly at both positions. Her organizing efforts, however,

were circumscribed by the coalition's campaign that stressed the value of a clean environment for wildlife and plants. The campaign ignored Butte's history and problematic economy, although it is possible that residents' needs for employment, which necessitates attracting industries to Butte, has also militated against residents' involvement in the clean-up. Even if the EPA's or environmentalists' assessment of public health risks is correct, their calculations of exposures and resulting illnesses are probability estimates only, whereas the effects of income loss or reduction are immediate and very concrete.

Given the failure of the coalition's environmental focus, Craig changed tactics and began to connect the contaminants to illnesses in Butte (Moore and Luoma 1990). This tactic also failed, Craig (1995) said:

> People told me if they walked across it [toxic waste] and immediately dropped dead, they'd pay attention. All you can say is cadmium may cause this, lead may cause that, etc.

The history of risk taking may also militate against public expressions of concern about the health effects of exposure. Similarly, the longevity of mining may have naturalized illnesses. One resident (Crain 1995), who studied agency records related to health effects and had her children tested, said Butte should not be compared to nonmining towns:

> I don't know about illnesses in the state. I look at other mining communities, like places in Colorado. We're going to be different than other places in Montana.

This statement simultaneously stresses the exceptionalism of Butte and other mining towns, and naturalizes mining-related health risks.

Environmentalists interpreted residents' failure to join the coalition's campaign and their attachment to their mining past as working-class hostility to environmentalism. Given the well-documented environmental degradation from Butte mines, many environmentalists in the state see mining companies and miners as proponents of pollution. Some social scientists have noted that environmentalists often discount the concerns of working-class people to provide for themselves and their families (Brown 1991; Buttel and Flinn 1978). Even when working-class worries are recognized, they tend to be dismissed as narrow self-interest by those who, because of their education, do not expect to find themselves in the same situation (Buttel and Flinn 1978). This bias against working-class people ignores both the contributions that such working-class communities as Love Canal, New York, and Woburn, Massachusetts, have made to environmental thought (Brown 1991), as well as the potential of workers as a base of support (Buttel and Flinn 1978). In Butte, the environmentalists' representation of miners and mining both reinscribes the historic suspicion of Butte and extends the contaminated label attached to Butte the place to Butte's working-class residents, constructing working-class bodies as sites of contamination.

In contrast to the tourism map produced by the Chamber of Commerce, the EPA map connotes professionalism and expertise. As such, it asserts a "professional" representation of Butte. Equally importantly, the map represents the biophysical world as knowable and controllable and valorizes science as the objective knowledge behind the technologies that allow the EPA to assert control over biophysical processes.[7] Although the Clark Ford-Pend Oreille Coalition has consistently charged that the EPA's cleanup plans are inadequate, it also valorizes science as *the* way of understanding the meaning of the contaminants in Butte. Despite these differences, both maps reinforce, and challenge, each other. It is thus important to unpack the intertextual linkages between these two maps and what that says for how Butte's working class has been portrayed in the historical struggle to produce the modern landscape of this urban place.

Creating Dialogue: Tensions at the Boundaries

Despite the differing representations of Butte's mining past (heroic or polluting) both maps foreground the importance of mining to Butte's identity and both maps' representational regimes rely on similar binary stems (urban/rural, expert/lay, safe/dangerous) to construct and fix their images of Butte. Fixity, however, is not possible because the tensions created by the instability of the binary systems illustrate the intertextual linkages to the maps' hegemonic readings of Butte's working-class history, readings that erase past and present struggles. Those struggles still reverberate within Butte, and Montana, today, as evidenced in the following sections. Past and present came into direct conflict when the EPA's remediation efforts jeopardized Butte's historic landscape. A similar struggle over identity, based in the past or the present, is taking place in both Montana and the American West as a region. The conflicts between expert and lay understandings of the meanings of contamination, tourism and contamination, and class differences are also inscribed in the Berkeley Pit, a site that appears on both maps, but with very different intention and meaning.

History or Remediation

In the mid-1980s, faced with the difficulties of inducing corporations to locate in Butte and produce jobs for laid-off residents, the notion of mining the mining landscape to attract tourists became attractive. As the EPA, ARCO, and environmentalists wrangled about the extent of cleanup, ARCO and Butte-Silver Bow officials began to negotiate for corporate investment in the preservation of Butte's historic sites. The plan to which they agreed, however, entailed preserving many of the areas the EPA and environmentalists deemed dangerously contaminated. Because the National Historic Preservation Act requires federal government agencies to approach any structure older than fifty years as a potential historic resource, the historic preservation plan represented mine dumps and slag heaps as historic resources. The EPA and environmentalists feared that in heavy rainfalls contaminated soils from the mine dumps and slag heaps would be washed down the steep slopes of Butte Hill toward Silver Bow Creek and then travel to the Cark Fork River and into Idaho.

The EPA withdrew its objections when local officials and ARCO developed land-use regulations that they maintained were sufficient to protect residents from the waste that will remain when cleanup activities are completed.[8] Environmentalists charged that ARCO and local officials used preservation to limit ARCO's liability by decreasing the magnitude of the areas to be reclaimed. Some argued that official willingness to accept funds from ARCO for historical preservation was a continuance of a history of seeking scraps from the corporate table:

> The further removed from local government, the better off you are. I've seen the local government here blackmailed. The economy's so vulnerable to blackmail. (Waring 1995)

In this reading, the historical development plan was an ARCO ploy to limit its cleanup liability by offering tourism as an alternative development plan. Similarly, local officials' desire to protect historical resources is merely an attempt to encourage development. I am hesitant, however, to dismiss local attempts to lure corporations to Butte by downplaying the contamination that remains and commodifying the mining landscape as mere "boosterism" (Logan and Molotch 1987) because the EPA has repeatedly assured residents that the cleanup is sufficient to remove any health dangers and, however sanitized, residents prize the mining history embodied in the landscape.

Development plans, however, are contested. Although local officials and residents seeking jobs use similar economically derived discourses that tend to affirm the jobs versus environment binary deployed by ARCO and other polluting corporations (Edelstein 1988), there are important differences related to class. Maney (1995), whose job consisted of retraining miners for alternative employment, said she would welcome more mining in Butte, not because of a commitment to mining per se but to allow those who left Butte in search of employment to return and because mining salaries are traditionally higher than those offered by some of the firms that officials were trying to induce into moving to Butte:

> we're [labor organizations] involved in the creation of a family wage, decent jobs—not six-dollars-an-hour crap. We're certainly concerned with the political climate, the whole economic war on the working class, and reclaiming our heritage and our right to speak for ourselves. . . . We're concerned not only about family wage, but the kind of job that males in our class can work and regain their sense of dignity, their sense of having worth.

Others (Dennehey 1995; Lynch 1995) do not preclude future mining but foresee a more diversified economic base. Public health director Dan Dennehey (1995) said that although Butte is likely mined as much as it can be, technological advances may ensure that mining continues to have a place in the state's economy:

> I think we can manage it environmentally but I don't think we can afford any more fiascos like Anaconda. . . . It's a huge state. There's room for more mining. Crown Butte [a proposed mine that environmentalists charge could damage Yellowstone National Park] is problematic, it could damage "The Last Best Place." In an area where there's low environmental impacts to the community and landscape, I think it's a possibility. If technology can make strip mines look better, it should be done. It's a siting issue. I don't want to see wilderness areas succumb to

mining. I don't want tailings where I hunt or fish. I think there's a happy medium between tourism and mining, concerning money and environmental impacts.

Dennehey brings together the tourism and EPA maps in an account that asserts the ability of technology to control biophysical processes. Although he implicitly posits a nature (wilderness)/culture (human activities) binary, he suggests that it can be mediated through the care in the siting of mines. His concerns are articulated at the state level through a debate about Montana's identity.

"The Treasure State" or "The Last Best Place"

Like Butte, both Montana and the American West are experiencing identity crises based in struggles over past and present. The "happy medium" that Dennehey seeks will be difficult to locate in Montana, which has not yet decided if it is, as its motto asserts, "The Treasure State," or "The Last Best Place." In the 1990s, in efforts to attract tourists, the state began to describe itself as "The Last Best Place," the title of an anthology of literature from and about Montana. At the same time, the state took actions to facilitate new mining operations. In 1995, the governor signed two bills that allowed more pollutants in Montana's water. The new standards increased the previous standard for each of the more than a hundred carcinogens, except arsenic, from a one-in-a-million statistical probability that people who drank the water over a lifetime would incur cancer to a probability of one in one hundred thousand. Significantly, the changes also limited appeals to the issuance of water permits. Prior to the change, anyone who submitted an official comment during a discharge permit hearing had standing to appeal a decision; the change stipulated that only someone with a property interest, water right, or direct economic interest in the permit had standing.[9] Because the changes will make it easier for mining companies to obtain discharge permits and constrain opposition, they reinscribe "The Treasure State" identity.

Although the tourism map only references other cities, the *Visitors' Guide* locates Butte in relationship to other mining towns and indicates continued mining potential for silver, sapphire, and phosphate in the nearby Sapphire Mountains. Simultaneously, the *Guide* signals "The Last Best Place" by references to wildlife watching and outdoor recreation.

It does not, however, indicate that the practices of "The Treasure State" might jeopardize "The Last Best Place." For example, the description of fishing in the area does not indicate that, when heavy rains disturb the sediment in Silver Bow Creek and the Clark Fork River, fish, which have a low tolerance for copper, have been killed in large numbers.

In many ways, the tension that exists in Montana around "The Treasure State" and "The Last Best Place" mimics the tensions that have emerged in recent years between the "Old" and the "New" West. The Old West is represented as the site of resource extraction, while the New is often represented as a mecca for recreation-minded tourists. As "The Mining City," environmentalists have mapped Butte onto the discarded Old West; it has not been given a place in the New West. As indicated by Dennehey's (1995) comments, by miners who hunt and fish, and by the *Guide*'s tactic of inserting Butte's mining practices and Superfund status into tourist areas, the boundaries between the "Old" and "New" West and "The Treasure State" and "The Last Best Place" are permeable.

I argue that the "The Treasure State" and the Old West exist as the constitutive outsider within the boundaries of "The Last Best Place" and the New West. The legacy of the Old West survives further in the ways in which Anaconda's domination of Butte and Montana is articulated through the subjectivities of Butte residents and in the centrality of mining as demon in environmentalists' strategies (Cantrill 1996). These binary categories of identity operate to exclude, by relegating to the past those who survived economically by practices that have become associated with "The Treasure State" and the Old West. The future in environmentalists' discourse is in "The Last Best Place" and the New West.

The Berkeley Pit: Ecological Disaster or Tourist Destination?

Past and present dangers are embodied in the Berkeley Pit, which appears on both maps. The meanings of the pit have been hotly disputed. On the tourism map, the pit is a tourist attraction; on the EPA map it is a site of contamination. Daily, the pit—a 1,789-foot-deep tiered crater covering eighty acres—receives roughly five million gallons of toxic groundwater from the 3,500 miles of underground mine tunnels beneath Butte Hill (USEPA 1993). While underground and, later, pit mining was ongoing, deep-level pumps kept groundwater from flooding the tunnels and the pit. In 1983 (ironically, on Earth Day), ARCO corporate spokesmen told Butte-Silver Bow officials that the company had shut off the deep-level pumps the preceding midnight and the pit was flooding with toxic water (Dailey 1995). The elevation at which the contaminated water will merge with groundwater has been a subject of dispute between ARCO, the EPA, and environmentalists, each of whom has advanced a different elevation as the critical interface.

Although many who worked in the mines argued that water in the Berkeley Pit presents a clear and present danger, regardless of elevation (Craig 1995; Daily 1995; Shea 1995), they were unable to convince the EPA to take immediate action to clean the acidic water. In 1995, however, 342 snow geese that had apparently stopped on their southward migration to rest in the waters of the pit were found dead. Although ARCO spokespersons denied that the acidic water caused the birds' deaths, autopsies found that the water was responsible. Despite the EPA's assertions of apathy on the part of Butte's people, residents were horrified by ARCO's denial. In a letter to the *Montana Standard,* one resident (Immonen 1995) wrote:

> My husband used to come home from work in the mines (even when the pumps were still going up on the hill) with his legs full of copper sores. We treated them each night with zinc oxide and wrapped them in plastic in the hopes of keeping them dry through the next shift. It never helped. He worked in water up to and over his ying yang, which is now speckled with arsenic burns.

In February 1996, CTEC and a Missoula-based group, Women's Voices for the Earth, cosponsored a Snow Geese Memorial, which was attended by representatives from statewide environmental groups and a small group of miners, the first time that environmentalists and miners had expressed a common concern. Also, for the first time, statewide environmentalists connected the contamination to public health issues. Despite the public outcry, the EPA has not altered its plans. The agency's concession to residents' fears was to construct "an eerie soundtrack to warn off migrating birds that might otherwise land in its chemical soup" (Goodman 1995).

Visitors to the Berkeley Pit (18 on the tourism map) walk through a long wood tunnel onto a viewing stand that overlooks the pit. When it works properly, tourists can press a button to activate a tape that gives them a physical description of the pit (without reference to the toxins in the water). Tourists can also shop for copper goods and the usual

plethora of tourist items—T-shirts, baseball hats, key chains, and refrig-
erator magnets—proclaiming the "Mining City" in the gift shop at the
Berkeley Pit.

Although the EPA's map can be read as challenging the tourism map's
valorization of Butte's mining identity, the agency's engineering orientation does not preclude future mining. Instead, it stresses the need to
develop technologies to treat mining residues prior to entry into the environment so that mining can continue to be a viable industry. Because
federal law supersedes local law, the EPA map also challenges local au-
tonomy. It is also noteworthy that, beyond the presence of Silver Bow
Creek, which flows westward from Butte, the EPA map isolates Butte
from the rest of Montana, whereas the tourism map indicates Butte in
relation to Billings, Helena, and Missoula.

Dialogues and "Histories"

The addition of Butte residents' voices not only enriches our understanding of both maps individually and together, but also demonstrates
how the meanings of Butte change when the class struggles that are
erased by both maps are inserted into the discussion. Their voices also
defy the valorization of the mining/contamination binary created when
the maps are read against each other. Although many residents prize the
mining history that exists within the waters of the Berkeley Pit, they also
fear its effects. For many residents, Butte's mining history is a trope of
class struggle. The survival skills of Butte's working-class people were
derived within an industrial milieu that produced a very particular
awareness of class, domination, and practices of resistance. A classical
marxist understanding of class as ownership of the means of production,
however, is not sufficient to explain the practices of domination and
resistance in Butte. Rather, I argue that class is relational and articulated
through a cultural milieu in which it is inextricably interwoven with
other subject positions such as ethnicity, gender, race, religion, and
sexuality. Equally important, the awareness of class in Butte developed
within the categories established by Anaconda's discourse in company
announcements and company press.

Because Anaconda traditionally wielded its authority along the axis
of class, some working-class people interviewed (Maney 1995; Shea 1995)
valorize class subjectivities over those of gender, race, and ethnicity. I
argue that many residents' love of local history, which is often articulated

as class struggle—miners against Anaconda management—entails more than a simple recounting of the past or valorization of the "glory days" of mining; it is a form of resistance that contests the discourses of Anaconda and its captive press, the sanitized history of the tourism map, and the EPA's cartography of toxins. The history of Butte that is so interwoven into the present is not an abstraction; it is an emotional reality, a terrain bounded by resistance and loss, a proud inheritance to be claimed by survivors, and a vital constituent of their identities. This history "is the burden of attitudes, mores, prejudices, loves and hatreds rooted in the economic, social, and political milieu which formed over 100 years ago" (Malone 1995: 217). It is produced and reworked daily in the spaces of these maps and in the sociospatial arrangements of the city.

Histories in Butte are very personal matters, to which Reavis's (1995) comments attest:

> I've never seen so many amateur historians in my life. You just ask a question and off they go. People call me and want me to talk about family histories and dates.

Family histories, especially those of long-term residents, are frequently genealogies of mining-related losses. The emotional burden of a family's history of struggle permeates this letter, written by a resident to the *Montana Standard*. The author argued for the preservation of Butte's remaining head frames, which he, like other Butte residents, calls gallows frames:

> Most of them [the miners] died at very young ages, like my dad who went to work in the mines at the age of 16 and died at the age of 40 in the county hospital. . . . These gallows frames are not only a picture of history, but are also memorials. I am positive they are tombstones.
>
> I do believe that to even think of destroying them for a profit is totally sacrilegious. (Bedovenac 1992)

The author highlights both the miners' struggles to stay alive and their frequent death at a young age. His reference to the county hospital signals miners' financial dependence on the county for medical care because company wages for hard, often lethal, work were no guarantee of economic security. In his account, the gallows frames become a trope for grief, transforming the history of mining into personal and, by the pluralization of tombstone, community loss. He opposes the gallows frames to Anaconda's profits and Butte's economic security by implying that no amount of profits or local security was sufficient to justify such losses. His assertion that the removal of the gallows frames for profit would be sacrilegious delineates the ground on which the frames stand as sacred, invoking the Christian practice of declaring the space of martyrs sacrosanct. It is not too much of a stretch to read this text as an assertion that Butte miners were sacrificed for corporate profit.

Implicit in this and other residents' accounts is "an ideological struggle to define the present" that entails "a struggle to define the past" (Scott 1985: 178). Despite their status as the excluded "other" in both maps, the past and present struggles of working-class residents exist in both map spaces. These mappings of identity and locality resonate on both state and regional scales in attempts to fix identities of Montana and the American West. A reading of these map spaces indicates that places—be they localities, states, or regions—exist only as processes, always changing across contexts.

Conclusions

Both maps can be read individually and deconstructed through the words of Butte's people. When those voices are brought to the tourism map, they affirm the mining identity and the naturalized mining landscape asserted by the map, yet they simultaneously challenge its sanitized representation of Company/working-class relations. Thus, their voices implicitly endorse the power relations that created the tourism map and the Chamber's goals of attracting tourists (and industries) to Butte, while contesting a continuance of the types of corporate/worker imbalances that created the landscape that many residents love. On the other hand, residents' experiences and voices challenge the EPA map by pointing to federal/local and expert/lay power imbalances that have resulted in the representation of Butte as contaminated and ignored the social history and economic plight of many residents.

The intertextual reading is strengthened by setting the two maps into a dialogue with each other to locate the tensions that exist within both maps. This dialogue destabilizes the valorization of mining in the tourism map and the contaminated label that denigrates Butte in the EPA map. In addition to exposing and challenging the binary systems that underlay the maps—federal/local, expert/lay, dangerous/safe—it demonstrates their complicity in erasing the class struggles inscribed into the mining landscape. When the dialogue between the maps is then brought into a critical engagement with residents' voices, the complicities and challenges that Butte residents bring to the maps are highlighted. In this way, we can see that each map is not merely the paper it was printed on, but is part of a larger map space (Del Casino and Hanna 2000) that is discursively and materially interrelated with a myriad of other moments and places.

The moment of conflict between history and remediation demonstrates the tension between past and present and tourism and contamination asserted in both maps. When residents' voices are added, we see these tensions embodied in the ways in which residents engage with the maps. Their attachment to local history and local officials' quest for corporations to locate in Butte to supply much-needed jobs exist in an uneasy tension with residents' awareness of local officials' acquiescence to corporate demands in the past that allowed abuses of miners and their families and their fears that these imbalances might continue into the present. We also see their attempts to negotiate these tensions expressed in Dennehey's desire to locate a middle ground between the mining practices implied in "The Treasure State" and the tourism denoted in "The Last Best Place," in the Chamber's location of mining within tourism areas, and in Craig's failed attempt to correlate a history of illnesses with the mining landscape.

The moment of conflict between "The Treasure State" and "The Last Best Place" challenges both the tourism map's and residents' assertions of Butte's uniqueness by placing mining practices within the context of other mining and natural-resource exploitation operations in Montana. It also highlights the ways in which environmentalists who seek "The Last Best Place" have deployed time and space to stigmatize Butte and its residents as embodiments of contaminated practices. In this moment, environmentalists relegate Butte and its people to the past by asserting a different meaning of space that excludes Butte's past and present social and spatial arrangements. This moment also foregrounds the complicity of the state with capital accumulation as expressed in the lowering of arsenic standards and constraint of opposition to the siting of mining operations. When the tension between "The Treasure State"/"Last Best Place" is considered within the moment of engagement between the "Old" and "New West," claims to exceptionalism are further challenged by its location within a larger region. This dialogue also indicates the instability of the binary by showing that just as "The Treasure State" is the constitutive other of "The Last Best Place," so the "New" West has been constructed to exclude the "Old."

The moment of the deaths of the snow geese in the Berkeley Pit brings together all of the complexities of these interrelated tensions. The deaths of the geese highlight the danger implied in the EPA's map and thus challenge the erasure of potential exposures to pollutants in the Chamber's map. The deaths and residents' intimate knowledges of the dangers associated with exposure to the waters of the pit illustrate the limits of the expert/lay boundary by undermining the EPA's self-representation as accurate assessor of risks. The ability of ground and surface water to move beyond the boundaries of the pit (and Butte) destabilizes notions of Butte as spatially separate from Montana and the region. The agency's failure to respond to the environmentalists and Butte residents' concerns about the pit as threat created a moment when environmentalists and miners came together with similar agendas. In this way, the binaries of "The Treasure State"/"Last Best Place" and "Old"/"New" West were undermined as Butte residents' identities as miners and valorization of working-class subjectivities took a back seat to fears about the water and environmentalists' constructions of residents as apathetic were challenged by the miners' presence at the Snow Geese Memorial service.

On a superficial level, the power relations that created both maps (as well as the subjectivities of residents who valorize class over against other subject positions) seem to have placed many Butte residents in the position of picking their poison: protecting their histories and culture while risking uncertain longer-term effects of contaminants that remain after cleanup, or reassessing potential public health problems related to exposure while risking immediate and tangible economic and cultural effects. But a deeper dialogic analysis exposes tensions, modes of resistance, and contingencies that call such a determinist reading into question. The mining landscape will remain but the meanings of the landscape are always subject to change.

Notes

1. Interviews were conducted from 1994 through 1996 during the EPA's planning process, which consists of identifying contaminants, assessing health risks related to exposure, developing remediation plans, and conducting public hearings to elicit responses to remediation plans.

2. I use the term *rural* hesitantly because I do not subscribe to the notion that there is a "rural" that is somehow physically and culturally distinct and separate from an equally unproblematic "urban"; instead, I see the "rural" and the "urban" as mutually constitutive. I follow Montanans in the use of the term. For difficulties associated with the term, see Cloke and Milbourne 1992, Jones 1995, and Murdoch and Pratt 1993.

3. Butte's mines were quite possibly the most dangerous in the world (Emmons 1990). Recent estimates indicate that some 2,200 men died in Butte's mines (Dobbs 1999).

4. From 1980 to 1988, Butte's population fell from 50,500 to 43,200 and unemployment skyrocketed (Malone, Roeder, and Lang 1993). The Our Lady of the Rockies project began with a man's promise to build a statue of the Virgin Mary in his backyard if his wife survived a serious illness. Finn (1998) reports that the idea of a statue was picked up by local businessmen as a way to attract tourists.

5. "Superfund" is a common reference to the federal Comprehensive Environmental Response, Compensation and Liability Act of 1980.

6. If taxpayer dollars were the sole source of funds for cleanup and health testing, the agency's prioritization might be reasonable. The Superfund law, however, mandates that parties who are held responsible for the contamination pay remediation costs.

7. Although it is beyond the scope of this chapter, the assumption that the biophysical world is knowable has been critiqued by a number of academics—for example, Gregory (1979), Haraway (1991), Pickles and Watts (1992), Rose (1993), and Whatmore (1999)—who maintain that because our knowledges are mediated by language, situated and partial, our understandings will always be incomplete and situated.

8. Because the contamination is so pervasive and many buildings in Butte have been constructed on mine tailings, it is not possible to remove all contaminants.

9. In the American West, water is a private property and water rights are sold with land. Luke (1997) provides an overview of environmental discourses.

7. Mapping Identities, Reading Maps

The Politics of Representation in Bangkok's Sex Tourism Industry

Vincent J. Del Casino Jr. and Stephen P. Hanna

In his book *The Power of Maps,* Denis Wood argues that maps, including tourism maps, "work." They work, he claims, by serving particular interests, not just those of their immediate authors, but of broader power alignments within society. They also work by "making present" the past, the future, and places distant from us in space. Finally, they work by "attaching the territory to what comes with it." In other words, maps tie space to characteristics that often define that space in particular contexts.

We argue that tourism maps "work" in other ways as well. Maps do not only serve interests by contributing to the social production of tourism spaces; they work in conjunction with the process of identity construction. Furthermore, maps do not merely make present what is distant in space and time, they are intertextually linked with the spaces, identities, experiences, and other texts of and about tourism that might not be revealed in a cursory reading of a map. As we argue in the Introduction to this volume, maps work because people use them in their experience of places. Tourism maps are not simply objects, but *parts* of the places to which people travel. They are thus inextricably linked to everyday experience. In addition, maps reference, or make present, a host of existing representations of tourism space. Any critical perspective of mapping must therefore investigate the multiple historical and spatial referents that are part and parcel of any tourism map. This compilation of referents comes together and constitutes what we call a map space.

In this chapter, we present an example of how to read the map spaces of tourism in a manner that recognizes a map's complex intertextuality. *Bangkok Stadtplan für Männer Presents the Nightlife,* a 1991 German sex tourism map of Bangkok, "works," in part through its linkages to a long history of producing Thailand as a feminized and sexualized space for Western tourists. Given the complex intertextual linkages between this map and the spaces and identities it represents and reproduces, our reading cannot be a simple investigation of how the social power inscribed on the map during production serves to reproduce existing social norms and values. As Sparke (1995) so eloquently puts it, we do not simply want to demythologize the map; rather, we want to interrogate the multiple and unequally contested meanings that are present within any map space. This demands the recognition that map spaces are much broader than the paper on which they are printed. They include the margins of the map and the various representations that it calls upon in its construction of tourism spaces and identities. It also demands that we recognize that a map space is an open and never completed process. Thus, any reading of a map, just like the map space itself, is always partial and incomplete.

Map Spaces as Texts

Most critical readings of maps, like recent readings of landscapes in cultural geography (Cosgrove 1984; Cosgrove and Daniels 1988; Duncan and Duncan 1988, 1992; Mitchell 1994; Nash 1996), rely on treating maps as social texts. Pickles (1992: 193), for example, argues that maps are textual "in that they have words associated with them, that they employ a system of symbols with their own syntax, that they function as a form of writing . . . , and that they are discursively embedded within broader contexts of social action and power." He employs hermeneutics to unpack the complex relationships between propaganda maps as texts and the "object-worlds" they portray. Harley (1988, 1989, 1990) calls for a deconstruction of maps and relies on Foucault and, to a lesser extent, Derrida to uncover the power relationships behind the map that ensure that it reproduces the sociospatial status quo.

Unfortunately, Harley and others who employ this formulation of deconstruction tend to produce readings that effectively close off a map's meaning. "Truths" about the social space reproduced through the map are revealed once and for all by the deconstructionist. Returning to Derrida (1972, 1988b), however, suggests that Harley's methodology is much more a "historicization and a Foucauldian sensibility toward the power relations underpinning, and expressed in, maps" (Sparke 1995: 4; see also Belyea 1992). Sparke calls this "demythologizing the map" and argues for critical readings that open up rather than reduce the complex interrelationships between map and space.

Critics of deconstruction may argue that such a call invites a total retreat from the political nature of Harley's project. But, as many authors have argued, deconstruction is a political project intended to subvert the foundational nature of Western philosophies. In Sparke's formulation of a critical cartography, elements of Derridean deconstruction are added to demythologization in order both to recognize the hegemonic nature of most maps and to keep open the possibility of other readings. We would argue that one such element is the destabilization of the oppositional binaries that underlie seemingly natural categories (Derrida 1972; Natter and Jones 1997).

This argument is paralleled by developments in identity theory. Over the past two decades challenges to essentialist identity politics in cultural studies, postcolonial and poststructuralist literary theory, and later in geography have posited that identities based on race, gender, sexuality, and/or class are not inherent or natural, but are constructed as categories through hegemonic discourses (Morrison 1992; Jackson and Penrose 1993; Bhabha 1994). In other words, identity categories are themselves representations (Natter and Jones 1997). As can be seen in the constitution of tourism identities, an other—the working nontourist for example—is constructed in opposition to leisured tourists. Because the sites of leisure for the tourist depend directly on the work of nontourists, however, tourism spaces always contain within them both the dominant identity, the tourist, and its submerged other, the tourism worker. Such constructions are articulated through hegemony: the employment of social power to make categories appear to be naturalized and fixed in space (Laclau and Mouffe 1985; Natter and Jones 1997).

The identity categories constructed through these representations are always partial, however. They never capture the complex differences that constitute a particular social actor. This allows, and is caused by, individuals who perform their identity within and beyond these categories (Butler 1988, 1990). In tourism spaces, tourism workers perform as part of the site and thus reproduce the tourism space and their identity as "host" through their actions. As individuals, they are to "become" the site, thus hiding what is, for them, work. At the same time, their performances can expose the partiality of the representational action through, for example, their resistance to the acts themselves. Their ad-libbing rewrites scripts and regulated work norms (Jarlov 1999). Thus, identity categories only imperfectly capture the identities of social actors performing within and beyond these categories, making the relationship between the category and any actor ambiguous and open to contestation.

The resultant tourism map spaces are thus tension-filled because they exist at a set of constructed boundaries between the exotic and the everyday, between resistance and regulation (Shields 1991b). Thus, while the maps and other representations deployed in tourism by entrepreneurs and government officials appear to fix and demarcate the boundaries between such dualisms, their ambiguous relationships to social actors performing their identities in tourism spaces ensure that these representations both legitimate and destabilize identity categories. Destabilizations of apparently authorial representations are thus possible because no one is merely a "tourist" or "tourism worker," but is instead a multiple subject constituted of many discourses and identities. Each actor exists in a variety of social spaces simultaneously—at the "center" of one category designation and at the "margins" of another (Rose 1993).

Reading Identities in Tourism Map Spaces

In the simplest sense, we can examine the tourism map as a product of hegemonic discourses, as Harley does. We can analyze it for the way it incorporates texts, drawings, or photographs to fix the identities of both tourism spaces and social actors in those spaces. These attempts, however, never fully inscribe the map with meaning, because the map is not limited by the boundaries set on it through production. Maps do not just fix meaning at the moment of production, but (re)present the ambiguities and partiality of space and identity categories. Thus, following Sparke, we do not simply demythologize a map. Instead, we examine the complex sets of social relationships that produce and reproduce the map and the space it is a part of as an ambiguous site of identity construction. Reading maps not just for the "exclusions" that Harley sought to expose, but for the intertextuality of the map, tourism space, and the identities of social actors, demonstrates the multiple meanings that are part of any identity category.

Therefore, we read maps not just as texts but as spaces. As such, a map space is not bound by the margins of the paper on which it is printed, but is inscribed with meaning through its intertextual linkages with other texts and spaces. In addition, map spaces are sites through which we can examine the processes of identity construction, and the historically and spatially contingent social relationships that constitute identity categories. To do this, we follow other identity theorists by arguing that all social actors perform within and beyond identity categories. Map spaces, which represent these performed identities, similarly reproduce the traces of the ambiguities that are part of all categorical designations. Hegemonic discourses that seek to fix oppositional markers—leisure and work or the exotic and the everyday, for example—expose the intertextuality of any set of oppositions. Thus, it is important to examine how identities are disciplined within map spaces. At the same time, because traces of the other are always hidden within any category, we must examine how these disciplinary representations expose the presence of exclusions, margins, and other ambiguities. It is our contention that this process is readable in any map space.

This definition of map space presents some methodological challenges. It is not enough to write a history of representing Thailand to provide context or background before claiming that the map, in this case *Bangkok, Stadtplan,* contains the same tropes we identify in the history. A map space does not contain meanings as much as it "makes present" images, memories, spaces, and other representations that readers use to interpret it (Wood 1992). Therefore, we employ a less linear method to trace some of the many intertextual connections through which *Bangkok, Stadtplan* contributes to the reproduction of spaces and identities. Beginning with the symbols or icons that make up the map itself, we identify the oppositional categories that this map attempts to fix by reading through the map to other well-known representations, both past and present, that are structured around the same dualisms. At the same time, we note how the map space—composed of *Bangkok, Stadtplan* and the other texts and spaces it recalls—reproduces the tensions and ambiguities between and within these oppositions. Further, we illustrate how these work to undermine the categories of space and identity that this map space is intended to fix and reproduce.

Ambiguous Identities in Tourism Map Spaces of Thailand

Using the theoretical framework and methods already outlined, we now explore the reproduction of tourism identities and spaces in *Bangkok, Stadtplan für Männer Presents the Nightlife,* a 1991 map produced to guide German sex tourists to and through the thoroughly sexualized city of Bangkok. This map of sex-tourism spaces, identities, and performances is cartoonish, off-color, and potentially offensive, making it a perfect example of the type of map dismissed or ignored by most cartographers and geographers of tourism. We believe, however, that reading this map as an unbounded space offers critical insights into the always partial attempts to fix the spaces and identities of tourism through the employments of oppositional categories. Although this is, of course, only one of many different map spaces constructing Thailand and Bangkok as tourist destinations, we demonstrate how this representation of Bangkok is interconnected with some of these other markers of Thai tourism identities, both past and present. Produced by tourism capital and the Thai government, these images are re-presented on the map, helping to define Bangkok, and to a certain extent all of Thailand, as a tourism space and to identify Thai people as the perfect exotic hosts for Western tourists. We do not claim to capture the totality of Thailand's representational history, however. Instead, we explore some of the common tropes that are deployed throughout the history of writing Thailand as a place and identifying it as a tourism site. These are made explicit by our reading "through" map icons and across the map's boundaries to these other representations. At the same time, we note how this map space fails to fully fix the categories it recalls and reproduces, creating ambiguities and the potential for alternative interpretations, contestations, and other performances of resistance.

The set of images presented in this map is only one piece in a larger series of guidebooks, videos, and maps designed to guide the tourist through the sex-tourism spaces of the Southeast Asian region. The map itself is a white-on-gray road grid overlaid and overwhelmed by a color-coordinated icon system designating the different forms of sexual entertainment (Figure 7.1). The map also has, on the back, a brief introduction to Bangkok, an advertisement for various videos on Southeast Asian sexual entertainment sites, and the names and descriptions of

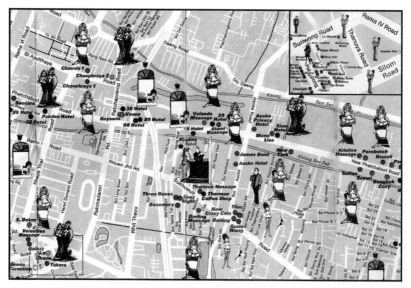

Figure 7.1. Map sections, *Bangkok, Stadtplan für Männer Presents the Nightlife* (Berlin: M. Dulk Verlag, 1991).

various forms of "entertainment." The map's cover is a reproduction of three women wearing tank tops and bikini bottoms working in a go-go bar. In essence this map is supposed to normalize Bangkok's function for exotic sex and demonstrate the safety of the space for the sex tourist. At the same time, the map images *fix* the tourist—normalizing the practices of the tourist as "free from his everyday constraints"—and ease his movement from one form of entertainment to another.

Bangkok, Stadtplan's effectiveness in fixing the everyday/exotic and discipline/freedom oppositions onto Thai spaces and identities is dependent on its explicit and implicit references to other popularly known representations employing these and other dualisms to reproduce Thailand's image for tourists. For example, the guidebook *Nightlife in Thailand* (1988) deploys a common trope of urban areas as spaces of sexual availability. It is intended to highlight what is and what is not "open" for tourists seeking nighttime pleasures. Figure 7.2 reproduces this trope into map form. Just as *Bangkok, Stadtplan* is intended to ease the tourist's movements to and through certain districts in Thailand's capital city, this representation of the guidebook's geography situates for the reader five major urban areas in Thailand where active "nightlife" is available. In addition, both maps normalize these sites as distinct from those found in the everyday lives of tourists. *Nightlife in Thailand* speaks to a wide audience, from those interested in five-star restaurants to go-go bars, all-night discos, and massage parlors, but seeks to make some experiences common to all who travel through Thailand's nightlife sites. For example, the authors of *Nightlife* argue that

> it is the go-go bars that most visitors to the city [Bangkok] really want to see. The name Patpong [a district in the downtown area] has become known the world over, so much so that coming to Bangkok and not seeing Patpong would be like going to Rome and ignoring the Coliseum. (Dingwall, Swabey, and Rice 1988: 24)

Thus, sex tourism has become a "normal" function of the everyday in Bangkok, and in other cities, as both *Bangkok, Stadtplan* and *Nightlife in Thailand* describe in detail. At the same time, the identity of these major urban tourism areas is constructed in opposition to an other, the rural. The rural exists as those spaces "ignored" in the *Nightlife* and *Bangkok, Stadtplan* maps, everything in between these major cities. The maps thus reproduce the tensions of a developing country actively engaged in opening up its urban areas to development, while demonstrating the lack of concern for the rural. It is only in the urban map spaces of nightlife, such as *Bangkok, Stadtplan,* that a tourist can find leisured cosmopolitan comforts in the site of an exotic other.

Bangkok, Stadtplan and other contemporary tourism map spaces of Thailand do not just reference each other. Ultimately, they become intelligible in the presence of a long history of disguising the tensions within the everyday/exotic, rural/urban, and other dualisms by fixing them as oppositions. G. William Skinner notes that as early as the fifteenth century Southeast Asia was constructed as a sexualized space for foreign visitors:

> Both Ma Huen and Fei Hsin [part of Chinese admiral Cheng Ho's mission throughout Southeast Asia during his famous 1405–33 expeditions] were greatly impressed by the independent status of Siamese women, and above all their predilection for Chinese men. According to Fei, "whenever [a Siamese woman] meets a Chinese man, she is greatly pleased with him, and will invariably prepare wine to entertain and show respect to him, merrily singing and keeping him overnight." The

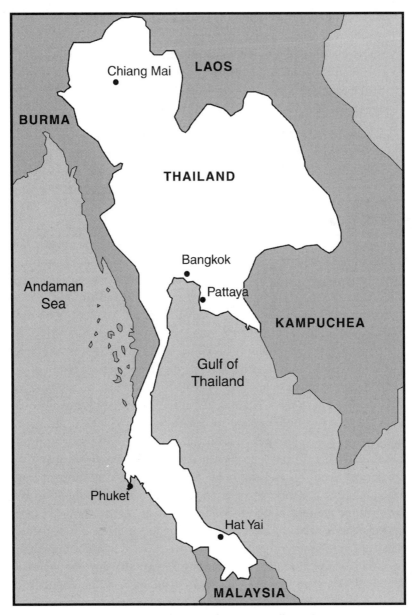

Figure 7.2. Nightlife attractions. Redrawn from Dingwall (1988).

> husband in such a case, according to Ma, is not perturbed but flattered
> that his wife should be beautiful enough to please the Chinese. From
> this idyllic account, it would appear that the Chinese had other reasons
> than trade for resorting to Siam. In any case, the fabulous stories told by
> the expeditionaries after their return to China greatly stimulated trade
> and emigration to Nan-yang [Southeast Asia]. (Skinner 1957: 3)

The sexual availability of Thai women for the Chinese marks this
space as an other within their geographical imagination. It is not just
Thailand, but all of Southeast Asia, that becomes a place that draws
Chinese men to the region for "resorting." One can argue that this same
myth motivates the large number of Chinese Malaysians and Singa-
poreans who today travel to southern Thailand for weekend vacations
in the cocktail bars and cabaret lounges of Hat Yai, the largest urban
center in the southern part of the country (Dingwall, Swabey, and Rice
1988). It is also possible that the early myths of the sexual availability of
Thai woman spread through the trade routes between Europe, Africa,
India, and China and reproduced Thailand's sexualized identity for both
Chinese and non-Chinese men alike.

Thus, it is not surprising that Western representations of the nineteenth and twentieth centuries also rely on and reproduce many of the
same dualisms, as they imagine Thailand as an exotic leisure paradise
and identify Thai people as sensual, beautiful, erotic, and sexually available. J. Antonio's *Guide to Bangkok and Siam* (1904), for example, paints
an image of a land and people sitting at the margins of civilization. He
positions Thailand's unique exotic nature between the modern and the
traditional, the West and the East. "In Siam to-day one sees a country
emerging from the darkness of an ancient barbarism and rapidly assimilating those western methods which alone can assure it a permanent
existence as a political entity" (Antonio 1904: 1). The emergence of
Thailand as a "modern" political entity is tempered by the iconography
of this "barbarous" society. This tension is reproduced in the representations deployed to identify Thailand. As an example, photographs of
Thai costumes highlight the multiple identities and class structure of
urban and rural Thai peoples in Antonio's text. The use of women as
models for these various fashions attaches Thailand to Western notions
of femininity and sexuality. Additionally, the image captions categorize
the styles as "traditional," "modern," and "hill tribe." "Traditional" de-
notes the clothing of the dominant central Thai people, while modern

dress incorporates the European styles worn in Bangkok by wealthy elites, both royal and bourgeois. This latter fashion statement signals that this country, or at least parts of it, is available and "safe" for Western travelers, whereas the traditional garb is a reminder of Siam's exotic nature and the hill tribe "costume" represents its barbaric side (see Del Casino 1996 for a more detailed discussion of nineteenth- and twentieth-century representations of Thailand).

Although tensions between the modern and the traditional are not as overt in *Bangkok, Stadtplan,* some of the map's entertainment icons call upon the East/West dualism directly to assure tourists that they can enjoy Western safety and comfort in the midst of Eastern exoticism. For example, the "nightclub and disco" icon (Figure 7.3) represents for the tourist a

Figure 7.3. Nightclub/disco icon, *Bangkok, Stadtplan für Männer Presents the Nightlife.*

comfortable and safe environment of simple leisured practices, practices that ironically can be had most anywhere. Because this is now in the tourism map space of Bangkok, however, it becomes an exotic, unique space of leisure apparently opposed to the leisure spaces of the West.

The "coffee-shop" icon in *Bangkok, Stadtplan* also reproduces the tensions between East and West, the everyday and the exotic (Figure 7.4). It appears to mimic an idyllic 1950s Western soda shop, and is therefore a "safe" and comfortable space in exotic "Oriental" Bangkok. The two men, both Caucasian, are engaged in conversation, as the third person, a "Thai" woman with Western features and clothing but "almond-shaped eyes," sits on the side staring at the two men. This reactionary moment represents the reason some Western men travel to Thailand: to reassert a position of dominance in a relationship with a women, to have a companion who is "seen and not heard." The map thus contains within it traces of Western feminism that, for the reactionary male tourist identified in this map space, mark Western women as "less available" and thus less exotic. Such traces of an imperfectly excluded other—Western feminism—ensure that this map space contains more than just the leisured activities of a Western masculine fundamentalism.

These icons' negotiations between the exotic and the everyday and East and West "make present" images used in other contemporary promotions of Thailand produced by the tourism industry. As an advertisement for the Siam International Hotel titled "Rudyard Kipling Never Stayed Here" states:

> Mr. Kipling never stayed with us at the Siam International Bangkok, because our hotel hadn't been built in his day. And as far as we know, he didn't venture as far East as Thailand. But if he had, we feel sure he would have had second thoughts about his immortal line: "East is East and West is West and never the twain shall meet."
>
> Because at the Siam International we've combined the best of the East with the best of the West. Our building is of spectacular Thai design. And our service is wholly Thai. So we do everything possible to make you comfortable and we do it all with a smile. Yet we offer you the very best of western comfort, cuisine, and entertainment. When in Bangkok you owe it to yourself to stay at the Siam International.

Thus, it is through the map's icons that the map space of Bangkok is a part of other representations and spaces of Thailand's tourism sites. In

Figure 7.4. Coffee-shop icon, *Bangkok, Stadtplan für Männer Presents the Nightlife.*

effect, these icons represent the disciplining of leisure through its confinement to particular places and specific tourist rituals. The "nightclub and disco" icon, therefore, fixes the identity of the tourist as a "red-nosed drunk," yet passive observer of the performances of particular acts designed to attract his attention (Figure 7.3). He engages in the regulated map spaces of tourism and acts within the bounds of an identity constructed out of its opposition to his "everyday."

The use of the exotic/everyday and East/West dualisms to fix the spaces of tourism in Thailand is practiced not only by Western tour companies and Thai capitalists, but by Thai government agencies and officials as well. At the suggestion of the World Bank, the Thai government embarked on a campaign in the 1960s to actively promote tourism as a form of sustainable development (Thanh-Dam 1990). First through the Tourism Organization of Thailand (TOT) and later through the Tourism Authority of Thailand (TAT), the Thai government produced texts and images that portrayed Thailand as both a site of exotic natural human and physical beauty and of ancient traditions, all of which are safely placed within a modern booming economy, a democratic society, and an anticommunist stronghold (Del Casino 1995). These official representations of Thai spaces and identities for the purpose of tourism lend meaning to *Bangkok, Stadtplan.*

Thailand Illustrated, a magazine that was published by the Department of Public Relations in Thailand beginning in the 1960s and through the 1970s, is an example of official attempts to fix Thailand as a tourism space. An examination of the magazine for the period 1967 to 1974 reveals some interesting representational consistencies and demonstrates that several ideological motivations lay behind the design of the magazine. Using representations of the royal family, archaeological sites, traditional customs, and beauty contest winners, the magazine supports tourism growth and promotes nationalism while demonstrating how these two projects are intertwined. Dignitaries, such as British royalty and California governors, are ushered through the pages of this text and place Thailand at the center of a developing Southeast Asian region. The linkage between tourism and nationalism, developed discursively through representation, is materially produced in government-sanctioned festivals, markets, entertainment districts, and particular cultural practices demonstrating the safe and accessible contexts for tourism travel (see Van Esterick 1994 for a discussion of the Miss World Pageant in Bangkok, which coincided with the massacre of student protesters just miles from the site of the pageant in 1992). Protests and other transgressive practices against the government are hidden by this celebration of nationalism through tourism. *Bangkok, Stadtplan* has similar erasures. Hidden behind the cartoon icons are slums and other establishments not related to the sex-tourism industry, thus promising a hassle-free environment for the tourist.

More obviously connected to the *Bangkok, Stadtplan* map space is *Thailand Illustrated*'s construction of Thailand as site of natural human beauty and sexual availability. Beauty contest winners and other Thai women are represented on 44 percent of the magazine's covers from 1967 to 1974. This is not surprising considering the economic importance of the developing sex-tourism industry at this time (Thanh-Dam 1990) and the role that feminine identities have played in the development of national identities (Katrak 1992; and Parker and Hendrick 1994). In addition, although the government has never officially sanctioned sex tourism, its long-term benign neglect of the industry coupled with its representations of Thailand, especially of Thai women, helps reproduce the country as a unique site for leisure activities and defines it as a space of sexual openness far away from the disciplining mores of Western society. Figures 7.5a and 7.5b ("A farmhouse in the central region of Thailand" and "A northern belle at Mae Klang Waterfalls, Chiang Mai") demonstrate the central role of Thai women in the *Illustrated*'s production of Thailand for tourists. The covers and the advertisements and photographs inside the magazine often depicted women in traditional roles and rural settings, but sacrificed accuracy for beauty by replacing farm attire with the finest sarongs (Figure 7.5a). The romanticized view

a   b

Figure 7.5. (a) A farmhouse in the central region of Thailand (*Thailand Illustrated,* vol. 185, 1971). (b) A northern belle at Mae Klang Waterfalls, Chiang Mai (*Thailand Illustrated,* vol. 163, 1971).

of the land, and of farming in particular, is also transferred directly to the female figure. Figure 7.5b, on the other hand, evacuates any pretense toward setting Thai beauty in a cultural context. Instead, a woman is placed in the physical landscape: tropical beauty and human beauty are fused. Unlike the first image, the women are removed from any form of economic or ritual activity, such as farming, and are juxtaposed with the landscape. Her wrap, a Thai bathing cloth, is as close to nude as one can get in this context: in the village no adult is ever seen without a wrap when bathing.

The tourism-development literature produced by the Thai government thus draws on images of a sexualized past and a set of ephemeral qualities—beauty, serenity, peacefulness, and exoticism—to mark Thailand as an exotic and erotic site. This process of representing Thailand through the image of women can also be noted in an advertisement for Thai International Airlines from 1971, which positions the following text above the smiling face of a young Thai woman:

> What could she learn in Sweden? Every one of Thai International's hostesses is taught the trade in Sweden. That means getting to grips with the technical details involved in serving over 100 people in the confines of today's big jets. It's a complicated business and they go to the best air hostess training centre in the world to learn it. Their side of the business you see is a different matter. *To a Thai girl friendliness, courtesy and willingness-to-please are second nature. It's something they are born to have.* Other airlines talk about girls trained to be friendly and helpful. To our girls any other way of doing things would be unthinkable. (Papineau 1977: back cover; emphasis added)

The Thai flight attendant is trained in the European tradition but embodies a pure Thai sexuality that is exemplified by "friendliness, courtesy and willingness-to-please." It is an attempt to naturalize this identity and fix it for the tourist.

Returning to the "coffee-shop" icon, we can see how *Bangkok, Stadtplan* reproduces this supposed sexual availability of Thai women (Figure 7.4). In Bangkok, the coffee shop is a commonly accepted place to meet freelance commercial sex workers. Thus, the passive woman depicted in this "innocent" scene is not just a 1950s throwback, but is available for sex as well. The almond eyes confirm her Thai identity, further assuring Western male readers that she is friendly, courteous, and willing to please. Nevertheless, women may transform this reactionary moment into a positive net effect for themselves. Playing a "role" for tourists allows them to earn income, for example, from men who may feel that they have "fallen in love." They are therefore not simply victims but agents performing identities (see Walker and Ehrlich 1992 for examples of interviews with and letters to commercial sex workers in Bangkok from their clients after clients have returned home; also Lysa 1998).

In this way, a tension is created within the most fundamental set of oppositional categories in tourism: work and leisure. The coffee shop, an apparently safe and readable leisure space for the tourist, is also a space of work for women, bartenders, and others performing identities. Leisure thus depends on its opposite, work, to sustain its meaning for tourists and nontourists alike. The map space is intended to annihilate work from its image, but the very production of any leisure space is dependent on its other, work, for its identity. The map space, and the material spaces it is tied to, are both leisure and work spaces simultaneously. Thus, attempts to fix the boundaries between the exotic and the everyday, leisure and work, expose the hegemonic discourses that seek to define and maintain these differences and reveal the ambiguous and blurry natures of these mutually constituting identity categories. This is brought forth even more strongly in the icon of the go-go dancer (see Figure 7.1). Her face maintains an obvious grimace. It demonstrates the outward reality of this industry and the difficulty that such a job brings to someone who must sell her body and emotions on a daily basis. Work, monotonous and sometimes depressing, is brought to the fore.

Also recalled in *Bangkok, Stadtplan* are some of its more immediate representational precursors. An informal set of writings that began to popularize the Thai sex-tourism industry in the 1960s highlights further the tensions existing within the dualisms—everyday/exotic and work/leisure—that are produced when these oppositions are employed to fix the identities of Thai tourism. For example, Andrew Harris's (1968) underground classic *Bangkok after Dark* became a fantasy guide for incoming European and North American sex tourists throughout the 1970s and served to reinscribe Thailand as a unique, yet safe, sexualized space. Harris echoes the sentiments of the Thai International advertisement in his opening chapter:

But even while the plane was still in the air, there were indications of
what lay ahead. . . . The two hostesses brought a continual procession
of drinks and food . . . they were coffee-colored creatures with almond-
shaped eyes who moved with a grace I had never seen before. . . . And
the girls were continually smiling—not the usual smiles of airline hostesses, but warm smiles that seemed to transform the cold airplane cabin.
(Harris 1968: 9)

Like the comforts of modern air travel and the "procession of drinks
and food" mixed with the exotic "coffee-colored creatures with almond-
shaped eyes" provided by the Thai flight attendant, the map space examined here exhibits similar tensions and demonstrates the intertextual
linkages between this space and other spaces. The Thai flight attendants
are both the exotic and the everyday. On the map, Thai women are represented with Caucasian-image icons that constitute their bodies as sites
of tension between "Eastern" and "Western" sexuality. The poses, clothes,
and hairstyles assert the comfortable—the safety of the everyday in a
Western context—but the "almond-shaped" eyes identify and maintain
the idea of the exotic. The performance of go-go and the deployment
of Caucasian-image icons demonstrates that these are acts designed to
fit into a particular set of preconceived notions of sexuality. The icons
therefore represent neither authentic nor inauthentic acts, but instead
demonstrate that the practices of social actors are within (and perhaps
beyond) particular category designations. Similar processes of identity
formation occur on the plane and in the map space. The performances
of these social actors also appear to "naturalize" Thai female sexuality as
exotic and other and expose the identification of a space of leisure as a
space of work as well.

Thailand is safe, not only because of the traces of a familiar West,
but also because it is a space outside the everyday routines of tourists.
Thus acts that might be deemed inappropriate are more manifest in this
unique and socially distant place. It is thus not surprising that this map
space, which claims to be distant and exotic, represents multiple ways in
which tourists can engage in activities not consistent with their everyday lives. Further, as a leisure space Thailand is available for a variety
of transgressions from the heterosexualized norms present in everyday
Western—and Thai—society. The image of the "transvestite" (Figure 7.6)
illustrates further how this map space represents the tensions present in

Figure 7.6. Transvestite icon, *Bangkok, Stadtplan für Männer Presents the Nightlife.*

any identity construction. Present in the Bangkok sex-tourism landscape are the possibilities to act outside heterosexualized spaces and within those spaces designed for "third" genders. This icon signals alternatives to heterosexual experiences for the tourist. It is not a Thai man in drag, but a German man, goatee and all, who stands in for the image of the transvestite. At the same time, this emancipatory moment demonstrates that sexuality is not only performed but also regulated through the confinement of particular practices to specific sites in the urban landscape. This moment of emancipation cannot exist outside of its other, regulation. They are mutually constituted.

The collision of the dualisms—exotic/everyday, authentic/inauthentic, emancipation/regulation, gay/straight—within the map spaces of tourism illustrates the mutual constitution of these oppositional pairs. The exotic icons are dependent on everyday images of leisure. This is necessary so that the tourist can read and act within a set of temporarily fixed identity markers. Similarly, the staged acts of the tourism workers highlight the performative nature of identity and demonstrate that these acts are neither authentic nor inauthentic. They are instead the result of the temporary suturing of particular performances to particular identity categories in a map space. Thus the representations that are intended to stand in their place are also constitutive of the temporary and performed identities of both tourists and nontourists in Thailand and represent the ambiguity of these spaces.

The ambiguous identities present in the map space also mean that the map itself is open to multiple interpretations and uses that reference alternative representations of Thailand that have always existed. Despite the power of the Thai government and capitalists (both international and national) to promote Thailand as site of tourism bliss, their images are called upon to attract the outrage of an international audience of activists and scholars as well. Thus, maps such as *Bangkok, Stadtplan* document and open up this space to both local and global criticism and to alternative uses (such as this essay). The map space's production and existence create their own negations and their own opposition. Women's groups speak out against sex tourism and Buddhist monks contest what they see as the growing commodification of Thai society and a loss of moral ethics. For example, the Asia Watch Women's Rights Project (1993) has published a scathing exposé on the trafficking of Burmese women, who are literally sold in Burma to Thai entrepreneurs and corrupt border police who sell these women to brothel owners in the southern and western parts of the country. In addition, groups in Thailand such as EMPOWER and Friends of Women have gained international recognition for their efforts to improve the position of women in Thailand and challenge the power of the sex-tourism industry. These challenges demonstrate that, once produced, any attempt to inscribe the map with meaning will be completely contingent on the reader himself or herself and how he or she chooses to deploy the embedded images.

The international attention garnered through such critical responses to the sexualized and commodified tourism spaces of *Bangkok, Stadtplan* and other representations has helped activists in Thailand continue to combat the uneven relationships between men and women, rich and poor. It, along with internal attention drawn to Thailand's AIDS epidemic, has helped force the Thai government to address commercial sex work and some of the economic inequalities that promote such an industry. The Thai government has reevaluated tourism and diversified its tourism economy, a trend that is evident in the tourism map spaces of Thailand. As an example, the shift in cover representation on Nelles Verlag's *Thailand* map from the image of a woman on the 1994 edition to that of a Buddhist monk on the 1998 edition illustrates how Thailand is being represented less as an exotic, overtly feminine site to one that is more focused on the "traditional" cultural attractions that Buddhist icons represent (Figures 7.7a and 7.7b).

One has to be careful, however, not to read counterhegemonic discussions as wholly "outside" the systems that inform dominant discourses. Through the reliance on models of colonialism, markers of wealth and poverty, and/or biological reductions of sexual difference, such counterhegemonic discourses reinscribe, to a certain extent, the dominant discourses and identity categories that often hide the voices of those peoples that they are hoping to illuminate. Groups, represented as an individual identity designation, such as "Thai female prostitutes," for example, can become the stand-in for a much more complex, dynamic, and individual experience of commercial sex work that varies across space, class, and ethnicity (see Cohen 1982 as an example of this form of reductionism). We can recognize, therefore, the ambiguities that exist in any set of representations and read such representations for both the absences they produce and those notions that are, perhaps, most present.

a   b

Figure 7.7. Thailand Nelles Verlag, from (a) 1994 and (b) 1998.

Further, as representations proliferate and sectors of the global tourism industry fight for a share of the market, these representations and the spaces they claim to represent are reinscribed with new meanings and juxtaposed with new spaces and images in order to maintain themselves as tourist sites. A quick look at Patpong, one of the most famous sex-tourism sites in Thailand and found as an inset on *Bangkok, Stadtplan,* illustrates these changes (Figure 7.1). By the late 1980s, the Thai government began efforts to shift its image as a sexualized space and diversify its tourist economy. Investments throughout the 1980s in beach resorts, eco-tourism, trekking, and shopping districts have altered the arrangement of the industry. Patpong has changed as well, masking its sex-tourism persona behind a government-sanctioned night market. Today, the entire site is covered with this market and serves as one of the major attractions for men, women, and couples in Thailand. As the schematic in Figure 7.8 shows, the once exclusively sex-tourism space of Bangkok is now a tourism shopping mecca, with hundreds of stalls fronting the neon signs of the go-go bars and sex-show shops. Only Thanon Thaniya, an area that sits next to Patpong and is designated euphemistically as "Little Tokyo," escapes this masquerade. Its less visible members clubs, many located on second-floor shops, are not as overt a demonstration of Thailand's sex-tourism history. It may have not been *Bangkok, Stadtplan für Männer Presents the Nightlife* per se that anchored the challenges that led to the covering of this space, but its existence and complex interrelationships to other representations, spaces, and identities made this shift possible.

Conclusion

It is no secret that Thailand depends heavily on tourism and tourism dollars to sustain its economy (Ulack and Del Casino 2000). That dependence has given rise to an enormous representational infrastructure, both within and beyond Thailand, through which some social actors,

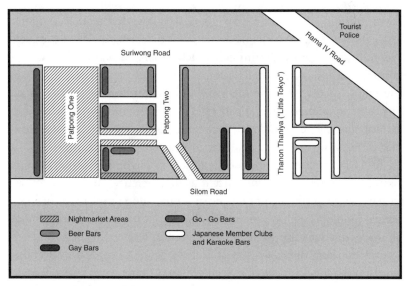

Figure 7.8. Schematic of the Patpong district and its surroundings. Revised from Del Casino (1995).

particularly entrepreneurs and governmental tourism officials, struggle to maintain Thailand's "exotic" appeal. This process of constructing Thailand as a tourism destination, both materially and socially, involves the isolation and deployment of key dualisms: the exotic is positioned against the everyday and leisure is negotiated as an opposite of work, for example. The representational practices of tourism entrepreneurs and government officials are intended to reify and naturalize these dualisms by drawing on a reconstructed history of Thailand's lands and peoples. Exoticism and leisure are thus "transferred" to social actors who are meant to perform a particular set of scripted practices as they work in and through tourism spaces. Through an examination of *Bangkok, Stadtplan* we have explored some of the ways in which such apparently fixed dualisms may be destabilized and (re)presented through a critical cartographic framework. We have "chipped away" at the rigidly constructed and hegemonic representation of Thailand and Thai sexuality as fetishized objects and exposed the ways in which the categories of Thainess, Thai femininity, and Western and Asian masculinity are socially and spatially constructed through representational practices.

In addition, our reading of *Bangkok, Stadtplan* is intended as an illustration of both a theoretical framework for understanding the relationships among maps, spaces, and identities and a methodological approach for examining any tourism map. Thus, we argue that neither a tourism space nor the map that claims to represent that space are final products; rather, both are processes through which social and spatial identities are constructed and contested. The complex intertextual linkages that make the maps, spaces, and the identities of tourism "work" actually make any tourism map an integral part of identity formation and the production of space. The boundaries between maps and spaces are, therefore, erased, resulting in what we call the map spaces of tourism.

Because a tourism map space is always an ongoing process as people simultaneously use and experience it as they practice tourism, it follows that no single reading can ever reveal a final and complete set of intertextual moments within a map space that enable it to work. Furthermore, all map users will approach the map from different directions and will bring with them their own sets of knowledges and experiences. In other words, different people will focus on different map icons and will make different intertextual connections with these symbols. Because of this, we choose not to simply place an entire map in a linear history of the production of tourism spaces and identities through representation. Instead, we employ a nonlinear reading method in which we trace out possible connections between a map icon and the representational field constructing tourism space and identities and then return to the map to trace another set of connections. We do not do this, however, to argue that representational strategies serving dominant interests are any less likely to succeed in reproducing hegemonic categorizations of space and identity. Rather, we argue that the precise ways that both hegemonic and resistant texts are invoked in the map spaces of tourism are always subject to change.

Bibliography

Adams, P., S. D. Hoelscher, and K. Till, eds. 2001. *Textures of Place: Reimagining Humanist Geographies.* Minneapolis: University of Minnesota Press.

Ahmad, I. 1993. Selling black history in Alabama. *American Demographics* (January): 48–49.

Akerman, J. 1993. Blazing a well-worn path: Cartographic commercialism, highway promotion, and automobile tourism in the United States, 1880–1930. *Cartographica* 30(1): 10–20.

Alabama Bureau of Tourism and Travel. 1993. *Alabama's Black Heritage.* 5th ed. Montgomery: Bureau of Tourism and Travel.

———. 1995. *Alabama's Civil Rights Journey.* Montgomery: Bureau of Tourism and Travel.

Alderman, D. 1996. Creating a new geography of memory in the South: (Re)naming of streets in honor of Martin Luther King Jr. *Southeastern Geographer* 36(1): 51–69.

———. 1999. Beyond the gates of Graceland: Memorial entrepreneurs and the scale politics of commemorating the King in Lauderdale Courts. Paper read at Southeastern Division of the Association of American Geographers, at Tampa, Florida.

———. 2000. A street fit for a king: Naming places and commemoration in the American South. *Professional Geographer* 52(4): 672–84.

American Visions. 1993. *Bama Bound: Preserving a Proud Past.*

Anderson, G., and P. Anderson. 1834. *Guide to the Highlands and Islands of Scotland including Orkney and Zetland; Description of Their Scenery,*

Statistics, Antiquities and Natural History: With Numerous Historical Notices.
London: John Murray.

———. 1856. *Handbook to the Inverness and Nairn Railway, and the Scenes Adjoining It, with the Time Tables, List of Fares, and Regulations of the Line.* Inverness: Courier Office.

———. 1865. *Handbook to the Highland Railway System from Perth to Forres, Keith, Inverness and Bonar Bridge.* Edinburgh: John Menzies.

Anderson, P. 1867. *Guide to Culloden Moor and the Story of the Battle, with Description of the Stone Circles and Cairns at Clava.* Edinburgh: John Menzies (1920 reissued edition consulted, published Stirling: Eneas Mackay).

Anonymous. 1890. *Inverness as a Tourist Centre.* Inverness: R. Carruthers and Sons, Courier Office.

———. 1947. *Inverness, Strathpeffer and the North of Scotland.* London: Ward, Lock and Company.

Anonymous (Larry Poag). N.d. (ca. 1990). *Poag's guide for 1880 Bodie.* N.p.: N.p. (in the author's collection or available for purchase at the Bodie Museum).

Antonio, J. 1904. *Guide to Bangkok and Siam.* Bangkok: Siam Observer.

Antze, P., and M. Lambeck, eds. 1996. *Tense Past: Cultural Essays in Trauma and Memory.* London: Routledge.

ARCO. N.d. Environmental Action Plan for the Upper Clark Fork River Basin, section S. Anaconda, Mont.

ARCO/Butte-Silver Bow Planning Department. 1993. Institutional Controls Strategic Framework Document. Butte, Montana. May 4.

Asia Watch Women's Rights Project. 1993. *A Modern Form of Slavery: Trafficking of Burmese Women and Girls into Brothels in Thailand.* New York: Human Rights Watch.

Auchmutey, J. 1997. Tributes to a cause: A roundup of the museums and monuments commemorating the movement that changed the South—and the nation. *Atlanta Journal-Constitution,* August 24, R2.

Azaryahu, M. 1993. From remains and relics: Authentic monuments in the Israeli landscape. *History and Memory* 5: 82–103.

Bassett, C., and C. Wilbert. 1999. Where you want to go today (like it or not): Leisure practices in cyberspace. In *Leisure/Tourism Geographies: Practices and Geographical Knowledge,* edited by D. Crouch, 181–94. London and New York: Routledge.

Bedovenac, N. 1992. Letter to the editor. *Montana Standard,* September 22.

Belyea, B. 1992. Images of power: Derrida, Foucault, Harley. *Cartographica* 29(2): 1–9.

———. 1996. Inland journeys, native maps. *Cartographica* 33(2): 1–16.

Benjamin, W. 1999. *The Arcades Project.* Translated by Howard Eiland and Kevin McLaughlin. Cambridge, Mass.: Belnap Press.

Benn, A. 1996. Black Panther Party organizer to speak in Selma. *Montgomery Advertiser,* June 7, B1.

Bhabha, H. K. 1994. *The Location of Culture*. London and New York: Routledge.

Billeb, E. 1986. *Mining Camp Days*. Las Vegas: Nevada Publications.

Birmingham News. 1992. Behind the scenes. *Birmingham News,* September 15, 7P, 26P.

Black, J. 1997. *Maps and Politics*. Chicago: University of Chicago Press.

Bland, J. 1999. Interview by O. Dwyer with Joanne Bland, Acting Director of the National Voting Rights Museum, June 23.

Bloch, M. 1996. Internal and external memory: Different ways of being in history. In *Tense Past: Cultural Essays in Trauma and Memory,* edited by P. Antze and M. Lambeck, 215–34. New York: Routledge.

Blunt, A., and G. Rose, eds. 1994. *Writing Women and Space: Colonial and Postcolonial Geographies*. New York and London: Guilford Press.

Bodie State Historical Park. 1955. Unit History Files, 1955 to present. Bodie, California.

Bonnett, A. 1996. Landranger 168. Colchester and Blackwater Area 1:50,000. *Transgressions* 2: 132–33.

Bourdieu, P. 1977. *Outline of a Theory of Practice*. Translated by R. Nice. Cambridge: Cambridge University Press.

Brendon, P. 1991. *Thomas Cook: 150 Years of Popular Tourism*. London: Secker and Warburg.

Britton, S. 1991. Tourism, capital, and place: Towards a critical geography of tourism. *Environment and Planning D: Society and Space* 9: 451–78.

Brown, P. 1991. The popular epidemiology approach to toxic waste contamination. In *Communities at Risk: Collective Responses to Technological Hazards,* edited by S. Couch and J. Kroll-Smith, 133–55. New York: Peter Lang.

Bruner, E. 1994. Abraham Lincoln as authentic reproduction: A critique of postmodernism. *American Anthropologist* 96: 397–15.

Burnham, D. 1995. *How the Other Half Lives: A People's Guide to American Historic Sites*. New York: Faber and Faber.

Burns, S., ed. 1997. *Daybreak of Freedom: The Montgomery Bus Boycott*. Chapel Hill: University of North Carolina Press.

Butler, J. 1988. Performative acts and gender constitution: An essay in phenomenology and feminist theory. *Theatre Journal* 40: 519–31.

———. 1990. *Gender Trouble: Feminism and the Subversion of Identity*. New York and London: Routledge.

———. 1993. *Bodies That Matter: On the Discursive Limits of "Sex."* New York and London: Routledge.

Buttel, F., and W. Flinn. 1978. Social class and mass environmental beliefs: A reconsideration. *Environment and Behavior* 10 (September): 3, 433–50.

Cain, E. M. 1956. *The Story of Bodie*. San Francisco: Fearon Publishers.

California Department of Parks and Recreation. 1979. *Bodie State Historic Park. Resource Management Plan, General Development Plan, and Environmental Impact Statement*. Sacramento: California Department of Parks and Recreation.

————. 1988 (revised 2001). *Bodie State Historic Park.* Sacramento: California Department of Parks and Recreation.

California Division of Beaches and Parks. N.d. (ca. 1963). *A Walk in Old Bodie.* Sacramento: Division of Beaches and Parks, Department of Parks and Recreation.

Cantrill, J. G. 1996. Gold, Yellowstone, and the search for a rhetorical identity. In *Green Culture: Environmental Rhetoric in Contemporary America,* edited by C. Herndl and S. Brown, 166–94. Madison: University of Wisconsin Press.

Carson, C. 1986. Civil rights reform and the black freedom struggle. In *The Civil Rights Movement in America,* edited by C. Eagles, 19–32. Jackson: University of Mississippi Press.

Chafe, W. H. 1980. *Civilities and Civil Right: Greensboro, North Carolina and the Black Struggle for Freedom.* Oxford: Oxford University Press.

Chambers, I. 1990. *Border Dialogues: Journeys in Postmodernity.* London: Comedia-Routledge.

Chapman, R. W., ed. 1924. *Johnson's Journey to the Western Island of Scotland and Boswell's Journey of a Tour to the Hebrides with Samuel Johnson, LL.D.* London: Oxford University Press.

Charlesworth, A. 1994. Contesting places of memory: The case of Auschwitz. *Environment and Planning D: Society and Space* 12: 579–93.

Clark, J. 1993. North and south, states accent black history. *Tennesseen,* September 14.

Cloke, P., and P. Milbourne. 1992. Deprivation and lifestyles in rural Wales II: Rurality and the cultural dimension. *Journal of Rural Studies* 8(4): 359–71.

Codrescu, A. 1990. *The Disappearance of the Outside.* New York: Addison-Wesley.

Cohen, E. 1982. Thai girls and farang men: The edge of ambiguity. *Annals of Tourism Research* 9: 403–28.

Cordiner, C. 1780. *Antiquities and Scenery of the North of Scotland in a Series of Letters to Thomas Pennant by the Reverend Chas. Cordiner, Member of St. Andrew's Chapel Banff.* London: N.p.

Cosgrove, D. 1984. *Social Formation and Symbolic Landscape.* London: Croom Helm.

————. 1989. Geography is everywhere: Culture and symbolism in human landscapes. In *Horizons in Human Geography,* edited by D. Gregory and R. Walford, 118–35. Totowa, N.J.: Barnes and Noble.

————. 1999. Introduction: Mapping meaning. In *Mappings,* edited by D. Cosgrove, 1–23. London: Reaktion.

Cosgrove, D., and S. Daniels, eds. 1988. *The Iconography of Landscape: Essays on the Symbolic Representation, Design, and Use of Past Landscapes.* Cambridge: Cambridge University Press.

Couch, S., and J. S. Kroll-Smith, eds. 1991. *Communities at Risk: Collective Responses to Technological Hazards.* New York: Peter Lang.

Cox, T. 1995. Interview with Odessa Woolfolk, president of the Board of Directors, Birmingham Civil Rights Institute. Birmingham, Alabama.

CPR. 1926. *The Ancient City of Quebec: Canadian Pacific Guide.* Montreal: Canadian Pacific Railway Company.

Craig, M. 1995. Interview by M. Curran. Victor, Montana, July 30.

Crain, E. 1995. Interview by M. Curran. Butte, Montana, September 21.

Crang, M. 1996. Envisioning urban histories: Bristol as a palimpset, postcards and snapshots. *Environment and Planning A* 28(3): 429–52.

———. 1999. Knowing, tourism, and practices of vision. In *Leisure/Tourism Geographies: Practices and Geographical Knowledge,* edited by D. Crouch, 238–56. London: Routledge.

Crang, P. 1997. Performing the tourist product. In *Touring Cultures: Transformations of Travel and Theory,* edited by C. Rojek and J. Urry, 137–54. London and New York: Routledge.

Cresswell, T. 1996. *In Place, Out of Place: Geography, Ideology, and Transgression.* Minneapolis: University of Minnesota Press.

Crouch, D. 1999a. Introduction: Encounters in leisure/tourism. In *Leisure/Tourism Geographies: Practices and Geographical Knowledge,* edited by D. Crouch, 1–16. London and New York: Routledge.

———, ed. 1999b. *Leisure/Tourism Geographies: Practices of Geographical Knowledge.* London: Routledge.

Daily, F. 1995. Lecture. Missoula, University of Montana. December 8.

Davis, T. 1998. *Weary Feet, Rested Souls: A Guided History of the Civil Rights Movement.* New York: W. W. Norton.

de Certeau, M. 1984. *The Practice of Everyday Life.* Berkeley: University of California Press.

———. 1985. Practices of space. In *On Signs,* edited by M. Blonsky, 122–45. Baltimore: Johns Hopkins University Press.

Del Casino, V. J., Jr. 1995. Creating "tourism space": The social construction of sex tourism in Thailand. M.S. thesis, Department of Geography, University of Wisconsin-Madison.

———. 1996. Mapping the tourist gaze or creating it: Revivifying notions of other. Paper read at Paper/Scissors/Rock: Interdisciplinary Graduate Student Conference on Nationalism, Empire and Post-Colonialism, at Queen's University, Kingston, Ontario, Canada.

Del Casino, V. J., Jr., and S. P. Hanna. 2000. Representations and identities in tourism map spaces. *Progress in Human Geography* 24(1): 23–46.

DeLyser, D. 1998. Good, by God, we're going to Bodie! Landscape and social memory in a California ghost town. Unpublished Ph.D. dissertation, Department of Geography, Syracuse University.

———. 1999. Authenticity on the ground: Engaging the past in a California ghost town. *Annals of the Association of American Geographers* 89(4): 602–32.

———. Forthcoming. Good, by God, we're going to Bodie! Ghost towns and the American West. In *Western Places, American Myths,* edited by G. Hausladen. Las Vegas: University of Nevada Press.

Dennehey, D. 1995. Interview by M. Curran. Butte, Montana, September 21.

Denzin, N. K. 1994. Postmodernism and Deconstructionism. In *Postmodernism and Social Inquiry,* edited by D. Dickens and A. Fontana, 182–201. New York: Guilford Press.

Derrida, J. 1972. Structure, sign, and play in the discourse of the human sciences. In *The Structuralist Controversy: The Languages of Criticism and the Sciences of Man,* edited by R. Macksey and E. Donato, 247–72. Baltimore: Johns Hopkins University Press.

———. 1988a. *Limited Inc.* Translated by S. Weber. Evanston, Ill.: Northwestern University Press.

———. 1988b. *On Grammatology.* Baltimore: Johns Hopkins University Press.

Diller, E., and R. Scofidio. 1994. Suitcase studies: The production of a national past. In *Back to the Front: Tourisms of War,* edited by E. Diller and R. Scofidio, 32–105. Caen: FRAC Basse-Normandie.

Dingwall, A., H. Swabey, and C. Rice. 1988. *Nightlife in Thailand.* Twickenham: Stepping Out Publications.

Dobbs, E. 1999. Mining the past. *High Country News,* June 11, 31.

Domosh, M. 1998. Those gorgeous incongruities: Polite politics and public space on the streets of nineteenth-century New York City. *Annals of the Association of American Geographers* 88(2): 209–26.

Donnachie, I., and C. Whatley, eds. 1992. *The Manufacture of Scottish History.* Edinburgh: Polygon.

Driver, F. 1995. Visualizing geography: A journey to the heart of the discipline. *Progress in Human Geography* 19(1): 123–34.

Duncan, J. 1990. *The City as Text: The Politics of Landscape Interpretation in the Kandyan Kingdom.* Cambridge: Cambridge University Press.

Duncan, J., and D. Gregory, eds. 1999. *Writes of Passage: Reading Travel Writing.* London and New York: Routledge.

Duncan, J., and N. Duncan. 1988. (Re)reading the landscape. *Environment and Planning D: Society and Space* 6: 117–26.

———. 1992. Ideology and bliss: Roland Barthes and the secret histories of landscape. In *Writing Worlds: Discourse, Text and Metaphor in the Representation of Landscape,* edited by T. Barnes and J. Duncan, 1–37. New York: Routledge.

Duncan, N., ed. 1996. *Bodyspace: Destabilizing Geographies of Gender and Sexuality.* London and New York: Routledge.

Dwyer, O. 2000a. Interpreting the civil rights movement: Place, memory, and conflict. *Professional Geographer* 52(4): 660–71.

————. 2000b. Memorial landscapes dedicated to the civil rights movement. Dissertation, University of Kentucky.

Edelstein, M. 1988. *Contaminated Communities: The Social and Psychological Impacts of Residential Toxic Exposure.* Boulder, Colo.: Westview Press.

Edensor, T. 1998. *Tourists at the Taj: Performance and Meaning at a Symbolic Site.* London and New York: Routledge.

Edney, M. H. 1993. Cartography without 'progress': Reinterpreting the nature and historical development of mapmaking. *Cartographica* 30(1): 54–68.

Emmons, D. 1990. *The Butte Irish: Class and Ethnicity in an American Mining Town, 1875–1925.* Urbana and Chicago: University of Illinois Press.

Eskew, G. 1998. *The Won Cause: Memorializing the Movement through the Birmingham Civil Rights Institute.* Atlanta: Georgia State University.

Fabiansson, N. 2001. The archaeology of the Western Front 1914–1918. http://w1.865.telia.com/~u86517080/BattlefieldArchaeology/ArkeologyENG_3B.html. June 1.

Falk, J. 1995. Factors influencing African-American leisure time utilization of museums. *Journal of Leisure Research* 27(1): 41–60.

Fees, C. 1996. Tourism and the politics of authenticy in a North Cotswald town. In *The Tourism Image: Myths and Myth-Making in Tourism,* edited by T. Selwyn, 121–46. Chichester: John Wiley.

Feifer, M. 1985. *Tourism in History: From Imperial Rome to the Present.* New York: Stein and Day.

Fentress, J., and C. Wickham. 1992. *Social Memory.* Oxford: Blackwell.

Finlay, R. 1994. Controlling the past: Scottish historiography and Scottish identity in the 19th and 20th centuries. *Scottish Affairs* 9: 127–42.

Finn, J. 1998. *Tracing the Veins: Of Copper, Culture, and Community from Butte to Chuquicamata.* Berkeley and Los Angeles: University of California Press.

Fletcher, I. 2000. *Ian Fletcher Battlefield Tours 2000: The Millennium Brochure.* Rochester: Ian Fletcher.

Floyd, M., K. Shinew, F. McGuire, and F. Noe. 1994. Race, class, and leisure activity preferences: Marginality revisited. *Journal of Leisure Research* 26: 158–73.

Foote, K. E. 1997. *Shadowed Ground: America's Landscapes of Violence and Tragedy.* Austin: University of Texas Press.

Foucault, M. 1980a. Two lectures, lecture one: 7 January 1976. In *Power/Knowledge: Selected Interviews and Other Writings, 1972–1977,* edited by C. Gordon, 78–92. New York: Pantheon Books.

————. 1980b. Two lectures, lecture two, 14 January 1976. In *Power/Knowledge: Selected Interviews and Other Writings, 1972–1977,* edited by C. Gordon, 92–108. New York: Pantheon Books.

Fuller, S. 1999. Interview by O. Dwyer of Sarah Fuller, Greater Birmingham Convention and Visitors Bureau. Birmingham, Alabama, June 22.

Gable, E. 1996. Maintaining boundaries, or 'mainstreaming' black history in a white museum. In *Theorizing Museums: Representing Identity and Diversity in a Changing World,* edited by S. Macdonald and G. Fyfe, 177–202. London: Blackwell.

Gable, E., R. Handler, and A. Lawson. 1992. On the uses of relativism: Fact, conjecture, and black and white histories at Colonial Williamsburg. *American Ethnologist* 98: 791–805.

Gallaher, C. 1997. Identity politics and the religious right: Hiding hate in the landscape. *Antipode* 29(3): 256–77.

Gillis, J. 1994. Memory and identity: The history of a relationship. In *Commemorations: The politics of National Identity,* edited by J. Gillis, 3–24. Princeton, N.J.: Princeton University Press.

Glasscock, C. 1937. Goodbye, God: I'm going to Bodie. *Pony Express Courier,* November 1, 6, 10, 14, and December 9, 10.

Glassman, J., S. Prudham, and J. Wainright. 2000. The battles of Seattle: Microgeographies of resistance and the challenge of building alternative futures. *Environment and Planning D: Society and Space* 8(1): 5–13.

Godlewska, A. 1995. Map, text, and image. The mentality of enlightened conquerors: A new look at the *Description de l'Égypte. Transactions of the Institute of British Geographers* 20(1): 5–28.

Goffman, E. 1959. *The Presentation of Self in Everyday Life.* Garden City, N.Y.: Doubleday.

———. 1974. *Framing Analysis.* Cambridge: Harvard University Press.

Gold, J., and M. Gold. 1995. *Imagining Scotland: Tradition, Representation, and Promotion in Scottish Tourism since 1750.* Aldershot: Scolar Press.

Gold, J., and S. Ward. 1994. *Place Promotion: The Use of Publicity in Selling Towns and Regions.* Chichester: John Wiley.

Gold, M. 2000. From preservation to interpretation: Presenting the sacred in a secular age. Unpublished M.A. thesis, Department of Geography, St. Mary's College, Strawberry Hill, London.

Goodman, E. 1995. A mess as a national monument? *Boston Globe,* October 23, A25.

Goodrich, J. 1985. Black American tourism: Some research findings. *Journal of Travel Research* 24: 27–28.

Goodwin, M. 1993. The city as commodity: The contested spaces of urban development. In *Selling Places: The City as Cultural Capital, Past and Present,* edited by G. Kearns and C. Philo, 145–62. Oxford and New York: Pergamon Press.

Gordon, A. 1997. *Ghostly Matters: Haunting and the Sociological Imagination.* Minneapolis: University of Minnesota Press.

Gregory, D. 1979. *Ideology: Science and Human Geography.* New York: St. Martin's Press.

———. 1994. *Geographical Imaginations.* Cambridge, Mass., and Oxford: Blackwell.

Gunther, J. 1947. In *Inside U.S.A.* New York: Harper and Brothers.

Halbwachs, M. 1980. *The Collective Memory.* Translated by F. J. Ditter and V. Y. Ditter. New York: Harper Colophon.

Hall, S. 1997. The work of representation. In *Cultural Representations and Signifying Practices,* edited by Stuart Hall, 15–64. London, and Thousand Oaks, Calif.: Sage.

Hall, T., and P. Hubbard. 1996. The entrepreneurial city: New urban politics, new urban geographies? *Progress in Human Geography* 20(2): 153–74.

Handler, R. 1988. *Nationalism and the Politics of Culture in Quebec.* Madison: University of Wisconsin Press.

Hanna, S. P. 1996. Is it Roslyn or is it Cicely?: Representations and the ambiguity of place. *Urban Geography* 17(7): 633–49.

Haraway, D. 1991. *Simians, Cyborgs, and Women: The Reinvention of Nature.* London and New York: Routledge.

Harley, J. B. 1964. *The Historian's Guide to Ordnance Survey Maps.* London: National Council of Social Service for the Standing Conference for Local History.

———. 1988. Maps, knowledge, and power. In *The Iconography of Landscape: Essays on Symbolic Representation, Design and Use of Past Environments,* edited by D. Cosgrove and S. Daniels, 277–312. Cambridge: Cambridge University Press.

———. 1989. Deconstructing the map. *Cartographica* 26(2): 1–20.

———. 1990. Cartography, ethics, and social theory. *Cartographica* 27(2): 1–23.

Harley, J. B., and K. Zandvliet. 1992. Art, science, and power in sixteenth-century Dutch cartography. *Cartographica* 29(2): 10–19.

Harris, A. 1968. *Bangkok after Dark.* New York: Macfadden Books.

Harvey, D. 1989a. *The Condition of Postmodernity: An Enquiry into the Origins of Cultural Change.* Cambridge, Mass., and Oxford: Blackwell.

———. 1989b. From managerialism to entrepreneurialism: The transformation in urban governance in late capitalism. *Geografiska Annaler* 71B: 3–17.

Hayden, D. 1995. *The Power of Place: Urban Landscapes as Public History.* Boston: MIT Press.

Healy, C. 1997. *From the Ruins of Colonialism: History as Social Memory.* Cambridge: Cambridge University Press.

Heffernan, M. 1995. Forever England: The Western Front and the politics of remembrance in Britain. *Ecumene* 2: 293–323.

Henderson, J. 1997. Singapore's wartime heritage attractions. *Journal of Tourism Studies* 8(2): 39–48.

———. 2000. War as a tourist attraction: The case of Vietnam. *International Journal of Tourism Research* 2: 269–80.

Hine, D. 1986. Lifting the veil, shattering the silence: Black women's history in slavery and freedom. In *The State of Afro-American History: Past, Present,*

Future, edited by D. Hine, 223–49. Baton Rouge: Lousiana State University Press.

Hoelscher, S. D. 1998. *Heritage on Stage: The Invention of Ethnic Places in America's Little Switzerland.* Madison: University of Wisconsin Press.

Holcomb, B. 1993. Revisioning place: De- and re-constructing the image of the industrial city. In *Selling Places: The City as Cultural Capital, Past and Present,* edited by G. Kearns and C. Philo, 1–32. Oxford and New York: Pergamon Press.

hooks, b. 1991. *Yearning: Race, Gender, and Cultural Politics.* London: Turnaround.

Howitt, W. 1840. *Visit to Remarkable Places, Old Halls, Battlefields, and Scenes Illustrative of Striking Passages in English History and Poetry.* London: N.p.

Immonen, B. 1995. Letter to the editor. *Montana Standard,* December 10.

Jackson, P., and J. Penrose. 1993. Placing "race" and nation. In *Constructions of Race, Place, and Nation,* edited by P. Jackson and J. Penrose, 1–26. London: UCL Press.

Jarlov, L. 1999. Leisure lots and summer cottages as places for people's own creative work. In *Leisure/Tourism Geographies: Practices and Geographical Knowledge,* edited by D. Crouch, 231–37. London and New York: Routledge.

Johnson, N. 1994. Sculpting heroic histories: Celebrating the centenary of the 1798 rebellion in Ireland. *Transactions of the Institute of British Geographers* 19: 78–93.

———. 1995. Cast in stone: Monuments, geography, and nationalism. *Environment and Planning D: Society and Space* 13: 51–65.

———. 1996a. Framing the past: Time, space, and the politics of heritage tourism in Ireland. *Political Geography* 18(2): 187–207.

———. 1996b. Where geography and history meet: Heritage tourism and the big house in Ireland. *Annals of the Association of American Geographers* 86(3): 551–66.

Johnson, R., and A. Johnson. 1967. *The Ghost Town of Bodie as Reported in the Newspapers of the Day.* Bishop, Calif.: Chalfant Press.

Johnston, L. 2001. (Other) bodies and tourism studies. *Annals of Tourism Research* 28(1): 180–201.

Jones, J. P., III 2000. The street politics of Jackie Smith. In *The Blackwell Companion to the City,* edited by G. Bridge and S. Watson, 448–59. Oxford: Blackwell.

Jones, J. P., III, and W. Natter. 1999. Space 'and' representation. In *Text and Image: Constructing Regional Knowledges,* edited by A. Buttimer and S. Brunn, 239–47. Leipzig: Leipzig Institute.

Jones, O. 1995. Lay discourses of the rural: Developments and implications for rural studies. *Journal of Rural Studies* 11(1): 35–49.

Karp, I., and S. Levine. 1991. Introduction: Museums and multiculturalism. In *Exhibiting Cultures: The Poetics and Politics of Museum Display,* edited by

I. Karp and S. Levine, 1–10. Washington, D.C.: Smithsonian Institution Press.

Katrak, K. 1992. Indian nationalism, Gandhian 'Satyagraha' and representations of female sexuality. In *Nationalisms and Sexualities,* edited by A. Parker, A. Russo, D. Sommer, and P. Yaeger, 395–406. New York and London: Routledge.

Kayser Neilson, N. 1999. Knowledge by doing: Home and identity in a bodily perspective. In *Leisure/Tourism Geographies: Practices and Geographical Knowledges,* edited by D. Crouch, 277–90. London and New York: Routledge.

Kearns, G., and C. Philo, eds. 1993. *Selling Places: The City as Cultural Capital, Past and Present.* Oxford and New York: Pergamon Press.

Kidd, C. 1993. *Subverting Scotland's Past: Scottish Whig Historians and the Creation of an Anglo-British Identity, 1689–c. 1830.* Cambridge: Cambridge University Press.

Kinnaird, V., U. Kothari, and D. Hall. 1994. Tourism: Gender perspectives. In *Tourism: A Gender Analysis,* edited by V. Kinnaird and D. Hall, 1–34. Chichester: John Wiley.

Kirmayer, L. 1996. Landscapes of memory: Trauma narrative and dissociation. In *Tense Past: Cultural Essays in Trauma and Memory,* edited by P. Antze and M. Lambeck, 153–98. New York: Routledge.

Kirschenblatt-Gimblett, B. 1998. *Destination Culture: Tourism, Museums, and Heritage.* Berkeley: University of California Press.

Kittredge, W., and A. Smith, eds. 1991. *The Last Best Place: A Montana Anthology.* Seattle and London: University of Washington Press.

Koonz, C. 1994. Between memory and oblivion: Concentration camps in German memory. In *Commemorations: The Politics of National Identity,* edited by J. Gillis, 258–80. Princeton, N.J.: Princeton University Press.

Kugelmass, J. 1996. *Missions to the Past: Poland in Contemporary Jewish Thought and Deed,* edited by P. Antze and M. Lambeck, 199–214. New York: Routledge.

Lachance, M., and G. Norcliffe. 2001. Geographies of globalization and protest: The summit of the Americas, Quebec City. Paper read at Canadian Association of Geographers, Montreal.

Laclau, E., and C. Mouffe. 1985. *Hegemony and Socialist Strategy: Towards a Radical Democratic Politics.* London and New York: Verso.

Lakoff, G., and M. Johnson. 1979. *Metaphors We Live By.* Chicago: University of Chicago Press.

Lamar, H., ed. 1998. *The New Encyclopedia of the American West.* New Haven: Yale University Press.

Laquer, T. 2000. Introduction. *Representations* 69: 1–8.

La Tempa, S. 1993. Rediscovering Black America. *Chicago Tribune,* February 14, section 12, 1–6.

Laurier, E. 1999. That sinking feeling: Elitism, working leisure, and yachting. In *Leisure/Tourism Geographies: Practices and Geographical Knowledge,* edited by D. Crouch, 195–213. London: Routledge.

Lee, G. 1998. Freedom's path: A journey on the road to civil rights. *Washington Post,* January 15, section E, 1.

Lefebvre, H. 1991. *The Production of Space.* Translated by D. Nicholas-Smith. Oxford and Cambridge, Mass.: Blackwell.

Lemelin, R. 1950. *The Plouffe Family.* Translated by Mary Finch. Toronto: McClelland and Stewart.

Lenman, B. 1995. The place of Prince Charles and the 45 in the Jacobite tradition. In *1745: Charles Edward Stuart and the Jacobites,* edited by R. Woosnam-Savage, 1–14. Edinburgh: HMSO.

Lennon, J., and M. Foley. 1999. Intrepretation of the unimaginable: The US Holocaust Memorial Museum, Washington, DC, and 'dark tourism.' *Journal of Travel Research* 38: 46–50.

———. 2000. *Dark Tourism.* London: Continuum.

Lettice, J. 1794. *Letters on a Tour through Various Parts of Scotland in the Year 1792.* London: T. Cadell.

Limerick, P. 1988. *The Legacy of Conquest: The Unbroken Past of the American West.* New York: W. W. Norton.

Limerick, P., C. Milner II, and C. Rankin, eds. 1991. *Trails toward a New Western History.* Lawrence: University Press of Kansas.

Linenthal, E. 1991. *Sacred Ground: Americans and Their Battlefields.* Urbana: University of Illinois Press.

Livesey, H. 1996. *Frommer's Montreal and Quebec City.* New York: Macmillan.

Livingstone, D. 1992. *The Geographical Tradition.* Oxford: Blackwell.

———, ed. 1999. *Geography and Enlightenment.* Chicago: University of Chicago Press.

Lloyd, D. 1998. *Battlefield Tourism: Pilgrimage and the Commemoration of the Great War in Britain, Australia, and Canada, 1919–1939.* Oxford: Berg.

Logan, J., and H. Molotch. 1987. *Urban Fortunes.* Berkeley: University of California Press.

Loose, W. 1979. *Bodie Bonanza: The True Story of a Flamboyant Past.* Las Vegas: Nevada Publications.

Lowenthal, D. 1975. Past time, past place: Landscape and memory. *Geographical Review* 65(1): 1–36.

———. 1998. *The Heritage Crusade and the Spoils of History.* Cambridge: Cambridge University Press.

Luke, T. 1997. *Ecocritique: Contesting the Politics of Nature, Economy, and Culture.* Minneapolis and London: University of Minnesota Press.

Lynch, J. 1995. Correspondence with M. Curran, October 25.

Lysa, H. 1998. Of consorts and harlots in Thai popular history. *Journal of Asian Studies* 57: 333–53.

MacCannell, D. 1989. *The Tourist: A New Theory of the Leisure Class.* New York: Schocken Books.

MacHaffie, P. 1995. Manufacturing metaphors: Public cartography, the market, and democracy. In *Ground Truth: The Social Implications of Geographic Information Systems,* edited by J. Pickles, 113–29. New York and London: Guilford Press.

Malone, M. 1995. *The Battle for Butte: Mining and Politics on the Northern Frontier, 1864–1906.* Helena: Montana Historical Society Press.

Malone, M., R. Roeder, and W. Lang. 1993. *Montana: A History of Two Centuries.* Seattle: University of Washington Press.

Maney, M. 1995. Interview by M. Curran. Butte, Montana, September 22.

———. 1996. Lecture: Women, labor, and community in Butte. Missoula, Montana, March 19.

Massey, D. 1993. Power-geometry and a progressive sense of place. In *Mapping the Futures: Local Cultures, Global Change,* edited by J. Bird, B. Curtis, T. Putnam, G. Robertson, and L. Tickner, 59–69. New York and London: Routledge.

———. 1999. Spaces of politics. In *Human Geography Today,* edited by D. Massey, J. Allen, and P. Sarre, 279–94. Cambridge: Polity Press.

McArthur, C. 1994. Culloden: A pre-emptive strike. *Scottish Affairs* 9: 97–126.

McCarthy, J. 1986. *Joyce's Dublin: A Walking Guide to Ulysses.* Dublin: Wolfhound Press.

McClintock, A. 1995. *Imperial Leather: Race, Gender, and Sexuality in the Colonial Contest.* New York: Routledge.

McGrath, R. 1984. *Gunfighters, Highwaymen, and Vigilantes.* Berkeley: University of California Press.

McKinsey, E. 1985. *Niagara Falls: Icons of the American Sublime.* Cambridge: Cambridge University Press.

McNaughten, P., and J. Urry. *Contested Natures.* London: Sage. 1998.

Merell, B. 1991. *Bodie 1880.* Map: N.p., N.p. (available for purchase at Bodie Museum, Bodie, California).

Mines, P. 1998. Travel in the black. *Atlantic Tribune,* May 15–31, 14–16.

Mitchell, L. S., and P. E. Murphy. 1991. Geography and tourism. *Annals of Tourism Research* 18: 57–70.

Mitchell, T. 1988. *Colonizing Egypt.* Berkeley: University of California Press.

Mitchell, W. J. T., ed. 1994. *Power and Landscape.* Chicago: University of Chicago Press.

Monk, J. 1992. Gender in the landscape: Expressions of power and meaning. In *Inventing Places: Studies in Cultural Geography,* edited by K. Anderson and F. Gale, 123–38. Melbourne: Longman Cheshire.

Monmonier, M. 1996. *How to Lie with Maps.* Chicago and London: University of Chicago Press.

Moore, J., and S. Luoma. 1990. Hazardous wastes from large-scale metal extraction: The Clark Fork Waste Complex, Montana. Presented at the Clark Fork River Symposium, Missoula. April 20.

Morris, A. 1984. *The Origins of the Civil Rights Movement: Black Communities Organizing for Change.* New York: Free Press.

Morrison, T. 1992. *Playing in the Dark: Whiteness and the Literary Imagination.* Cambridge: Harvard University Press.

Morton, H. 1929. *In Search of Scotland.* London: Methuen.

Mouffe, C. 1992. Democratic politics today. In *Dimensions of Radical Democracy: Pluralism, Citizenship, Community,* edited by C. Mouffe, 1–16. London and New York: Verso.

———. 1993. *The Return of the Political.* London and New York: Verso.

Mueller, C. 1990. Ella Baker and the origins of participatory democracy. In *Women in the Civil Rights Movement: Trailblazers and Torchbearers, 1941–1965,* edited by V. Crawford, J. Rouse, and B. Woods, 51–70. Brooklyn: Carlson Publishing.

Mumford, L. 1938. *The Culture of Cities.* New York: Harcourt Brace Jovanovich.

Murdoch, J., and A. Pratt. 1993. Rural studies: Modernism, postmodernism, and the post-rural. *Journal of Rural Studies* 9(4): 411–27.

Nabbefeld, J. 1992. Institute should have strong impact on city economy. *Birmingham News,* November 15, 14P.

Nash, C. 1996. Reclaiming vision: Looking at landscape and the body. *Gender, Place, and Culture* 3: 149–69.

National Association Tour. 1997. *Tour Operators' Market Assessment Plan for the African American Market.* Washington, D.C.: National Tour Association Development Council.

Natter, W., and J. P. Jones III. 1997. Identity, space, and other uncertainties. In *Space and Social Theory: Interpreting Modernity and Postmodernity,* edited by G. Benko and U. Strohmayer, 143–61. Oxford and Cambridge, Mass.: Blackwell.

Neisser, U. 1982. *Memory Observed: Remembering in Natural Contexts.* San Francisco: W. H. Freeman.

Nietzsche, F. 1985. *The Uses and Abuses of History.* Translated by A. Collins. New York: Macmillan.

Nora, P. 1989. Between memory and history: Les lieux de mémoire. *Representations* 26 (spring): 7–25.

Norrell, R. 1986. *Reaping the Whirlwind: The Civil Rights Movement in Tuskegee.* New York: Vintage Books.

NTS (National Trust for Scotland). 1965. *Culloden.* Edinburgh: National Trust for Scotland.

O'Connor, D. 1998. Cinematic regimes of light/power/knowledge: The political economy of secrecy. Unpublished Ph.D. dissertation, Department of Sociology and Anthropology, Carleton University, Ottawa.

O'Reilly, D. 1996. Massacre trail lures sightseers. *The European,* November 14–20, 3.

O'Rourke, E. 1978. *The Highest School in California: A Story of Bodie, California.* Sacramento: Spilman Publishing Company.

Papineau, A. 1977. *Papineau's Guide to Bangkok: City of Enchantment,* 10th ed. Singapore: Andre Publications.

Parker, P., and M. Hendricks. 1994. *Women, Race, and Writing in the Early Modern Period.* London: Routledge.

Partners für Berlin. 1996. *Schaustelle Berlin Program-Journal, 25 (Juni 25).* Berlin: Partners für Berlin.

———. 1997a. *Schaustelle Berlin: Volles Program, Ausgabe 2/97, 15 (Juni 31).* Berlin: Partners für Berlin.

———. 1997b. *Schaustelle Berlin: Volles Program: Das Neue Berlin Entdecken: Discover the New Berlin, 15 (Juni 31).* Berlin: Partners für Berlin.

———. 1999. *Das Neue Berlin erleben, Discover the New Berlin: Schaustelle Berlin: Programheft 2, Alle Termine 2, 19 (Juli 4).* Berlin: Partners für Berlin.

———. 2000. *Schaustelle Berlin: Das Programmheft, 3 (Juni bis 3).* Berlin: Partners für Berlin.

Payne, C. 1990. "Men led, but women organized": Movement participation of women in the Mississippi Delta. In *Women and Social Protest,* edited by G. West and R. L. Blumberg, 156–65. Oxford: Oxford University Press.

Pearce, D. 1995. *Tourism Today: A Geographical Analysis.* Essex: Longman.

Peleggi, M. 1996. National heritage and global tourism in Thailand. *Annal of Tourism Research* 23: 432–48.

Pennant, T. 1771. *A Tour in Scotland, 1769.* Chester: John Monk.

Peters, A. 1990. *Peters Atlas of the World.* New York: Harper and Row.

Philipp, S. 1993. Racial differences in the perceived attractiveness of tourism destinations, interests, and cultural resources. *Journal of Leisure Research* 25: 290–304.

———. 1994. Race and tourism choice: A legacy of discrimination? *Annals of Tourism Research* 21: 479–88.

———. 1995. Race and leisure constraints. *Leisure Sciences* 17: 109–20.

Philo, C., and G. Kearns. 1993. Culture, history, capital: A critical introduction to the selling of places. In *Selling Places: The City as Cultural Capital, Past and Present,* edited by C. Philo and G. Kearns, 1–32. Oxford and New York: Pergamon Press.

Pickles, J. 1992. Text, hermeneutics, and propaganda maps. In *Writing Worlds: Discourse, Text, and Metaphor in the Representations of Landscape,* edited by T. J. Barnes and J. S. Duncan, 193–230. New York: Routledge.

Pickles, J., and M. Watts. 1992. Paradigms of inquiry? In *Geography's Inner World,* edited by R. Abler, M. Marcus, and J. Olson, 168–91. New Brunswick, N.J.: Rutgers University Press.

Pile, S. 1996. *The Body and the City: Psychoanalysis, Space, and Subjectivity.* London and New York: Routledge.

———. 1997. Introduction. In *Geographies of Resistance,* edited by S. Pile and M. Keith, 1–32. London and New York: Routledge.

Pile, S., and N. Thrift, eds. 1995. *Mapping the Subject: Geographies of Cultural Transformation.* London and New York: Routledge.

Porter, G. 1996. Seeing through solidity: A feminist perspective on museums. In *Theorizing Museums: Representing Identity and Diversity in a Changing World,* edited by S. Macdonald and G. Fyfe, 105–26. London: Blackwell.

PR News. 1993. Case study no. 2333: Intensive media campaign fuels support for civil rights facility. *PR News,* January 25, 4–5.

Prentice, R., ed. 1976. *The National Trust for Scotland Guide.* London: Jonathan Cape.

Ray, J. 1995. Interview by M. Curran. Butte, Montana, October 24.

Reavis, M. 1995. Interview by M. Curran. Butte, Montana, November 29.

Reid, S. 1994. *Like Hungry Wolves: Culloden Moor, 16 April 1746.* London: Windrow and Green.

Rickard, T. 1932. *A History of American Mining.* New York: McGraw-Hill Book Company.

Ricoeur, P. 1976. *Interpretation Theory.* Forth Worth: Texas Christian University Press.

Ritzer, G., and A. Liska. 1997. 'McDisneyization' and 'post-tourism': Complementary perspectives on contemporary tourism. In *Touring Cultures: Transformations of Travel and Theory,* edited by C. Rojek and J. Urry, 96–109. London and New York: Routledge.

Roberts, S., and R. Schein. 1993. The entrepreneurial city: Fabricating urban development in Syracuse. *Professional Geographer* 45(1): 21–33.

Rojek, C. 1993. *Ways of Seeing: Modern Transformations in Leisure and Travel.* London: Macmillan.

Rojek, C., and J. Urry. 1997a. Transformations of travel and theory. In *Touring Cultures: Transformations of Travel and Theory,* edited by C. Rojek and J. Urry, 1–19. London and New York: Routledge.

———, eds. 1997b. *Touring Cultures: Transformations of Travel and Theory.* London and New York: Routledge.

Rose, G. 1993. *Feminism and Geography: The Limits of Geographical Knowledge.* Minneapolis: University of Minnesota Press.

Ross, M. 1995. Seven stacks of the neversweat. In *Look for Me in Butte.* Nevada City, Calif.: A Smokestack Recording (compact disc).

Roy, P. 2001. À terre, le mur de la honte! *La Presse* April 21, A3.

Ruffins, F. 1998a. Culture wars won and lost, part II: The national African-American museum project. *Radical History Review* 70: 78–101.

———. 1998b. Mythos, memory, and history: African-American preservation efforts, 1820–1990. In *Museums and Communities: The Politics of*

Public Culture, edited by I. Karp, C. Kreamer, and S. Levine, 506–611. Washington, D.C.: Smithsonian Institution Press.

Russell, C. 1927. Bodie, dead city of Mono. *Yosemite Nature Notes,* December 31.

Ryden, K. C. 1993. *Mapping the Invisible Landscape: Folklore, Writing, and the Sense of Place.* Iowa City: University of Iowa Press.

Sack, K. 1998. Museums of a movement. *New York Times* June 28 (travel section 12), 22.

Samuel, R. 1994. *Theatres of Memory,* vol. 1, *Past and Present in Contemporary Culture.* London: Verso.

Sandage, S. 1993. A marble house divided: The Lincoln Memorial, the civil rights movement, and the politics of memory, 1939–1963. *Journal of American History* 80: 135–67.

Saunders, N. 2001. Matter and memory in the landscapes of conflict: The Western Front, 1914–1999. In *Contested Landscapes: Movement, Exile, and Place,* edited by B. Bender and M. Winer. Oxford: Berg.

Savage, K. 1994. The politics of memory: Black emancipation and the Civil War monument. In *Commemorations: The Politics of National Identity,* edited by J. Gillis, 127–49. Princeton, N.J.: Princeton University Press.

Savard, P. 1971. *La Ville de Québec au Miroir de la Littérature 1860–1900.* Quebec City: Société Historique de Québec, Séminaire de Québec.

Sayer, A. 1985. Realism and geography. In *The Future of Geography,* edited by R. J. Johnston, 159–73. London: Methuen.

Schein, R. 1997. The place of landscape: A conceptual framework for interpreting an American scence. *Annals of the Association of American Geographers* 87(4): 660–80.

Scott, J. 1985. *The Weapons of the Weak: Everyday Forms of Peasant Resistance.* New Haven: Yale University Press.

Seaton, A. 1999a. From thanatopis to thanatourism: Guided by the dark. *Journal of International Heritage Studies* 2: 234–44.

———. 1999b. War and thantourism: Waterloo, 1815–1914. *Annals of Tourism Research* 26: 130–58.

———. 2000. Another weekend away looking for dead bodies . . . : Battlefield tourism on the Somme and in Flanders. *Tourism Recreation Research* 25: 63–77.

Semmel, S. 2000. Reading the tangible past: British tourism, collecting, and memory after Waterloo. *Representations* 69: 9–37.

Shaw, G., and A. Williams. 1994. *Critical Issues in Tourism: A Geographical Perspective.* Oxford: Blackwell.

Shaw, G., S. Agarwal, and P. Bull. 2000. Tourism consumption and tourist behaviour: A British perspective. *Tourism Geographies* 2(3): 264–89.

Shea, J. 1995. Interview by M. Curran. Butte, Montana, October 24.

Sherman, M. 1998. Tourism blazes a new trail. *Montgomery Advertiser,* April 13, 6B.

Shields, R. 1991a. *Imaginary Sites between Views Exhibition Catalogue.* Banff: Watler Phillipps Gallery, Banff Center for the Arts: 22–26.

———. 1991b. *Places on the Margins: Alternative Geographies of Modernity.* London: Routledge.

———. 1992a. Die masken des konsumenten. lebensstil konsum. *GDI-Impuls, Journal of the Gottfried Duttweiller Institute* 21: 3–20.

———. 1992b. A truant proximity: Presence and absence in the space of modernity. *Environment and Planning D: Society and Space* 10(2): 181–98.

———. 1997. Flow. *Space and Culture—The Journal* 1 (July): 1–12.

———. 1998. Raumkonstruktion und Tourismus. *Voyage: Jahrbuch für Reise und Tourismusforschung* 2: 53–72.

———. 2000. Virtual Spaces? *Space and Culture—The Journal* 4/5 (March): 1–12.

Sked, P. 1997. *Culloden.* Edinburgh: National Trust for Scotland.

Skinner, G. W. 1957. *Chinese Society in Thailand: An Analytical History.* Ithaca, N.Y.: Cornell University Press.

Smiley, F. 1998. Interview by O. Dwyer, Birmingham, Alabama, July 20.

Smith, D. 1987. *The Everyday World as Problematic: A Feminist Sociology.* Boston: Northeastern University Press.

Smith, G. 1925. Bodie: Last of the old-time mining camps. *California Historical Society Quarterly* 4(1): 64–80.

Smith, V. 1998. War and tourism: An American ethnography. *Annals of Tourism Research* 25: 202–27.

Sparke, M. 1995. Between demythologizing and deconstructing the map: Shawnadithit's New-Found-Land and the alienation of Canada. *Cartographica* 32(1): 1–21.

———. 1998. A map that roared and an original atlas: Canada, cartography, and the narration of nation. *Annals of the Association of American Geographers* 88(3): 463–95.

Sprague, M. Forthcoming. *Up Home in Bodie.* Las Vegas: University of Nevada Press.

Spratlen, T. 1986. Affluent blacks as travelers and tourists: Group characteristics and targeting advertising themes. Paper read at Tourism Service Marketing: Advances in Theory and Practices, Proceedings of the Special Conference Series on Tourism Service Marketing, at Cleveland, Ohio.

Spritzer, D. 1993. Exploring African-American history. *Travel Weekly,* October 14, G3–G4.

Stewart, J., and F. Ruffins. 1986. "A faithful witness": Afro-American public history in historical perspective, 1828–1984. In *Presenting the Past: Essays on the History and the Public,* edited by S. Benson, S. Brier, and R. Rosenweig, 307–38. Philadelphia: Temple University Press.

Sturken, M. 1997. *Tangled Memories: The Vietnam War, the AIDS Epidemic, and the Politics of Remembering.* Berkeley: University of California Press.

Tagesspiegel, Der. 1997. Was its dieses Jahr neu an der Schaustelle? June 14.

———. 1998. *Sommer '98 in Berlin: Schaustelle, Kuturveranstaltungen und Neues aus der Stadt.* Beilage des "Tagesspiegels" in Kooperation mit "Partner für Berlin."

Taylor, D. 1993. *Identity in Ethnic Leisure Pursuits.* San Francisco: Mellen Research University Press.

Taylor, J. P. 2001. Authenticity and sincerity in tourism. *Annals of Tourism Research* 28(1): 7–26.

Terdiman, R. 1993. *Identity in Ethnic Leisure Pursuits.* Ithaca, N.Y.: Cornell University Press.

Thanh-Dam, T. 1990. *Sex, Money, and Morality: Prostitution and Tourism in Southeast Asia.* London and Atlantic Highlands, N.J.: Zed Books.

Till, K. Forthcoming. *The New Berlin: Memory, Politcs, Place.* Minneapolis: University of Minnesota Press.

Toole, K. 1959. *Montana: An Uncommon Land.* Norman: University of Oklahoma Press.

———. 1972. *Twentieth-Century Montana: A State of Extremes.* Norman: University of Oklahoma Press.

Toupin, G. 2001. Les activistes font une brèche. *La Presse* April 21, A1.

Travel Industry Association of America. 1993. *African-American Travelers: Dimensions of the African-American Travel Market.* Washington, D.C.: Travel Industry Association of America.

———. 1996. The minority traveler: TravelScope survey. Washington, D.C.: Travel Industry Association of America.

Tunbridge, J., and G. Ashworth. 1996. *Dissonant Heritage: The Management of the Past as a Resource of Conflict.* Chichester: John Wiley.

Turner, V. 1974. *Dramas, Fields, and Metaphors.* Ithaca, N.Y.: Cornell University Press.

TWE (Tours with Experts). 2001. *Military History, 2002 Preview: Retracting the Paths of History.* Liverpool: Tours with Experts.

Ulack, R., and V. J. Del Casino Jr. 2000. Tourism. In *Southeast Asia: Diversity of Development,* edited by R. Ulack and T. Lienbach, 192–211. Englewood Cliffs, N.J.: Prentice Hall.

Urry, J. 1990. *The Tourist Gaze: Leisure and Travel in Contemporary Society.* London: Sage.

———. 1991. *The Tourist Gaze.* London: Sage.

———. 1995. *Consuming Places.* London: Routledge.

USEPA. 1991. *Draft Baseline Risk Assessment, Mine Flooding Operable Unit, Silver Bow Creek/Butte Area* National Priority List *Site.* Golden, Colo.

Valentine, G. 1999. Consuming pleasures: Food, leisure, and the negotiation of sexual relations. In *Leisure/Tourism Geographies: Practices of Geographical Knowledge,* edited by D. Crouch, 164–80. London and New York: Routledge.

Van Esterick, P. 1994. Beauty and the beast: The cultural context of the May massacre, Bangkok, Thailand. Working Paper No. 10, Thai Studies Project. Toronto, Canada.

Van Loan, C. 1915. Ghost cities of the West. Bad, B-a-d Bodie. *Saturday Evening Post,* September 25, 18–58.

Victoria, Q. 1968. *Our Life in the Highlands (Republication of Two Volumes from 1868 and 1884).* London: William Kimber.

Walker, D., and R. S. Ehrlich. 1992. *'Hello My Big Big Honey!': Love Letters to Bangkok Bar Girls and Their Revealing Interviews.* Bangkok: Dragon Dance Publications.

Ward, S., and J. Gold. 1995. Introduction. In *Place Promotion: The Use of Publicity and Marketing to Sell Towns and Regions,* edited by J. Gold and S. Ward, 1–17. New York: John Wiley and Sons.

Waring, G. 1995. Interview by M. Curran. Butte, Montana, October 21.

Warner, M. 1985. *Monuments and Maidens: The Allegory of the Female Form.* London: Weidenfeld and Nicolson.

Warren, S. 1999. Cultural contestation at Disneyland Paris. In *Leisure/Tourism Geographies: Practices and Geographical Knowledge,* edited by D. Crouch, 109–25. London and New York: Routledge.

Wedertz, F. 1969. *Bodie 1859–1900.* Bishop, Calif.: Sierra Media.

Weinstock, S. 1995. Interview by M. Curran. Butte, Montana, July 31.

Weyeneth, R. 1995. Historic preservation and the civil rights movement of the 1950s and 1960s: Identifying, preserving, and interpreting the architecture of liberation: A report to preservation agencies, part I. *CRM Bulletin* 18(4): 6–8.

Whatmore, S. 1999. Hybrid geographies: Rethinking the human in human geography. In *Human Geography Today,* edited by D. Massey, J. Allen, and P. Sarre, 22–40. Cambridge: Polity Press.

White, R. 1991. *It's Your Misfortune and None of My Own: A New History of the American West.* Norman: University of Oklahoma Press.

Wills, G. 1992. *Lincoln in Gettysburg: The Words That Remade America.* New York: Simon and Schuster.

Winter, J. 1995. *Sites of Memory, Sites of Mourning: The Great War in European Cultural History.* Cambridge: Cambridge University Press.

Wittig, M. 1988. The straight mind. In *For Lesbians Only: A Separatist Anthology,* edited by S. Hoagland and J. Penelope, 431–39. London: Onlywoman.

Wöber, K. 1997a. A database on the travel demand for European urban tourism destinations. In *International City Tourism: Analysis and Strategy,* edited by K. Grabler and J. Mazanec, 15–25. London: Pinter.

———. 1997b. International city tourism flows. In *International City Tourism: Analysis and Strategy,* edited by K. Grabler and J. Mazanec, 39–53. London: Pinter.

———. 1997c. Introducing a harmonization procedure for European city tourism statistics. In *International City Tourism: Analysis and Strategy,* edited by K. Grabler and J. Mazanec, 26–38. London: Pinter.

Wood, D. 1991. Maps are territories. *Cartographica* 28(2): 73.

———. 1992. *The Power of Maps.* New York and London: Guilford Press.

———. 1993. Maps and mapmaking. *Cartographica* 30(1): 1–9.

Wood, D., and J. Fels. 1986. Designs on signs: Myth and meaning in maps. *Cartographica* 23(3): 54–103.

Woodward, D. 1991. Maps and the rationalization of geographic space. In *Circa 1492: Art in the Age of Exploration,* edited by J. Levenson. 83–87. New Haven: Yale University Press for the National Gallery of Art.

Woodward, M. 1988. Class, regionality, and leisure among urban black Americans: The post–civil rights era. *Journal of Leisure Research* 20: 87–105.

Wright, J. K. 1942. Map makers are human: Comments on the subjective in maps. *Geographical Review* 42(4): 527–44.

Yardley, J. 1992. Black history, civil rights luring tourists to the South. *Atlanta Journal Constitution,* November 13, A1, A6.

Young, J. 1988. *Writing and Rewriting the Holocaust Memorials: Narrative and the Consequences of Interpretation.* Bloomington: University of Indiana Press.

———. 1993. *The Texture of Memory: Holocaust Memorials and Meaning.* New Haven: Yale University Press.

Zukin, S. 1995. *The Cultures of Cities.* Oxford: Blackwell.

Contributors

Mary Curran is assistant professor of geography at Eastern Connecticut State University. A human/cultural geographer, she is interested in human-environment relations, especially those involving disputes about "natural" resources. She is currently researching a debate about industrial hog farming in Kentucky.

Vincent J. Del Casino Jr. is assistant professor of geography and liberal studies at California State University, Long Beach, and has recently been visiting research fellow in the Department of Human Geography at the Australian National University. He has published works on tourism in *Progress in Human Geography* with Stephen Hanna and with Richard Ulack for Prentice Hall's recent edited volume on Southeast Asia. He has written about social/health geography, organizational geography, and ethnographic methodologies in *The Professional Geographer, Geoforum,* and *Geographical Review.*

Dydia DeLyser is assistant professor of geography at Louisiana State University. She has published in *Annals of the Association of American Geographers, The Geographical Review,* and several edited volumes. Her book *Ramona Memories* is forthcoming.

Owen J. Dwyer is assistant professor of geography at Indiana University, Indianapolis. His research interests lie with public spaces, the civil rights movement, and memorial landscapes. He has recently published in *The Professional Geographer* and *Social and Cultural Geography.*

John R. Gold is professor of urban geography in the School of Social Sciences and Law and Oxford Brookes University in Oxford, England. His major research interests are landscape representation, the production and consumption of cultural spectacle, and the impact of architectural modernism on urban reconstruction. His most recent books are *Place Promotion: The Use of Publicity and Public Relations to Sell Towns and Regions; Imagining Scotland: Tradition, Representation, and Promotion in Scottish Tourism since 1750; The Experience of Modernism; Landscapes of Defense;* and *Cities of Culture: Tourism, Promotion, and Spectacle.*

Margaret M. Gold was formerly principal lecturer in geography and European studies at Thames Valley University, London, and is now senior lecturer in arts management at the University of North London. Her major research interests are the ideological construction of heritage, the memorialization of the past, and the conflict between the sacred and the secular in tourist spaces. Her most recent books are *Imagining Scotland: Tradition, Representation, and Promotion in Scottish Tourism since 1750* and *Cities of Culture: Tourism, Promotion, and Spectacle.*

Stephen P. Hanna is assistant professor of geography at Mary Washington College, Fredericksburg, Virginia, where he teaches cartography, economic geography, and geographies of tourism. He has published on space and representation in *Urban Geography* and *Historical Geography* and, with Vincent Del Casino, wrote an article on tourism maps for *Progress in Human Geography.*

Rob Shields works in the fields of cultural geography, architecture, and new media. He is editor of *Space and Culture* and author of *Places on the Margin: Alternative Geographies of Modernity; Lefebvre; Love and Struggle: Spatial Dialectics;* and *The Virtual.* His edited books include *Lifestyle Shopping: The Subject of Consumption; Cultures of Internet: Virtual Spaces, Real Histories, Living Bodies;* and *Social Engineering* (with Adam Podgorecki and Jon Alexander).

Karen E. Till is assistant professor of geography at the University of Minnesota. She is coeditor of *Textures of Place: Exploring Humanist Geographies* (Minnesota, 2001) and has publishe d numerous book chapters and articles about her research on social memory and urban landscapes in such journals as *Society and Space, Ecumene, Historical Geography, Geographical Review,* and *Urban Geography.* She is finishing the book manuscript *The New Berlin: Memory, Politics, Place* (Minnesota, forthcoming).

Index